JT
8-2-14

SHARE VALUATION MANUAL

Share Valuation Manual

Roland Gurney

Gower

Published by
Gower Publishing Company Limited,
Gower House,
Croft Road,
Aldershot,
Hants GU11 3HR,
England

Gower Publishing Company,
Old Post Road,
Brookfield,
Vermont 05036,
U.S.A.

British Library Cataloguing in Publication Data

Gurney, Roland
Share valuation manual.
1. Corporations - Valuation - Great Britain
I. Title
332.63'221'0941 HD2845

Library of Congress Cataloging-in-Publication Data

Gurney, Roland.
Share valuation manual.
Bibliography: p.

1. Corporations–Valuation–United States–Handbooks, manuals, etc. 2. Corporations–Valuation–Law and legislation–United States–Handbooks, manuals, etc.
I. Title.
HG4028.V3G87 1987 657'.48 86-13692

ISBN 0 566 02678 3

Printed and Bound in Great Britain by
Redwood Burn Limited, Trowbridge, Wiltshire.

For my children Sacha, Oliver, Francesca and Alexis with love and affection

For Elizabeth for all her patience, understanding and love for which this book like all my writings is but part return

R. G.

Contents

Illustrations

Tables

Preface

This manual is designed to guide the reader through the intricate maze of the subject. It considers all the elements necessary to achieve a satisfactory valuation of any shareholding in any unquoted public or private company for any commercial or fiscal purpose.

Concepts are illustrated throughout by a wealth of specific examples. The text combines commercial, accountancy and legal approaches since all of these are involved in the valuation process.

It is my hope that the book will prove a useful and authoritative guide to anyone concerned with share valuations, notably accountants, directors, investors and analysts.

Roland Gurney

Table of significant share valuation cases

Arenson v Arenson [1977] AC 405

Attorney-General v Jameson (1905) 2 Ir.R 218

Attorney-General for Ceylon v Mackie (1952) 2 All ER 775

Buccleuch (Duke of) v IRC [1967] 1 All ER 129

Buckingham v Francis (1986)

Collier v Mason [1858] Vol.119 RR 394

Courthope, re [1928] 7 ATC 538

Crabtree v Hinchcliffe [1972] AC 707

Crossman v IRC [1937] AC 26

Dean v Prince [1954] 1 All ER 749

Delavenne v Broadhurst (1931) 1 Ch 234

Ebrahimi v Westbourne Galleries [1973] AC 360

Ellesmere (Earl) v IRC [1918] 2 KB 735

Findlay's Trustees v IRC (1938) 22 ATC 437

Glass v IRC (1915) SC 449

Goldcoast Selection Trust v Humphrey (1948) 27 AC 459

Holt v IRC (1953) 32 ATC 402

IRC v Clay [1914] 3 KB 466

John Smith's Tadcaster Brewing Co. Ltd, re [1952] 2 All ER 751

1 Introduction

Modern share valuation theory and practice has its origins in the statutory requirements of the old estate duty legislation (1894) as interpreted in the courts and reincarnated in the capital transfer tax (CTT) and capital gains tax (CGT) rules, embodied in Finance Acts 1975 *et seq*. and the Capital Gains Tax Act 1979. This grafted a statutory hypothesis of notional open market value on the often complicated restrictive structures and constitutions granted to private companies by Victorian statutes from the Joint Stock Companies Act of 1856 and the Companies Act of 1862. Commercial values since then have been based on a similar willing buyer and willing seller in free negotiation concept, but of course involve no statutory hypothesis so take full account of actual circumstances of the parties to the transaction. As will be seen later this comes close to some fiscal valuations where there is no express statutory basis of valuation.

PRINCIPLES

The valuer, for whatever purpose, is engaged in essentially a practical task but some fundamentals do emerge.

- The purpose of the valuation itself is of paramount importance since the same size of holding may command vastly different values — perfectly legitimately and meaningfully — for different purposes, notoriously for different taxes for example. Both buyer and seller may pitch different prices in different situations and this affects the ultimate concluded price.
- Subject to this it is one of the axioms of share valuation that different sizes of holding will require differentials in value if they possess different legal rights and powers. These may also be expressed in differences in access to

information concerning the company's past performance, current standing and future projections and these will translate into valuation changes.

- The company's articles and memorandum of association are critical contractual and constitutional documents that must be interpreted before the valuation can sensibly proceed.
- The company operates in a given business sector and its performance must be monitored against that context as well as the wider world of investment.
- The company will be more or less sensitive to economic indicators and the investment climate generally. The conditions prevailing at the valuation date should be examined and stated by the valuer.
- Changes in taxation, policy, technology and even fashion may cause fundamental re-rating of business prospects and the valuation must directly or indirectly reflect these.
- The valuation must also take account of the rich variety of circumstances and relationships embodied in the company, its directors, shareholders, employees and customers or clients. It should always be remembered that in the small to medium sized enterprise one individual may well hold several different titles.
- Valuation is of course both an art and a science. Accordingly, it contains elements of both objective analysis and subjective judgement. Nevertheless, the valuer's main task is to arrive at a reasonably accurate value for the purpose in hand and not to plead a special case.
- Mathematical exactitude in valuation is an impossible objective and a valuation range of acceptable values should always be established as a negotiating tool.
- Valuation is, above all, a dynamic process — reflecting the real world of the market-place — but unquoted shares will tend to fluctuate less than their stock exchange counterparts. This is due to the greater speculative element in quoted equity demand combined with the underlying stability of demand prevalent for private company shares.

THE SHARE VALUER

The professional share valuer is likely to fall into one of the following categories:

- A solicitor involved in estate and probate work who may be relatively inexpert. Solicitors often used to deal with the old assets valuations for estate duty that could take on legal complications of intricate complexity but generally needed little accounting ability. They are far less likely to get involved in open market valuations, whether statutory or commercial.

- A stockbroker asked for advice who may possess considerable experience of handling larger companies but much less of small to medium concerns.
- A banker in connection with security who may well be concerned mainly with break-up values if the enterprise fails rather than with the going-concern values of a successful venture.
- A merchant banker who may well be biased towards flotation prices and bid values. His experience will again be primarily of the larger private and public unquoted companies.
- A finance house which will be experienced in dealing with substantial minority holdings in medium to large companies selected with a view to medium to longer capital growth.
- An auditor who is often called in to determine the fair value required under a company's articles of association. His valuation in this capacity will not necessarily be the same as a statutory open-market valuation or a commercial transaction price.
- An accountant who is the person most likely to be asked to undertake a professional valuation of unquoted shares. He may well have, as auditor, inside knowledge of the company's affairs going back many years but this is not always an advantage in coming to terms with all the hypothetical aspects of the statutory open-market valuation. Some of the knowledge will be largely or wholly irrelevant and what is not may distort the auditor's vision of what is essentially an objective process, balancing different factors in the valuation equation.

The share valuer may also have to call on the valuation expertise of other valuers such as chartered surveyors for property valuations, patent and trade mark agents, copyright experts, machinery and plant valuers, livestock and bloodstock valuers, mineral rights valuers and specialists in particular sectors, notably those with a peculiar trade or customary basis for valuing goodwill such as pharmaceutical chemists, the hotel business, TV rental and dairy companies amongst others. Whether he does this or has the capacity to handle the valuation point himself depends very much on the size of holding, the amount prima facie at stake and the nature of the particular valuation point involved. It may also depend on the share valuer's own resources. The big city firms have their own share valuation departments and access to a wide variety of sources. A partner in a small provincial practice will have far less at his command.

There is of course a final category of professional valuer, namely the members of the shares valuation division of the Inland Revenue who deal with share valuations for that Department for all fiscal purposes. They are chosen for their presumptive ability to do this work and are given extensive in-house and on-the-job training. They have naturally a wealth of business information enabling them to undertake detailed comparability studies of sectors and companies. Over the years they will build up substantial expertise (the average stay in the division will be a minimum of four to five years) and beyond a certain level they can be called upon by the Department to demonstrate this in hearings before the General or Special Commissioners. In this respect they also have two great advantages in working full-time on nothing but share valuation (in probable contrast to their professional counterparts) and possessing records of past decisions at such tribunals. It is therefore not altogether surprising that the Revenue usually wins at such hearings. The other records kept by the division are details of past transactions in the company's shares so that these are immediately accessible to the examiners dealing with a new case.

Naturally there are specialists within the division handling such matters as copyrights, patents and trade marks, or special classes of valuation such as those under share option schemes. An examiner in the division has fairly wide valuation scope and is also expected to do his work cost-effectively and not undertake academic exercises so that in theory a combination of a reasonable approach and detailed valuation submission should lead to early negotiated agreements. In practice the negotiations can drag on for years with both sides becoming increasingly frustrated until an interview settles the deadlock or the case goes to appeal. Valuation apart, negotiation itself involves special skills and the valuer should at every stage refer for express instructions from his client pointing out the issues and tax at stake.

Finally, it should always be remembered that apart from breaking through the paper barrier of interminable point-scoring correspondence a telephone does at least get the case-file out of the examiner's working arrear! One thing examiners will not do is answer hypothetical questions about hypothetical transactions. The Department does not run it as a part-time share valuation service for tax avoidance specialists.

UNDERLYING ASSUMPTIONS

Many underlying assumptions pervade share valuation theory and practice. These need not be spelt out but they will affect the outcome so the share valuer should be aware of them. In particular he should be quick to detect the preconceptions and biases lurking on the other side of the negotiating table. Examples of such basic economic concepts are as follows:

Risk aversion

Investors wish to maximise net returns but minimise risk so they will require a higher return to compensate for higher risk.

Opportunity cost

Investors undertake a given investment only after carefully weighing up not only the pros and cons but alternative investment opportunities foregone by purchasing the shares in question. This is specially relevant in view of the locked-in nature of much unquoted company investment and the common lack of a dividend policy among private companies primarily due to the need to expand through retained profits rather than through equity capital or loan finance.

Theory of value

This differentiates value from price. Essentially, value is either utility or exchange value. To justify a higher price than a base figure (say par value) must involve an increase in marginal utility to the prospective purchaser. The purpose of valuation techniques is to establish a rationale for this increase.

Diversification and specialisation

Multi-national corporations carry both these to the nth degree. However, the smaller firm may be better placed to exploit special opportunities arising through market gaps.

Theory of the firm

There will be substantial differences between small firm and large company development and these are explored at length later in the book.

Portfolio theory

Investment specialisation can offer greater returns — just as diversification can minimise risk — up to a point.

Efficient market hypothesis

The Stock Exchange prices, yields and ratios embody all the information available to the market at a given point in time. This is especially significant in arriving at the impact of socio-economic and macro-economic factors on share prices.

Monopoly and monopsony

These concepts will only have a very limited application to an unquoted company. However, in a given sector they may serve to further differentiate private and public companies in terms of products and markets and performance.

Stock market fluctuations

Unquoted shares will not show the same patterns of highs and lows within a relatively short term but will be far more likely to give due weight to fundamental factors such as earnings, assets and dividends.

Bid and flotation premiums

On the other hand, where an unquoted company is perceived to be a bid or flotation candidate a substantial premium would be expected for the shares, and the size of this could certainly be ascertained with reference to comparable quoted special situations.

Stages in share valuations

Preliminary

- A valuation request is received from a client.
  Ascertain:
  (a) the purpose of the valuation;
  (b) the status of the company;
  (c) the holding to be valued.
- Obtain:
  (a) three years' accounts or five if results
  fluctuate substantially;
  (b) the articles and memorandum of association;
  (c) updating statements;
  (d) supplementary information;
  (e) terms of leases;
  (f) management accounts and budgetary statements;
  (g) profits projections
  (h) assets valuations if justified.

Information assembly

- Determine the legal position of the shares (their class rights).
- Determine the legal and tax status of the company (whether private or public, limited or unlimited, close or otherwise).
- Consider the precise purpose of the valuation (whether statutory or commercial, if the former the tax involved).
- Determine the special valuation requirements (for instance the peculiar provisions of a particular tax or duty).
- Analyse the company accounts in a tabular form so its past and present can be seen clearly in graphic lucidity.
- Apply the appropriate valuation techniques.
- Arrive at a preliminary valuation range of acceptable figures.
- If goodwill is involved (and fundamentally it will be if the company is a profitable going concern) special valuation methods may be required.
- If a special class of company is involved (for example a farming or property company) again special principles apply.

Formulating the valuation

This involves two main stages:

- The preliminary valuation range must be narrowed down to a firm figure after adjusting, if necessary, for other elements, including any later available information and the precious gift of common sense.
- The valuation must be rationally justified in a readily comprehensible form for the client and any professional adviser or Revenue personnel who may happen to see it. This entails a professional layout and valuation models or model valuations are included later in this book with this precise requirement in mind.

Of course if the share valuer is not a professional it will still improve his valuation expertise if the appropriate procedure is followed to ensure that his approach is at least methodologically professional and therefore more likely to be correct. It will also improve his chances of communicating the end result to his colleagues and others involved in the business.

Finally a non-professional valuer who grasps the valuation methods set out in this text will be in a much better position to both appreciate and criticise the valuations done and submitted by the professionals in whatever capacity. On all these grounds the effort required has to be a worthwhile exercise.

In actually formulating the valuation the following principles should invariably be observed.

The basis of valuation This must be established and stated with due care in fiscally and factually correct terms.

Implicit assumptions These should be spelled out not left to the client to detect.

Alternative valuation approaches It is important that these are considered and listed even if ultimately dismissed.

Valuation ranges These should be stated and the ghost of spurious mathematical exactitude laid to rest.

Qualifications of value It may be that the valuation in question is based very much on the peculiar context of the transaction in point and would be unlikely to apply for any other purpose. If so, this qualification or caveat should be expressly stated just like an auditor's qualification of statutory accounts or a surveyor's reservations in his survey.

The level of information This will vary according to the stated client requirements, the tax involved, the consideration passing if any, statutory information standards, company accounting procedures and so on. The astute valuer actively involved in negotiations, whether with the Revenue or another professional adviser or commercial concern, will hold some ammunition in reserve. It is not necessarily a sensible idea to exhaust all one's powder and shot at the first salvo.

Report conclusion This will submit a recommended final figure together with all the supporting evidence. It is normal procedure to include the accounts on which the valuation is based and any accompanying professional asset valuations, directors' opinions, or chairman's statements as appendices so that the smooth progression of the valuation logic is left undisturbed by statistical bulk.

How to use this book This book aims to explain to the reader in as lucid and yet comprehensive a manner as is possible sufficient of the theory behind a professional share valuer's approach to enable him to undertake the task of valuation himself. It intends therefore to act as a practical primer to assist both the valuation expert and the non-professional. The expert should find numerous points of interest and assistance in specific areas while the whole subject is made accessible to someone new to the field who wants a view of the subject as a whole as well as a 'do-it-yourself' guide. With these twin goals in mind the text contains both in-depth discussion of principles and practices and prolific examples and illustrations. In the course of many years experience in share valuation and business consultancy the author has encountered myriad instances of confusion and misconception on the subject of unquoted share values. It is hoped that this work can contribute substantially to improving the situation, both in the professions and among the boards of directors they advise. By using it, professional practice should add to its expertise and directors or investors themselves should get a good idea whether they can do the job themselves or whether to call in the full-time professional.

2 Occasions for valuing unquoted shares

The basic valuation divide is between those involving the statutory open market valuation and those which do not. There are, perhaps surprisingly, a large number of various occasions when valuations of unquoted shares may be required:

- When a statutory open market valuation is required for any fiscal purpose. This is subject to so many special provisions and so much judicial interpretation that it requires a separate explanation (see chapter 6).
- When there is a sale at full arm's length between unconnected persons, possibly acting on professional advice. Such valuations will follow normal investment and valuation criteria, but will be made in the restricted market for unquoted shares and not import the hypothetical statutory open market.
- When a sale takes place within the family the adviser may be consulted by both parties to advise on a fair value acceptable to all of them. He may thus stand more in the role of independent arbitrator than a partisan defender of a client's interest. He should state as objectively as possible the valuation criteria and his consequential reasonable valuation. He should also be fully cognisant with the financial requirements of all the parties affected by the transaction. If relinquishment of control by the elder of the younger generation is contemplated, the implications for CTT and CGT must again be borne in mind.
- When the fair value has to be determined by the auditors under the company's articles the auditor will be well acquainted with the company's financial affairs and will qualify his valuation by stating that he acts in

this case as an independent arbitrator. Such a fair value is normally determined only once a year and not at specific valuation dates. The auditor must also be careful not to state detailed reasons for his valuation unless he wishes to have them critically examined, as in the leading case of *Dean* v *Prince* (1954) Ch 409 where Harman, J. stated:

> The plaintiff was extremely dissatisfied with that valuation. She would in my judgment nevertheless have been powerless in the matter if the auditors had declined to expand their views. They should have remembered that silence is golden in a matter of this kind and that, short of fraud or dishonesty, which no one attributed to the auditors in this case, there was no way of questioning that certificate if the auditors declined to give reasons for the result at which they had arrived.

The auditors in that case were saved by the vulnerability of the company's asset position due to the covenants on its property, as well as the fact that it had made losses.

- When there is a takeover bid, valuations by three different parties may be required: for the shareholders (in both companies) to evaluate the bid, the board to oppose the bid and the bidding board. Such valuations require detailed information — gathering of a prospectus-type and stand between the arm's length sales and new issue prices.
- When shares are offered as a security for a loan. The valuation criteria in this case will be the minimum price obtainable for the shares in the actual restricted market as compared with the best possible price in the statutory open market.
- When shares are being critically examined for whatever investment reason. In this case the valuer is concerned with pointing out the pros and cons of making an investment in the company by way of purchase of that particular holding. The exercise will be as much one of investment analysis as of actual share valuation.
- When a will bequest stipulates a holding of shares of a certain value which must then be ascertained to determine the number of shares passing to the legatee, apart that is from any specific fiscal criteria employed in the statutory valuation which can be safely ignored.
- When shares are sold to employees under share option or incentive schemes. A professional adviser can be called in on these occasions and the advice he gives should reflect his client's specific requirements as well as the relevant valuation criteria.
- When shares are allotted on a capital restructuring. The value of the shares allotted will take into account the revised capital position of the company although of course historic results will also be relevant.

- When a rights issue is made the valuation will point out the value of the rights to assist the prospective purchaser in deciding whether or not to buy.
- When directors have to consider whether to wind up or continue trading, the valuer may have to decide the respective relative value of the company on a break-up or a going-concern basis.
- When tax planning requires equalisation or other alterations to estates the valuer may be called in to determine the respective values of the spouses' holdings in the company. This will normally be for CGT or CTT purposes and of course the relevant fiscal provisions and the statutory open market provisions would have to be given full play.
- When gifts are made with taxation considerations in mind. Again the valuer must take into account the prospective fiscal impact of the transfers in determining the open market value of the subject matter of the gifts.
- When institutional investors are financially backing an unquoted company and take a minority stake, normally 25 to 30 per cent. In this case the valuer will determine his valuation of the shares, not on the notional statutory basis, but on the basis of the value of the shares in the restricted market. Moreover, he will also be concerned expressly with the flotation value and security aspects of the holding in question. Finally, he may have to take into account the investment requirement of the particular institution.
- When trust funds or other similar investors buy significant holdings in unquoted companies the valuer will proceed on a similar basis to the above point.
- When a company can purchase its own shares under the Companies Act 1981. This must be preceded by alterations to its articles and, if necessary, its memorandum. The share valuer will again decide a fair value for the shares in the actual restricted market rather than proceed on statutory open market lines.
- When enterprises are nationalised. Such rare events will entail valuation with specific and detailed reference to the precise terms of the nationalisation as well as the exact circumstances of the company in question and the industry in general to which the usual valuation techniques can then be applied as appropriate.
- On a corporate demerger when a larger company may be broken up by mutual agreement into two or more constituent parts and run accordingly on separate lines with different managements the valuer must take into account the specific statutory requirements of the demerger legislation in the Finance Act 1981, as amended. He will also possibly reverse the logic of merger and show that the parts may be as great as, or greater than, the whole. This could easily be the case where a hotchpotch of companies

with a poorly co-ordinated holding company is split up into a series of successful subsidiaries given their independence from ill-informed central direction possibly on the basis of local management buy-outs.

- On a management buy-out the valuer may have to assess the future earning potential of the company and its assets on the basis of the changed organisational structure. In doing this he will look critically at the management's own projections. These may well have been prepared with applications for corporate finance from venture capital institutions in view. He will also of course examine the prospects for business success from industry information, both at the local and national levels.
- On a purchase of assets or even a going concern from a receiver the valuer must estimate the impact of the receivership on the company and its business relationships as well as the future performance of the business, possibly on a piecemeal basis.

3 Nature of a share

A share gives its owner proportionate ownership of the company, but not of its assets which are owned by the company itself. Ever since *Salomon* v *Salomon* (1897) AC 22, it has been clear that the company has a separate legal existence apart from its ownership.

Shares must have a nominal value since the capital clause of any memorandum must state 'the divisions thereof into shares of a fixed amount' and therefore a par value of, for example, £1 or £5. Each issued share should have a number unless all of them are fully paid and rank equally (CA 1948, s.74).

Shares must be allotted by directors only as authorised by a company in general meeting or an appeal. They may not be issued at a discount (FA 1980, s.21) and an attempt to do this indirectly through debentures with exchange rights for ordinary shares was prevented by injunction in *Moseley* v *Kitty Fontein Mines* (1904) 2 Ch 108. Issue at a premium is, however, in order and results in transfer to a share premium account in the balance sheet (treated as capital except for bonus issues) under Section 56, Companies Act 1948. Relief from this provision is given by Section 36 to 41, Companies Act 1981 if 90 per cent of the equity is obtained, since premiums then need not be credited to the share premium account.

CLASS RIGHTS

If class rights are defined by a procedure for the normal variation, this must be followed. If a special resolution is necessary, then the minority can appeal to the court (CA 1948, s.72) if holders of 15 per cent of the issued capital reply within 21 days of the special resolution. If there is no variation procedure provided for, then the variation must be made by unanimous consent of all the members of the company. If the memorandum prohibits variation of rights, then this can be affected only by recourse to a Section 206, Companies Act 1948 reconstruction. If the class rights are variable as stated in the articles or the memorandum, then the variation procedure must be followed. If there is no power of variation in the articles then either the articles must be amended by a suitable special resolution or an extraordinary resolution at separate meetings of each class of shares under Section 72 must be obtained. Under Section 143, Companies Act 1948 and Section 33, Companies Act 1980 the creation of special rights or the variation by a special resolution must be given public notice unless the recent requirements are already met by filing of the articles and memorandum or copy of the special resolution in question. It is to be noted that the mere issue of shares in priority to existing shares is not a variation of rights within the Section (s.72 CA 1948) as seen in the case of *White* v *Bristol Aeroplane Co. Ltd,* (1953) 1 Ch 65, where there were 600 000 preference shares and 3.3 million ordinary shares. It was held that the issue of a further 600 000 preference shares as bonus issues to the ordinary shareholders did not constitute a variation of rights, but only something affecting their enjoyment. A similar principle was applied in the case of *Re John Smith's Tadcaster Brewery* Co. Ltd (1953) Ch 308 where it was held that the issue of fully-paid bonus shares out of undistributed profits would not affect the rights of the holders of the existing ordinary £1 shares.

A share confers rights and imposes liabilities under the general contractual framework of the company's memorandum and articles as well as the specific provisions of the Companies Acts and the decisions in company case-law. The rights include:

- The right to vote (unless expressly excluded as with non-voting ordinary or most preference shares except in special circumstances such as on a winding up or when dividends are in arrear).
- The right to attend meetings.
- The right to receive statutory accounts.
- The right to dividends as declared (though not in excess of that recommended by the directors — Table A, Article 114) of the Companies Act 1948.
- The right to transfer shares (subject to any restrictions in the articles). The restrictions may be very severe indeed and were upheld in the Court of Appeal in *Re Smith & Fawcett* (1942) 1 All ER 542 where the surviving director-shareholder who held 4001 shares (50 per cent) relied on his absolute and uncontrolled discretion to refuse to register the transfer of the deceased's 4001 shares by the executor son unless the latter would sell 2000 shares at a named price. If grounds for refusal are stated, however, then these may be challenged, and refusal to register the transfer to persons of whom they do not approve must be for reasons personal to the transferee, not as in *Re Bede Steamshipping Co. Ltd* (1917) 1 Ch 123, on the grounds

that small parcels of shares should not be sold to persons with no acquaintance with the company's business. The board must also act positively and not as in *Re Copal Varnish Co.* (1917) 2 Ch 349 where one director stayed away from meetings to prevent a quorum. Moreover the refusal must be within a reasonable time and this will prima facie not exceed the two months' registration period under Section 78, Companies Act 1948.

The other main type of restriction is the preemption clause requiring shares for transfer to be offered first to the directors or other members at a price often called the 'fair value' determined by a specified formula or by the directors or by the auditors. The Companies Act 1980 (Sections 17 and 18) also provides that a company issuing new shares for cash must first offer them to existing shareholders or, under the articles, those of a particular class in proportion to the existing shares held.

- The right not to be oppressed as a minority (CA 1948, s.210 applying before CA 1980).
- The right not to be unfairly prejudiced (CA 1980, s. 75).
- The right not to be bought out if part of a holding greater than 10 per cent (CA 1948, s.209).
- The right to petition the court to cancel an alteration of the company's objects if part of a 15 per cent holding (CA 1948, s.5).
- The right to block a special or extraordinary resolution (if part of a holding greater than 25 per cent).
- The right to day-to-day control, including the appointment of directors and declaration of dividends, if part of a holding greater than 50 per cent.
- The right to winding up control including any special or extraordinary resolution if part of a holding of 75 per cent or greater.
- The right to absolute control if part of a holding of 90 per cent or more.

A share also confers substantial liabilities:

- If the company is an unlimited company, the shareholder may have an unlimited liability for the company's debts, on the occasion of a winding up, as great as a sole trader or a partner.
- Forfeiture arises (Articles 33, 39, Table A, CA 1948) if the shareholder does not pay any call or instalment, but only under the express power usually found in the articles as any other reason for forfeiture represents an unlawful reduction of capital. Such a forfeiture must be exercised for the company's benefit and not merely for the benefit of an individual shareholder — *Re Esparto Trading Co.* (1879) 12 Ch D 191 (forfeiture exercised for the benefit of two director-shareholders).

Surrender avoids the formalities of forfeiture, but is not a provision in the Acts or in Table A, Companies Act 1948. Shares may be sold, but the purchaser becomes liable to the amounts unpaid and cannot vote until he has paid. If not sold within three years, the shares must be cancelled (CA 1980, s.38).

- A private company has a lien on shares for money owed to the company by any member for any reason. This can be enforced by sale or by withholding dividends or by refusal to register a transfer.

  By Section 38, Companies Act 1980, a lien of a public company on its own shares is void.
- A shareholder of a limited company is liable to calls on partly-paid shares. He also has limited liability for the company's debts to the extent that the shares remain unpaid for.
- If a member knowingly receives an unlawful distribution (for example indirectly out of undistributable reserves such as the capital redemption reserve fund) he is liable to repay it to the company.

The case-law shows the following exceptions, protecting minorities:

- *ultra vires* or illegal acts which cannot be majority-sanctioned (*Ashbury Railway Carriage and Iron Co.* v *Riche* (1875) LR 7 HL;
- use of a fraudulent power on the minority (*Menier* v *Hooper's Telegraph Works* (1874) 9 Ch App 350 — a contract indirectly secured for the benefit of the majority);
- a resolution procured by a trick (*Baillie* v *Oriental Telephone and Electric Co.* (1915) 1 Ch 503 — resolution obtained without proper disclosure of total amount of directors' fees of £45000);
- discrimination against the minority (*Clemens* v *Clemens* (1976) 2 All ER 268 — an effective reduction of a 45 per cent holding to a helpless minority);
- use of majority influence against the 'interests of justice' (*Prudential Assurance Co. Ltd* v *Newman Industries Ltd* (1979) 3 All ER 507 — a takeover planned by the directors on the basis of a valuation itself based on misleading information from the directors);
- execute an act requiring a special resolution passed.

There is also statutory protection of minorities under:

- Section 210, Companies Act 1948 providing relief from oppression for minorities before the Companies Act 1980 — see *Scottish CWS* v *Meyer* (1959) AC 324 where a series of oppressive acts by the Co-operative Society devaluing a subsidiary progressively resulted in an order to buy out the minority at £3.75 per share.

- Section 75, Companies Act 1980 for conduct of a company's affairs in a manner prejudicial to the minority in circumstances where a winding up would not be justified when the court may make such order as it thinks fit, including regulation, injunction, proceedings or share purchase.
- Section 222(f), Companies Act 1948 where the court considers it just and equitable to order the winding up of the company.
- On a Section 287 application to the court (under the Companies Act 1948) by a minority shareholder.
- On a Section 209, Companies Act 1948 application by a shareholder with a minority holding not exceeding 10 per cent to order the compulsory acquisition of his shares.
- Under Section 137, Companies Act 1948 the minority have a right to a poll.
- 5 per cent shareholders: Under Section 140, Companies Act 1948 these shareholders have a right to compel the company to give notice of resolutions and to circulate statements.

  10 per cent shareholders:

  (a) Under Section 132, Companies Act 1948 these shareholders have a right to compel the directors to hold an extraordinary general meeting.

  (b) Under Sections 164 and 172, CA 1948, the Department of Trade and Industry may, on petition from such shareholders, investigate the company's affairs and its ownership respectively.

  (c) Under Section 44, Companies Act 1981 these shareholders may apply to the court to cancel a special resolution offering financial assistance to purchase shares.

  (d) Major shareholders may requisition a company investigation of its share ownership and ask the court to restrict shares where replies are unsatisfactory (under CA 1981, ss.74 and 76).
- 15 per cent shareholders: These shareholders may apply to the court to cancel a special resolution altering the company's objects and cancel a variation of class rights (under CA 1948, ss. 5 and 72, respectively).

DIVIDENDS

- Dividend payments are now regulated by Sections 39 to 45, Companies Act 1980 so that distributions of public or private companies other than investment companies can only be made out of realised profits (whether revenue or capital) less realised losses on a continuing basis so that losses must be paid off before any further distribution. Furthermore, a public company can only distribute if its net assets equal its share capital and distributable reserves. The availability of distributions is then determined on the basis of the relevant accounts.

- A preference shareholder cannot compel payment of a dividend even where there are more than sufficient profits.
- Dividends are recommended by directors and declared in general meeting whereupon a debt due to the shareholders is created. Interim dividends require only a director's power under the articles and not approval in general meeting so that they create no such debt.
- Dividends, unless the articles so provide otherwise, must be paid in cash (see *Wood* v *Odessa Waterworks Co.* (1889) 42 Ch D 636 where a company was restrained from giving debentures in lieu of cash).

MEETINGS

These are of three kinds:

- The annual general meeting which the company is statutorily obliged to call and which is called by the Department of Trade and Industry under Section 131, Companies Act 1948 in default of this.
  This is to determine such ordinary business as dividends, the accounts, the directors' and auditors' reports, appointment of directors and auditors and fixing the auditors' remuneration.
- An extraordinary general meeting — Section 132, Companies Act 1948. This is simply any general meeting other than the annual general meeting. It is required to pass an extraordinary general resolution (see below).
- Class meetings are held under Section 5, Companies Act 1948 and are required to determine variations of class rights.

RESOLUTIONS

These are:

- Ordinary resolutions which apply except in so far as either statute or the memorandum or articles require a special or extraordinary resolution to transact business. They are passed by a simple majority.
- A special resolution requires a 75 per cent majority and normally 21 days' notice (less if 95 per cent agree). A special resolution is required for a variety of significant reasons, such as the following:

(a) to alter the objects in the memorandum;

(b) to alter the articles (CA 1948, s.10);

(c) to commence a winding up (CA 1948, s.222);

(d) to sanction a sale of the company (CA 1948, s.287);

(e) to authorise financial assistance in the purchase of shares (CA 1981, s.43);

(f) to authorise off-market purchases of the company's own shares (CA 1981, s.47).

- An extraordinary resolution is required, for example under Section 32, Companies Act 1980, to vary class rights, and under Section 278, Companies Act 1948 for a creditors' voluntary winding up. A 75 per cent majority is required to pass one.

DIRECTORS

- A director is in company law 'any person occupying the position of director by whatever name called' (CA 1948, s.455).
- The director is now one of the relevant particulars on a company's creation (CA 1976, s.21).
- A director may be appointed for life under the articles and, if this is done before 18 July 1945, he cannot be removed.
- The articles may permit the appointment of alternate directors to act in a director's absence.
- The director is entitled to remuneration only if the articles so permit (see *Hutton* v *West Cork Railway Co.* (1883) 23 Ch D 654). If there is no fixed amount of remuneration, then evidently he cannot sue on a *quantum meruit* (see *Re Richmond Gate Property Co. Ltd* (1965) 1 WLR 335).
- The articles may permit assignment of the director's office.
- The articles of a private company may permit a director to nominate his successor.
- The Companies Act 1981 creates the concept of shadow directors, that is any person in accordance with whose instructions a director is accustomed to act.
- A register of directors' interests must be kept for inspection.
- Financial control rests with the board and cannot be usurped, for example by an attempted declaration of dividends in General Meeting (see *Scott* v *Scott* (1943) 1 All ER 582).

- Management of the company is conducted essentially through board meetings.
- A managing director may be appointed under the Articles. He is readily removable by the board, though damages for dismissal may result, as in *Southern Foundries* v *Shirlaw* (1940) AC 701 where it was held that the dismissal of the managing director was effective, but he was entitled to very substantial damages of £10 000.

4 The private and public company background

The first Companies Act allowing companies incorporation by registration rather than special Acts of Parliament or Royal Charter was the Joint Stock Companies Act 1844 and since then there have been Companies Acts in 1855, 1856, 1862, 1900, 1907, 1908, 1929, 1947, 1948, 1967, 1976, 1980 and 1981. The significant Companies Acts that concern the share valuer at present are, of course, the Companies Acts for 1948 to 1985. Until the Companies Act 1980, private companies were defined as companies with restrictions on transfer of their shares and with membership restricted to a maximum of 50 members. Public companies were defined negatively as simply all companies that were not private companies statutorily defined. The statutory and other restrictions on transfer under a private company's articles were a very significant factor in depressing the market value of the shares. They could range from articles incorporating Table A, Companies Act 1948 with the directors' discretionary refusal to register a transfer of shares to others, for instance imposing automatic accrual to the existing shareholders on the death of any member, and a whole spectrum of possible restrictions in between. Indeed, in many cases, the restrictions were such that there would be effectively a non-existent market for the shares, or a transfer at a minimal fair value, or even without payment. The restriction on the size of the company's membership was also another inhibiting factor on its potential growth.

THE PRESENT POSITION

As at the start of 1984, there were some 880 000 private companies, some 15 000 public but unquoted companies and some 4000 public quoted companies, sometimes called listed companies. The concept of a private company has now been reversed by the Companies Act 1980. Instead of being positively defined with reference to a statutorily imposed restriction on transfer, it is now defined as any company that is not a public company. The latter is in turn now positively defined as a company when it has:

- a minimum of seven members;
- an authorised capital of £50 000 (CA 1982, s.4(2);
- the designation plc (CA 1980, s.2).

A public unquoted company is still possible subject to the new statutory minimum limits. The new tax relief for new business ventures and the possibility of a company now purchasing its own shares, as well as the removal of the need for a private company to impose restrictions on transfer in its articles, have given new potential dimensions to the valuation of unquoted shares. In particular, by widening the possible extent of the market since the company is now a prospective purchaser. There is also the unlisted securities market as another half-way house between unlisted and listed status. However, it is doubtful whether companies or their shareholders will be rushing into the arena to change their existing memorandum and articles wholesale. Nor will the new venture's income tax relief generate an investment boom in new technology companies and so on, aside from a general economic revival. The size and significance of the stock market as the investment climate on which private companies operate must always be considered.

DIFFERENCES BETWEEN PRIVATE AND PUBLIC COMPANIES

It is useful to tabulate the differences between a private and public company.

- Before 1980 private companies had a statutorily imposed restriction on transfer.
- Private companies need only have one director, a public company must have at least two.
- Private companies need only have one member, a public company at least three.
- Private companies are invariably close companies for tax purposes, public companies are invariably not.
- Private companies cannot offer their shares to the public, public companies can. Indeed it is now an offence under the Companies Act for private companies to attempt to do so.
- Private companies do not generally pay dividends, public companies generally do.

- Private companies can suffer shortfall assessments on their investment income, public companies who are generally not close companies cannot be so assessed.
- Private companies may have only £2 issued capital, a public company must have at least £50000 authorised capital of which at least one-quarter must be fully-paid.
- A private company cannot achieve the same growth by acquisition as a public company as it has no ready market for its shares.
- A private company, if unlimited, need not lodge statutory accounts, a public company cannot escape this requirement.
- A private company's shareholders are unlikely to be institutional investors, the public quoted companies have a preponderance of institutional investors.
- A private company may retain substantial profits since it does not have the same dividend pressure as a public company.
- A private company has much greater restricted borrowing powers than a public company and hence a greater need to generate growth through internal funding.
- A private company's market is more restricted so it cannot achieve the same market share as a corresponding public company.
- A private company's size is generally so much smaller that it cannot achieve the same degree of either economies of scale or diversification of product as a public company.
- A private company is unlikely to achieve the professional management with the guaranteed succession of a public company.
- The rules of the City Code on takeovers and mergers apply to public companies, not private companies.
- The share prices in private companies will not fluctuate as violently as those of public companies.
- A public company may not accept payment for its shares by an undertaking to do work (CA 1981, s.20(2)).
- The non-cash consideration of a public company must be valued independently and a report made to the company within six months preceding the allotment (CA 1980, s.24).

Of course, no company shares may be allotted at a discount (CA 1948, s.21). Thus in the case of *Ooregum Goldmining Co. of India Ltd* v *Roper* (1982) the court decided that an attempt to issue £1 preference shares with 75p credited as fully paid-up was unlawful.

5 The statutory open market valuation

The statutory open market valuation may well be the most frequent type of share valuation to be encountered by the share valuer. It has many peculiar features which have emerged over the long line of decided cases on what must be among the most frequently interpreted of all fiscal provisions, and these propositions illustrate its multi-faceted nature.

- The classic concept is of a hypothetical willing buyer and hypothetical willing seller in free negotiation in a hypothetical transaction: see Ploughman, J. in *Re Lynall* as approved by the House of Lords in *Lynall* v *IRC* (1972) AC 680.
- The hypothetical purchaser cannot therefore be presupposed to be a family member. *Ex hypothesi* he cannot be supposed to be a director. On the other hand, 'that is not to say that directors as such are to be ignored. All likely purchasers are deemed to be in the market.' (Harman, L.J. in *Re Lynall* (1970) 1 Ch. 138.)
- The open market is the whole world of potential purchasers. As the Lord Chancellor stated in the House of Lords in the *Crossman* v *IRC* (1937) AC26 case:

  > In fixing those figures [the adjudicated share values] it appears from the judgment that Lord Plendor did not exclude anybody or include anybody in particular; he considered the matter generally. In my opinion that is the right way to arrive at the value in the open market.

- The kind of likely purchasers were considered by Sir Henry Benson in his expert testimony in the *Lynnall* case and included in his fairly exhaustive categories:

  (a) the existing shareholders;

(b) competitor companies;

(c) industrial holding companies;

(d) financial conglomerates;

(e) institutional investors;

(f) higher-rate taxpayers;

(g) directors of the company;

(h) merchant banks;

(i) preventure of capital lenders such as Estate Duty Investment Trust (EDITH) and Industrial and Commercial Finance Corporation (ICFC);

(j) the public at large.

- The longer nature of the investment and the motives behind it were considered by Dankwerts, J. in *Re Holt* (1953) 32 ATC 402 when he said:

> I think that the kind of investor who would purchase shares in a private company of this kind ... would be different from any common kind of purchaser of shares in the Stock Exchange and would rather be the exceptional kind of investor who had some special reason for putting his money into shares of this kind. He would in my view be the kind of investor who would not rush hurriedly into the transaction.

- Hindsight is not allowable in assessing the relevant valuation factors. As Dankwerts, J. said in the *Re Holt* case:

> It is necessary to assume the prophetic vision of a prospective purchaser at the moment of the death of the deceased and firmly to reject the wisdom which might be provided by the knowledge of subsequent events.

- Unless the open market criteria are in any case satisfied, past share prices are not appropriate measures of the statutory open market value. At the very least a differential of around 10 per cent should be applied to the restricted market price to arrive at a statutory open market value: see *McNamee* v *Revenue Commissioners* (1954) IrR 214. Moreover, such private treaty sales are not themselves open market sales within the statutory definition — see Lord Reid's speech in the *Lynall* case.

- The impossibility of placing the property on the open market at the valuation date is not strictly relevant: see *Duke of Buccleuch* v *IRC* (1967) 1 All ER 129 where 119000 acres of farmland were to be valued and it was generally accepted that there was no actual market for such a large acreage.

- It is irrelevant that a sale in the open market is actually prohibited by the articles or even by statute: see *Re Aschrott Clifton* v *Strauss* (1927) 1 Ch 313.

- A covenant not to sell would not necessarily make it an open market value: see *British Motor Trade Association* v *Gilbert* (1951) 2 All ER 641. The actual conditions affecting the property at the valuation date may not prevent an open market valuation: see *IRC* v *Graham's Trustees* (1971) SLT 46.
- The seller is as hypothetical and therefore as anonymous as the purchaser: see *Salomon* v *C of C and E* (1966) 3 WLR 36.
- The open market value is the best possible price achievable in the circumstances: see *Re Hayes Will Trust* (1971) 1 WLR 758.
- The property will be put on the market in such a way as to achieve the best possible price: see *Ellesmere* v *IRC* (1918) 119 LT 568.
- A valuation higher than a previous Stock Exchange marking is not necessarily an unfair one: see *Re Presscaps Ltd* (1949) 1 All ER 1013.
- A reasonable valuation could vary 10 per cent either side of a true open market price: see *Re Claridge, Holt & Co. Ltd* (1900). This concept of the valuation range of acceptable values is of very great practical significance in day-to-day negotiations. In particular, it can be used to anticipate or resolve situations that would otherwise be deadlocked without there being necessarily very much at stake in terms of tax.
- Acquisition by partners on a death will not prevent an open market value of the deceased's share: see *Dean* v *Prince* (1954) 1 All ER 749.
- Extremely restrictive articles of association will not eliminate the possibility of an open market valuation: see *Re Thornley* (1928) 7 ATC 178 where the shares were held by father and son and the articles provided for: conversion to preference shares of the ordinary shares held by either as at the death of the other; and an automatic offer of sale to the survivor of them.
- Testamentary options are not a test of open market value: see *Lord Advocate* v *Woods Trustees* (1910) 1 SLT 186.
- The statutory open market value has a similar application for all taxes. Thus the phraseology is very similar for IHT under Section 38, Finance Act 1975 and CGT under Section 150, CGTA 1979. Both statutory provisions were based on the old estate duty open market valuation under Section 7(5), Finance Act 1894. The ratio for this proposition is also confirmed in the leading case of *Crabtree* v *Hinchcliffe* (1972) AC 707 decided at the time of the *Lynall* case. The value may also be applied for stamp duty purposes (*Stanyforth* v *IRC* (1930) AC 339) and *semble* for income tax purposes.
- Purchase at open market value may enable the executors to override the value for estate duty purposes: see *Mason* v *Stroud* (1971) 215 EG 1303.

- Differentials must be maintained for different sizes of holdings where these carry differing legal powers: see *Ocean Coal Co. Ltd* v *Powell Duffryn Steam Coal Co. Ltd* (1932) 1 Ch 654. This proposition is the primary axiom of share valuation theory and practice.
- The price fixed by the articles can be as much an appreciatory as a depreciatory factor: this was a significant element in the decision in the *Crossman* case. The reason behind this is that the right to sell is only one of the collection of rights attaching to a shareholding and the right to buy at the articles' price may prove equally important.
- Restrictive clauses in the articles have been upheld by the courts in *Re Smith & Fawcett* (1942) 1 All ER 542. They are therefore a material factor in the valuation and can be given effect so that they determine to some extent the range of the market. The principle originally laid down in *A-G* v *Jameson* (1905) 2 IrR 218 is that the purchaser acquires the shares in the notional open market and then holds them subject to the articles.
- Different bases of valuation vary according to circumstances and, if necessary to arrive at a reasonable market value, even a minority holding may be valued on an assets basis: see *A-G (Ceylon)* v *Mackie* (1952) 2 All ER 775. This is, of course, when an earnings-based valuation would be either impossible or, at best, misleading.
- Judicial guidance and expert testimony on the valuation of different sizes of holdings is available in *Holt* v *IRC* (6.25 per cent), *IRC* v *Crossman* (10 per cent), *Salvesen's Trustees* v *IRC* (1930) 9 ATC 43 (33.33 per cent), *Re W.F. Courthope* (1928) 7 ATC 538 (48 per cent) and *McConnell's Trustees* v *IRC* (1927) SLT 14, a full control (99 per cent) holding. The most recent leading case on share valuation, *Lynall* v *IRC*, involved a 28 per cent influential minority-holding in a company on the verge of flotation.

THE RELATIONSHIP BETWEEN THE STATUTORY OPEN MARKET AND THE ACTUAL MARKET

This may come close to identity where there is a reasonably active market in the shares and a wide variety of potential purchasers. For practical purposes these actual transactions may then furnish the best possible evidence of the open market value if conducted in each case fully at arm's length, and may well be treated as such by the Revenue. These may then prove preferable to any theoretical formulations of value, any of which will necessarily involve the introduction of at least one arbitrary figure somewhere along the line. Such a case is not, however, the norm. Much commoner are articles restricting transfers to existing shareholders and giving them first option at a favourable pre-emption price. The latter will often be the fair value determined annually by the company's auditors. This is by no means decisive of the statutory open market value. Indeed in the leading *Crossman* case, the market value is held to be around $1\frac{1}{2} \times$ the articles price, in spite of extremely restrictive articles.

In the relatively rare extreme case there may be effectively no market at all since the articles may provide for automatic accrual to existing shareholders on a shareholder's death. In this event the open market value is virtually independent of the actual market which is effectively non-existent. It must then be determined on the *Crossman* assumptions that the purchaser would be entitled to have his purchase registered by the directors and would then hold his shares subject to the articles. In this case the restrictions also have an obverse side since the purchaser would in future be entitled to buy other shares at the favourable articles price or enjoy the right to automatic accrual. Clearly the restrictive nature of the articles is in fact merely one of very many valuation factors which have to be taken into account. It cannot preclude the value attaching to the shares if the other valuation criteria apply and suggest that there could be an open market purchaser who would be prepared to pay a positive price.

Similar principles apply if the only actual market comprises existing shareholders who, at the relevant time, and where it is established, are in fact unable or unwilling to buy the shares in question. This means in effect that there is no actual market. The hypothetical open market still exists, however, and a hypothetical price can therefore by negotiated as to what a purchaser would pay for locked-in, longer-term investment of this sort with little prospect of a short-term income or capital return and with little possibility of realising his capital investment should he suddenly require it. In fact such a purchaser fits the judicial description of a characteristic purchaser of unquoted private company shares envisaged in the case of *Re Holt*.

STATUTORY INFORMATION STANDARDS

These are set out in paragraph 13, Schedule 10, Finance Act 1975 for IHT and Section 152, Capital Gains Tax 1979 for CGT. The amending legislation purports to restore commercial reality to the statutory open market valuations by importing information standards founded on the practice of parties in actual market transactions, since their Lordships have effectively severed this connection in the *Lynall* case. At the same time, the basic open market concept that no potential buyer should be excluded is retained and the information deemed available is not defined too precisely in legalistic terms. An appeal to the market base and to different practices for different trades and businesses is thus more than theoretically possible. The legislation necessarily implies that the prospective purchaser will be approved by the particular board and information reasonably requested will be made available.

Subsection (3) of Section 152 emphasises the information a prudent purchaser in a full arm's length private treaty sale would require. This is because the hypothetical seller can in any case impart all the published information he possesses as holder of the shares in question and the company's articles may in fact limit the information which he as a shareholder could demand from the company and pass on to the purchaser. Since the purchaser is also entirely anonymous, his requirements must be objectively determined. In effect, both parties to the transaction are statutorily deemed to possess all the relevant information such a sale would involve if they are both to be willingly engaged in the negotiations. This point was made most cogently in a Court of Appeal whose ratio was embodied in the new statutory provision. There is, moreover, nothing restrictive or exclusive in this Section (and the corresponding IHT paragraph). The private treaty information standards extend the available information beyond the published information and other narrower tests. It merely supplements the information a purchaser could obtain by other means, for example through his professional agents, or by local knowledge of development schemes. Furthermore, the Section does not require directors to ascertain matters outside their knowledge, for example the true ownership of nominee holdings. This would appear to apply, for instance, to financial information which the management accounting systems might not make available even to the board. Nor does the Section provide any basis or guidelines for assessing the significance of the information objectively available. Ultimately, therefore, the issue of the extent of disclosure and its importance in the context of the share valuation can only be determined as regards any given company and its peculiar circumstances by expert witnesses before the Special Commissioners or on appeal before the court.

However, the most reasonable approach is evidently to suppose that boards of directors will disclose further information to the prospective purchaser, varying the two objective criteria: the size or influence of the holding as a proportion of the voting share capital; and the amount of outlay the purchaser is potentially incurring. Thus a purchaser of an influential minority holding of between 25.1 and 49.9 per cent of the voting capital — the kind of holding concerned in the *Lynall* case — would reasonably expect fairly full disclosure of material information about the company's past, present and future prospects and performances. A purchaser of 50 per cent of the voting capital, or of the controlling interest, would reasonably expect full disclosure of all such particulars. Equally, a purchaser of 25 per cent or less that nevertheless involved him in a prospective outlay of say £50000 would perhaps expect a fairly full disclosure by virtue of that fact. This view receives support from the uncontradicted expert witnesses for the Crown — Sir Henry Benson and Mr J.M.G. Andrews — in the *Lynall* case.

The information a prudent purchaser might reasonably require, within the terms of the relevant legislation, would comprise general information such as the history and prospects of the industry (as suggested in the *Salvesen* and *Holt* cases) and the industrial and commercial impact of contemporaneous economic, political, social and fiscal events and the following specific items:

- the company's history and prospects, including interim results;
- the provisions in the company's articles of association relating to costs, rights and shares;

- the prospects of a directorship;
- the identities, ages and holdings of other shareholders (in order to assess possibilities of transactions and possible influence in the company's affairs since the other shareholders are not excluded from the hypothetical open market and their holdings are not hypothetical but actualities);
- statutory accounts for at least three years before the date of valuation and in the case of a cyclical business possibly five years could be justified;
- particulars of market values of assets if materially different from book values;
- particulars of any flotation, quotation, takeover, merger, sale of the company or any other similar factor that might enhance the value of the shares;
- particulars of an investment or property company's portfolio of securities of properties.

The significance of the legislative emphasis on the prudent purchaser's position is threefold. Firstly, the vendor shareholder's possible special knowledge is thereby excluded. Secondly, there may be restrictions under the articles on disclosures by the vendor. Thirdly, the prudent purchaser's position has been well documented in them by the courts. The additional reference to 'at arm's length' precludes any argument modifying the statutory standard on the grounds that the prudent purchaser might possibly be a member of the family who would reasonably require less information.

THE CASE OF THE SPECIAL PURCHASER

The existence of the person with a particular interest in acquiring the property — the so-called special purchaser — creates problems in determining statutory open market valuations since, while it is judicially established that the special purchaser's price is not the open market price (see *Crossman* v *IRC* (1937) AC 26), it is equally well established that the special purchaser must be considered (*Robinson Bros. (Brewers) Ltd* v *Houghton and Chester-le-Street Assessment Committee* (1938) AC 321).

As the statutory open market is one from which no particular vendor or purchaser is excluded, by implication the special purchaser is not excluded. While his price is no more an appropriate measure of open market values and the fair value than under the company's articles of association is, it is a moot point how far that price is to be affected in the statutory valuation. The decided cases suggest that, depending on the circumstances, the range may vary from fairly full reflection to a pretty minimal one. Certainly the courts in the leading case of *Crossman* dismiss the possibility that the holding would be of particular interest to a trust corporation on the grounds that such a sale would not satisfy the open market criterion and should not be taken into account. However, the extremely restrictive articles imposed by the company in that case could arguably have deterred such a purchaser from buying the shares anyway. Moreover, Lord Plender's professional valuation, which was accepted by the courts, supposedly took all purchases into account and on this footing no further account had to be taken of the special purchaser price.

An additional weakness of using the *Crossman* case as an argument against reliance on the special purchaser element when higher value is required (for example in CGT Budget day election cases or for acquisition values based on open market price) is that the essential ratio concerned how effective a limitation the articles price was on the statutory open market value. Since the observation on the special purchaser's element was strictly *obiter* it was of an extremely persuasive value, given the approval of *Crossman* in *Lynall.*

The alternative arguments on this matter are as follows:

- The special purchaser need pay only a nominal amount (possibly only one bid) over the open market price of that otherwise obtained in his absence. The special purchaser's price should therefore only have a nominal impact on the statutory open market value. This argument has some validity where the spread of shareholdings is wide and the influence of any potential purchaser is greatly diminished — rather like the potential influence of any given firm in the economic theory of perfect competition. However, it may well lack force in the context of close-controlled private companies. In particular, the common experience with such companies is that the existing shareholdings will, invariably be in many cases, special purchasers anxious to prevent the entry of the outside shareholder, described as the detested intruder in one well-known judicial comment.

- Special purchasers may be known to speculate and this would force the price upwards and might indeed come close to the special purchaser's price in the knowledge that a ready profit could still be made by onward sale to the special purchaser. In such a situation the open market price might be just one bid below the special purchaser's price. Such a case was *IRC* v *Clay* (1914) 3 KB 466 and the associated case of *Glass* v *IRC* (1915) SC 449.

- In a specific situation where, say, the distribution of existing shareholdings (whose owners are, after all, in the open market) is 40 per cent to one and 40 per cent to another while 20 per cent is held by a third party as shares to be valued, there will then be two shareholders bidding for control, each of whom could therefore be said to be willing to pay the special purchaser's price. In this case a willing vendor would be unlikely to accept much less than a special purchaser's price. This is certainly an argument for a premium over the open market value that would otherwise apply. The extent of its validity might well depend on the actual circumstances of the parties in question.

- In any special purchaser situation — and in most cases this element will be absent — the availability, willingness and capability of the special purchaser must be demonstrated as a question of fact, just like a potential takeover, merger or liquidation or other value-enhancing factor. Granted this is so, the open market price might well approach the special purchaser's price. Failing such evidence, the special purchaser element might well justify little if any increment over the statutory open market value determined on the usual basis. These possibilities cover, of course, the entire spectrum of open market value.
- One particular application of this element is the argument that the notional disposal and reacquisition expressly provided in the Budget day election necessarily imparts a special purchaser element. The taxpayer is deemed to reacquire the shares at market value. This existing holding is a given fact and not a hypothetical element in the hypothetical transaction. Therefore, if he reacquires a small minority holding that, together with the existing holding, gives him control, he will pay the premium for control that will attach to the minority holding in this context. The idea is that the statutory provision embodies the concept of a market where the effective sale is between the taxpayer and himself as a willing vendor and special purchaser, respectively. This overlooks the fact that the reacquisition is expressly stated to be at market value which is not specifically defined in this context, so that the main valuation provision under Section 19, CGTA 1979 must apply. There is no express or implied modification of that provision, hence it is the open market value of the asset in question, that is the holding itself in view of the isolation that must be considered. There is certainly no restriction on the market to a statutorily imposed concept of a sale between the taxpayer and himself in a dual role. Evidently, the deemed provision is merely machinery for implementing the Budget-day valuation at 6 April 1965 market value to apply as a notional acquisition value where this may prove advantageous to the taxpayer.

OTHER MODIFICATIONS OF OPEN MARKET VALUE

- For both IHT and CGT there is no magnitude allowance in that there is no reduction in the value of the shares on the grounds that the whole holding — which may be very substantial indeed and the appearance of which on the open market would normally depress the open market price — is put on the market at the same time (CGTA 1979, s.3 (2), and proviso to s.160, IHT Act 1984). This factor is thus simply disregarded for valuation purposes and this adds to the hypothetical nature of the transaction embodied in the open market value. However, this modification of market value may itself require qualification since the characteristic locked-in nature of unquoted private company investment means that a substantial holding would necessarily mean a smaller class of interested investors. Arguably, the size of the holding in the leading case of *Salvesen's Trustees* v *IRC* (1930) 9 ATC 1943 (decided under the old estate duty regime which contained a similar provision in Section 60, Finance (1909–10) Act 1910) was a material factor in the valuation of a 33 per cent influential minority holding at £3 per share, representing a very substantial 70 per cent discount of the net asset value.

- For IHT valuations on a death, any changes that may have occurred by reason of a death are to be taken into account by virtue of paragraph 9, Schedule 10, Finance Act 1975. Thus any adverse effect of the death of a founding chairman or other driving force behind the company is a valuation factor. On the other hand, cogent evidence of the personal goodwill attributable to him would be required. Later accounts would have to be produced which might not necessarily be advantageous. Moreover, such a death might entail reorganisation that could enable a locked-in shareholder to have a better chance to realise his investment and this could increase the value of the shares. Finally, the company itself could possibly have replaced the deceased at less cost. This may be a factor where the director's remuneration is arguably excessive.
- Options to purchase, or other restrictions on disposal, are taken into account for IHT purposes, but only if for consideration, and if the contract was a chargeable transfer an allowance should be made for the value transferred (FA 1975 para. 5(1), sch. 10).

COMMERCIAL VALUATIONS

It is clear that whether a statutory valuation or a commercial valuation is required is crucial in determining the valuation approach. As the open market valuation receives detailed treatment elsewhere the elements of commercial valuations should be outlined here.

A critical distinction is sometimes drawn between value and price based on the difference between what might be called the intrinsic worth of the shares in question and the price they might fetch if actually sold in the real market. Concepts of intrinsic worth recall the fundamentalist approach of one school of investment analysis which evaluates the shares of quoted companies on the basis of available data and projections from these expressed in such basic valuation and analytical tools as dividend yield, earnings yield, price earnings ratio, net asset value and equity market capitalisation, as compared with current share price. These are of course amenable to mathematical expression but in arriving at a realistic price, what is what commercial valuations are all about, the share valuer must make several drastic adjustments. He is still of course aiming to arrive at the classic market balance between the price position of the buyer and that of the seller. To achieve commercial realism he must take far greater account of subjective factors and facts specific to that particular situation as it affects both the proposed parties to the transaction. If there is a special market premium due to the existence of a special purchaser then this must be given full weight. In fact the negotiated price would be very likely to approach the special purchaser's price, since, after all, the special purchaser would be there as a potential market maker. On the other hand, the distinctly depressive factors on share price in private companies can also be given full play. These include extremely restrictive articles which may effectively mean there is virtually no market in the shares or a resale price likely to be no more than par. Such factors if spelled out and properly interpreted could justify little or no premium over par value. On the other side there may be positive value in such factors as: the family nature of the company and therefore the determination of the other shareholders to pay a high enough price to keep out non-family purchasers; the directors and their intimate knowledge of the workings of the business and its prospective potential expressed in their subjective evaluation of it when buying or selling; the active involvement of particular persons in the company with special talents or abilities that enhance its profits potential, and so on.

In arriving at realistic values for commercial purposes the valuer should take full account of these various subjective factors but he will still go through the normal valuation process, taking on board any special situations or unusual company elements and applying the valuation techniques analysed elsewhere. He will still be using comparability studies and equity indices just as he will be using similar capacity for analysis, comparison and assessment in weighing up the factual, statistical and other evidence, persuading himself and then his clients, co-directors, or colleagues as to the correctness of his conclusions. He may be acting under specific instructions by one party to the transaction to arrive at the lowest reasonable value to get the prospective purchaser the best value for money, if not a bargain basement price. Conversely, he may be advising the seller on the highest initial opening bid price or the lowest acceptable value within reason. In such cases he will be marshalling his valuation expertise into presentation of as powerful a case as possible within his professional competence. He is not in that situation as an arbitrator or judge. He is professionally-paid advocate, not far removed from a barrister operating in the rarified atmosphere of an appeal court.

To illustrate the difference in approach required of a commercial valuer as opposed to the statutory open market approach, I have included one example of such a professional valuation in Chapter 13. I trust this will prove both enlightening and eye-opening.

CONCLUSION

The fundamental difference between open market and commercial valuations is that commercial valuations will be more realistic because they will move in accordance with the subjective elements affecting the shares rather than the hypothetical and often highly artificial statutory requirements. It follows that some appreciatory factors will be exaggerated, such as special purchaser features, but for the most part it is the depreciatory incidents affecting private company shares, such as restrictive articles and lack of marketability, that will come into prominence. It also follows that many, if not most, commercial valuations will stand at a lower level than would apply if they came about as statutory valuations. It will also be appreciated that where controlling interests are concerned, the articles' restrictions may be irrelevant and the narrow market argument can be rebutted by the fact that the private company can go public if other criteria for flotation, if only on the USM, are evidently satisfied. The same will apply where the company is effectively run as a partnership so that the director/shareholders would only sell as a going concern so that the value of even a minority director's stake should be valued as the arithmetic proportion of the value of a 100 percent holding if a commercial valuation is involved.

6 Valuations for takeovers and mergers

Some 15 000 companies alone (some 90 per cent of them unquoted) were acquired by quoted public companies during the 22-year period, 1954–75. The pace of such activity reflects the prevalent economic climate and, in particular, the stock market and other capital markets at the time. Thus the peak merger booms coincided with the stock market booms of 1952–55, 1967–68 and 1971–73. Conversely, the recessions of 1974–76 and 1980–81 had an adverse impact on the takeover market, but this has now recovered with the 1982–83 stock market recovery.

In valuing for the purposes of takeovers and mergers, initial enquiry demands:

- analysis of the advantages and disadvantages of mergers/takeovers in general and the merger/takeover in particular;
- examination of the kind of merger/takeover involved; and
- determination of the values of the acquired and the acquiring company, both before and after the merger/takeover.

ADVANTAGES AND DISADVANTAGES

The advantages include:

- better planning for the expanded group of companies;
- economies of scale, particularly important in mass production industries and services;
- savings in stock levels and purchases due to greater buying power and computerised distribution;

- financial efficiency due to overall supervision with a common banker;
- easier access to capital markets by virtue of greater size;
- savings in overheads and other administrative expenditure;
- improved research and development;
- diversification of product for the acquiring company, or for both;
- improved management succession;
- possible improved marketability of shares through new flotation prospects;
- better control of the market, possibly leading to market leadership of the group.

The disadvantages include:

- more impersonality, though the personal touch may still be maintained;
- possible loss of trade names, though these may be retained;
- taxes and fees and other incidental costs;
- monopoly or monopolistic tendencies and practices;
- empire building due to expansion for its own sake;
- personality clashes and incompatabilities — though if a merger/takeover proceeds these are presumably resolvable;
- some unfortunate case histories — for example, Letraset Ltd after taking over Stanley Gibbons Ltd, where the acquired company consistently underperformed for a number of years;
- possible undervaluation or overvaluation of the acquired company. This could result in a takeover version of the Amersham public issue which was, as events proved, a massive undervaluation.

TYPES OF MERGER/TAKEOVER

- Horizontal mergers/takeovers — the commonest kind — where a company in a similar kind of business is acquired.
- Vertical mergers/takeovers — where a company above or below the production or service point is acquired, for example a supplier acquires a buyer or vice versa.
- Conglomerate mergers/takeovers — a phenomenon of the 1960s and 1970s, notoriously for example Slater-Walker. The knitting together of incredibly diverse companies with a financial and legal common link only.

THE VALUES OF THE COMPANIES

The values of the companies depend initially, in part, on the way the merger/takeover proceeds. This can be in one of three ways.

- By a holding company, whether new or existing, acquiring both companies. In this event, public companies may often change their status to private companies and be held by a public-quoted holding company.
- By a complete amalgamation using a new or existing company to absorb both companies totally.
- By so-called pooling arrangements, involving common activities and shared profits in a fixed ratio. This is relatively rare and found only in large-scale enterprises such as nuclear power construction groups or in link-ups by, for example, royalty agreements in fibres and textiles and licensing provisions, as in aircraft and engineering.

The valuation process

The steps involved will be as follows:

- Preparation of an assets and liabilities statement including, if necessary, consolidation of subsidiaries.
- adjustments for market values of assets, including fixed assets, current assets and trade investments as well as intangibles such as goodwill, patents and copyrights.
- Tabulation of historic profit and loss accounts for, say, the past five years.
- Revision to take account of extraordinary items, directors' remuneration at a commercial rate and so on.
- Scrutiny of the memorandum and articles — though an acquirer achieving full control can change all these.
- Significant points from the chairman's and the directors' reports.
- Forecast profits or ascertained maintainable pre-tax profits for the current trading year.
- Determination of the risk-adjusted rate of return.
- Current ratio and other significant business ratios for the company.
- Relevant data on comparable quoted companies.
- Relevant industry data.
- Any available technical or product literature.
- Details of any recent 'arm's length' transactions.

- Relevant new issue statistics.
- Selection of the valuation basis or bases appropriate (see Chapters 8 and 9).
- Application of the valuation basis or bases to the particular holding/ company.
- Addition of any premium considered necessary to achieve the required level of control.

The valuation in this case will be the starting point for the bid. The process should be applied to:

- the acquired company's shares;
- the acquiring company's shares; and then
- the resulting group's shares to compare the figures and see whether the merger/takeover makes sense in both financial and valuation terms from the point of view of the respective boards and the shareholders.

The vast majority of takeover and merger bids are in fact uncontested, either on the original terms or because of revised offers. Only relatively few bids which happen to be hotly contested ever hit the headlines. It should also be borne in mind that the City Code on takeovers and mergers affects only those of public limited companies.

Example

Offer to acquire the 30000 issued £1 ordinary shares in ABC Ltd, a trading company specialising in the retail of timber and other DIY products. The shares are held equally by X, Y and Z, directors all in their thirties. The company's net assets are £750000, including £200000 for a freehold property (professionally valued in 1977 with the excess placed in a capital reserve). The latest pre-tax profits were £200000 after directors' remuneration of £75000 paid equally to X, Y and Z. Earnings per share were £3.33 on a fully-taxed basis. The company was incorporated from a partnership in 1977. The profits over the last three years have been on a steadily rising level. No dividends have ever been paid. Relevant quoted sector companies (and price earnings ratio) are: Gibbs & Dandy (7.3); and Lovell Y.J. (8.0). Sector companies that show exceptional and therefore non-comparable price earnings ratios are: Magnet & Southerns (27.2); Sharpe & Fisher (11.4); and Travis & Arnold (14.0).

The price earnings ratio for this company should be lower than the $7\frac{1}{2}$ quoted average ($7.3 + 8.0 \div 2$) and a price earnings ratio of, say, 6 is suggested. This represents a 20 percent discount on the quoted figure. The full going-concern value would be on a higher price earnings ratio of at least 10 (equivalent to a multiplier of 5 applied to the pre-tax profits level) giving £33 per share or £1m for the company. For the 33 percent holdings under offer (exercising collective control) a valuation at £20 per share in the range £18–£20 per share is suggested. A premium for collective control would bring this to, say, £22.50 per share. This would be a basic negotiating position for the bidding board. This board of the biddee company would no doubt produce a higher projected pre-tax profits figure, reconsider the historic lack of dividends and requisition an up-to-date professional property valuation as well as more detailed comparability statistics. Moreover, the bidding board may regard the acquisition as a special purchase. There may be intangible or synergistic reasons why ABC Ltd would fit into the group structure. This may increase the bid price during preliminary negotiations or on a counter-bid by a third party.

7 Analysis of company accounts

Companies must submit annual statutory accounts to the shareholders. Their purpose is to account to their proprietors for the use of funds. How the money has been used is explained in the profit and loss account, and the state of the company's finances is contained in the balance sheet. It must be appreciated, however, that the profit and loss account's effectiveness is limited to the period which it covers and by the accounting convention under which it is drawn up, while the balance sheet at best captures the company's position at one moment in time and is again subject to the particular accounting conventions under which it is prepared. Both accounts are relatively static descriptions of essentially dynamic organisms — modern corporations. The standard of information required by statute, before the Companies Act 1967 embodied some of the major recommendations of the Jenkins Committee, was in many cases minimal. In particular, a company with exempt private status need not file any accounts at all with the Registrar of Companies House, so it was altogether free of public scrutiny. As stated, this has since been abolished and is now a privilege enjoyed only by unlimited companies.

The Companies Act 1948 requires:

- Statutory profit and loss accounts and a balance sheet to give a true and fair view of the company's profit and loss and state of affairs, respectively (s.148).

- Group accounts where there are subsidiaries (s.150–151) with three exceptions (in each case where the directors' opinion is that):

  (a) it is impracticable or of no real value, or would involve disproportionate expense;

  (b) results would be harmful or misleading;

(c) the business of the company was, in each case, so different that they cannot be reasonably treated as a single undertaking.

- A directors' report stating *inter alia*:
  (a) the company's affairs;
  (b) the dividend (if any);
  (c) the amount carried to reserves.
- The accounts or an annexed statement must show:
  (a) aggregate directors' remuneration;
  (b) aggregate directors' pensions;
  (c) aggregate directors' compensation for loss of office.
- The statutory accounts must also show:
  (a) loans to officers;
  (b) loans to any persons who thereafter become an officer by the company or a subsidiary or under a guarantee from or on a security provided by the company or a subsidiary;
  (c) the amount of any such loans made before the financial year, but outstanding at the end of it (s.197).

The Companies Act 1967 requires in addition:

- Any subsidiary's name, country of incorporation and proportion of shares held (s.3).
- Similar information for associates (exceeding 10 per cent) (s.4).
- Name and country of incorporation of the company's holding company (s.5).
- The following details of earnings:
  (a) chairman's emoluments;
  (b) directors' emoluments by salary bands starting at £2500;
  (c) waivers of directors' emoluments;
  (d) employees' earnings greater than £10000 per annum.
- Directors' report which will state (s.12):
  (a) names of directors;
  (b) principal activities of the company and its subsidiaries;
  (c) any significant change in the fixed assets and significant market

values thereof in the company or its subsidiaries;

(d) reasons for any issues of shares, stocks or debentures and the amounts thereof and the consideration received;

(e) contracts in which any directors are interested;

(f) particulars of arrangements under which directors can acquire benefits by means of share acquisitions in the company or other companies;

(g) details of directors' shareholdings in the company or in other companies in the group;

(h) other matters material for appreciation of the state of the company's affairs by its members (s.16);

(i) proportions of turnover among classes of businesses, and contributions of each class of business to the profits or losses;

(j) average number of persons employed by the company and its subsidiaries;

(k) critical donations in excess of £50;

(l) exports, and a statement that there are none if the turnover exceeds £50 000;

(m) details of service contracts;

(n) changes in directors' holdings;

(o) anyone with in excess of 10 per cent of the voting rights in the company.

EXAMINATION OF THE PROFIT AND LOSS ACCOUNT

The share valuer should note, on a separate preliminary sheet, the basic financial aspects of the company's performance for the past three to five years depending on the nature of the company's business and in particular how cyclical it is. Before that he should read the directors' report at the beginning of the statutory account.

This will normally show:

- The company's registered office.
- The board of directors with their shareholdings (beneficial and nominee as well as family holdings) for the current and previous year.
- Notice of significant changes in share capital (e.g. bonus issues, company acquisitions, or sales of properties) between the end of the accounting period and the date of the report.

- The nature of the company's business.
- The market value of the fixed assets (normally freehold property) if significantly different from balance sheet book values. However, there is frequently a disclaimer in this report, either that the market value is of little significance as the company is a going concern, or the cost of valuation would be disproportionate to its significance to the shareholders.
- The proposed dividends, if any (and details of any interim dividends paid) with particulars of any dividends waived.
- The amount of exports, if any.
- The amount of turnover, if not exempt from disclosure.
- The profit or loss for the period compared with the previous year.
- Whether or not the directors consider the company's position is satisfactory.

In addition there may be a chairman's report, not necessarily supplied with the statutory accounts. This may be extremely valuable if the chairman explained in detail the company's performance and the impact of government policies and economic and industry trends with some forecast for the future. This could be used with caution by a prudent prospective purchaser, or be worth little if minimally informative, as suggested in many cases.

BALANCE SHEET

The most relevant balance sheet will be that closest in time to the date of valuation. However, past balance sheets should also be analysed since these will disclose the history of the company's use of its funds and its particular financial strengths and weaknesses. They will also put the present balance sheet into a proper perspective, disclosing for example whether the latest characteristics, say, a liquidity or excessive cash, are temporary or recurrent phenomena. Balance sheet analysis will follow the practice used by investment experts in categorising the company's financial features.

The items should be grouped under the following relevant headings which may or may not be evident from the balance sheet itself.

Fixed assets

These comprise:

- Land and buildings whether freehold or leasehold. The basis of valuation should invariably be market value.
- Machinery and plant. The basis of valuation in this case should be market

value, but the book value may be taken unless the assets in question are substantial in nature.

- Office equipment and fixtures and fittings. The basis of valuation will usually be the book value.
- Motor vehicles (unless held as stock by a car dealer or a garage). The basis of valuation should normally be market value which can be checked from trade journals or from a trade valuation. However, if these are not of a substantial nature then the book values can be followed.
- Livestock, for example a dairy herd (in a farming company). The basis of valuation will be market value but again if not substantial in nature then the book values could be followed.
- Tools and utensils. These will normally be taken at the book value.
- Machinery, for example tractors and implements. These should be valued at their market value, but again the book value can be followed if the amounts involved are not substantial.

In short these items are normally kept permanently in the business and used to generate profits.

Current assets

These comprise:

- Stock-in-trade, valued at cost or realisation whichever is lower.
- Work-in-progress, valued at cost.
- Trade debtors and pre-payments, included at book value unless proven bad debts.
- Loans to associates and subsidiaries, included in at the book value, unless known to be doubtful or bad debts.
- Marketable securities, to be valued at book or market value as appropriate, according to the amounts involved.
- Cash-in-hand and cash at the bank which will, of course, be appropriately included at book value.
- Trade investments which may require a market valuation.

Also included are directors' current accounts which will be included at the face figure. The same will apply to building society accounts and recoverable advance corporation tax as well as loans to directors and participators and premiums paid on endowment policies.

Current liabilities

These will invariably be included for valuation purposes at the book figure. Such items include:

- short-term loans (under five years);
- bank overdrafts;
- trade creditors;
- loan stock holders;
- corporation tax due;
- directors' loans and accounts;
- loans from associate companies, subsidiaries or parent company;
- amounts due under a lease or purchase;
- minority interests in subsidiaries.

The company balance sheet portrays the position at one moment in time. It is generally made to fulfil such obligations to account shareholders and inform them of the financial position at the end of the year. It has, however, many limitations from the share valuer's point of view. Examined critically it does nonetheless supply much useful information on the company's financial state as at the accounting date. The following limitations and other points should be borne in mind in the critical analysis of balance sheets.

- The vast majority of balance sheets of unquoted companies will be prepared under the historic cost accounting convention. This means that most, though not all, the items will be in at original cost. In many cases this will mean the market value would be different.
- Assets subject to depreciation may be under- or over-depreciated. Consequently, the company's statutory profits may be overstated or understated.
- Intangible assets such as goodwill may, or may not, be accounted for. Either way they are unlikely to be included at market value unless this is negligible or the acquisition was relatively recent and at an arm's length transaction market price.
- Some tangible assets may be excluded, although they may have a market value. Examples would notably be leases at less than rack rent and farming tenancies.
- Investments in subsidiaries may be included at directors' estimated value or at cost which will probably, in either case, have to be checked from the accounts of the subsidiaries in question.

- Trading stock and work-in-progress will probably be included at low cost or net realisable value and cost plus overheads, plus attributable raw materials. In either case, the market value may be lower, especially on a break-up basis which may involve substantial write-offs. If a property dealing or development company is concerned these items will require valuation by a professional surveyor. If a farming company is involved, a professional valuer may well be required again. The Shares Valuation Division could call on the services of the district valuer and the livestock valuer, respectively, if they considered the size of holding or amount at stake justified this.
- Cash items require no valuation, but loans, debentures and amounts due from parent company or subsidiaries do.
- Debtors may require a discount in a break-up situation or if there is a history of bad debts (normally indicated in the profit and loss account as write-offs), or if cogent evidence of specific bad or doubtful debtors is deduced. But factorisation is possible and 75 to 80 per cent cash can be guaranteed in this way, although discounts larger than 20 percent should be exceptional only.
- Machinery and plant, motor vehicles, fixtures and fittings are typical fixed assets that normally require no revaluation, but, if substantial, an open market valuation may well be rewarding. Again, in the case of machinery and plant, the Revenue have a specialised valuer in this field. Motor vehicles can be checked from trade guides, such as *Glass's Motorists' Guide*.
- Freehold property may be included at a figure substantially below market value, for example at 1960 cost. The 1967 Companies Act requires directors to state their opinion of the market value of the freehold property if materially different from the balance sheet figure. However, this is often either ignored outright or the report may refer to cost of valuation as not being justified, although in the opinion of the directors the freehold property is substantially in excess of the balance sheet figure. It is of course possible that the property is in at valuation and the excess is included in the balance sheet in the company's reserve. The date of valuation may then have to be ascertained and the revaluation (if any) made accordingly. If a small minority is involved, either the directors' valuation would be accepted or a revaluation by capitalising rents received would preclude the need for any actual property valuation. A leasehold property may be over-depreciated as a wasting asset and have a much higher market value. This too may require professional valuation.
- Trade investments are often holdings in an associated company which gives the company an interest in the supplier or buyer otherwise connected. These are rarely substantial and can usually be accepted at cost or directors' valuation without further query. If substantial, the holding

should be checked and the associated company investigated to establish its trading links and the company's dependants on it.

- The treatment of deferred taxation is a controversial matter, though to some extent less so since SSAP16. This released significant amounts of deferred tax in the company's reserves in shareholders' funds, allowing provision on the liability method, so that no provision is necessary where no liability is anticipated in the foreseeable future.

  The main items of deferred taxation are as follows:

(a) A potential corporation tax charge, on sale, on the excess of balance sheet written-down values of fixed assets over the tax written-down values. This arises frequently with the first-year allowance for machinery and plant. Normally, however, a progressive company will continue investing in machinery and plant and other fixed assets so that any items replaced that might incur such liability will be more than offset by further capital allowances. If a break-up basis applies, however, this must be allowed in full.

(b) A potential corporation tax charge on capital gains from excess of sale proceeds over the balance sheet values of fixed assets. Here again the likelihood of such disposals taking place must be considered. In the case of a trading company valued as a going concern, the likelihood is remote and the allowance for such contingent tax should therefore normally be small. This can be justified on the grounds of the judgments in *Re Sutherland* [1961] 40 ATC 318.

    There is also the possible prospect of roll-over relief on the acquisition of further assets and, of course, the chance that there may be further CGT reliefs, or even its abolition, before any such contingent liability actually accrues. Of course, if a property trading company is concerned, the likelihood is much greater and a full allowance could possibly be called for. The same goes for any other property company since its property is not essential for its trade which can be sold and the proceeds invested whenever the market is considered right. A standard allowance often given is 50 per cent of the contingent tax for property companies, but each case is dependent on its merits. There are property companies whose last disposals date from the 1930s, and even exceptionally from much earlier than that. Clearly in such cases the contingent tax allowance should be as nominal as say 5 per cent of the possible tax, as with any trading company.

Trading profit

This applies only to trading companies. The terms 'operating profit', 'trading profit' and 'pre-tax profit' may well in fact coincide in such companies.

Net profit before tax

This should exclude any extraordinary items if these have been included above the line. In assessing goodwill, investment and other non-trading income should be eliminated.

Corporation tax

This will show the notional corporation tax payable as assessed by the accountants subject to agreement with the Inspector of Taxes. Adjustments may, of course, be made in future years to take account of the corporation tax actually paid. This deduction may also reflect deferred taxation arising out of accelerated capital allowances, stock relief and other corporation tax reliefs. Thus, the company's actual cash flow may not be affected at all by the incidence of the corporation tax notional charge. The share valuer must assess, as far as possible, the likely corporation tax to be paid by the company in any given tax year. This is critical since it is the actual tax payable, not the notional tax charge, which will determine the company's profitability and its retained profits and thus the amount of shareholders' funds.

Net profit after tax

This figure may be the same as the pre-tax figure if the tax charge is zero and may even substantially exceed the pre-tax profit if there is a tax repayment due to capital allowances or losses brought forward, and the like. The company does, of course, have the advantage of the beneficial cash flow in that event. To achieve consistency between companies, it may be necessary to assume a notional full tax charge in that case and deduct at 52 or 42 per cent (small companies rate) as the case may be.

Net earnings per share

This may be stated — some companies even state it for a five-year period. If not, it should be deemed by taking the net profit after tax (adjusted as appropriate) and deducting preference dividends and any other prior dividends or prior charges so as to determine the earnings attributable to the ordinary share capital. The earnings per share are then simply the net earnings divided by the number of ordinary shares in issue. Thus £100 000 post-tax earnings and £25 000 issued ordinary shares will show a figure of £4 earnings per share.

Dividends paid

These will, after April 1973, be stated net as paid by the company. They can be listed net for averaging purposes and then grossed up to reflect the advance corporation tax credit. The present grossing up factor is 10/7 (effective from 6 April 1979). Note should be made of waivers by directors or other shareholders. These may benefit recipient shareholders, but the net cost for the company may also be reduced. Thus the declared rate may need reduction to the rate at which the dividend was actually paid.

Dividend cover

This should be noted and represents the net earnings for the ordinary shares divided by the net dividend paid. Thus earnings of £50 000 and a net dividend of £25 000 gives a cover of 2. Once again, the earnings exclude extraordinary items, but may include non-trading items such as rent received, dividends from quoted companies, bank interest, and so on, since the investor is concerned primarily with the amount of cover and not its source. The share valuer will by now have completed the top half of his notation.

Depreciation

Different industries and assets have different rates applied. In general, the accounts method may be followed. Depreciation as a deduction against trading profits has, however, a substantial impact on pre-tax profits. Exceptionally, the rates used may be too high or too low and the profits may be consequently understated or overestimated. Moreover, the 100 per cent free depreciation provisions of capital allowances after 27 October 1970 may create imbalances in the tax charge. Tax written-down values may be zero while accounts values may still be substantial. This may affect future profits adversely and the possibility must be noted.

Extraordinary items

These should be scrutinised. If evidently non-recurrent items, they should be deducted from the profits since they can be of no possible benefit or detriment to a potential purchaser. However, such items may be recurrent as part of a business cycle (for example, periodic capital transactions of buying and selling of fixed assets at a profit or loss). If regular enough, such items, even if treated as extraordinary in the statutory accounts, should be taken as profits. They are, after all, added to the distributable profits and may be received as dividends or as a benefit in the shape of retained profits to be distributed in due course as dividends (from reserves), bonus issues, or in the form of a capital surplus on a winding up or as a positive valuation factor in a takeover or merger.

Taxation

The individual company's tax charge is likely to be distorted by a variety of allowances, reliefs and other factors. Since the professional share valuer will not have access to the company's tax file (unless he is in the fortunate position of his Revenue counterpart who can easily requisition this) he cannot see the company's particular tax profile. The significance of the tax charge is, of course, to determine the company's distributable profits (that is, its net earnings attributable to the ordinary shares or available as cover for the preference shares). The share valuer must therefore decide on a treatment of taxation that will give him:

- a meaningful investment yardstick of comparison with other comparable companies;
- a reasonably straightforward basis of calculation;
- a relatively consistent system for year-to-year inter-company comparisons;
- a useful measurement of management performance;
- an adequate definition of distributable profits;
- an acceptable analysis of the company's cash flow and retentions;
- a method of average profits determination that can be used without further adjustment in earnings-based valuations.

In applying this criteria, it should be borne in mind that there have been three systems of corporate taxation within the last 18 years:

- before 6 April 1965 — income tax and profits tax;
- from 6 April 1965 to 6 April 1973 — classical corporation tax;
- from 6 April 1973 — mainstream corporation tax and advance corporation tax (the imputation system).

Table 7.1 illustrates the main fiscal effects of each system. The pre-imputation corporation tax system penalised distributions whereas the present mainstream corporation tax plus advanced corporation tax system is largely neutral as between distributions and retentions.

The share valuer will see that low tax charges lead to swollen deferred taxation provisions in both profit and loss accounts and company balance sheets. Neither provision is necessarily realistic. On a going-concern basis their deduction may well give a misleading impression as to the company's available profits and reserves. Since SSAP16, the large deferred taxation provisions have been written back wholesale into company profit and loss accounts and balance sheets, thus inflating earnings and shareholders funds. This has been accelerated by the treatment of stock relief clawback in the

Table 7.1
Corporate taxation: main fiscal effects of each system

	£
Pre 6 April 1965	
Pre-tax profits	100000
Income tax @ 41.25%	41250
Profits tax @ 15%	15000
Net dividend	43750
= gross	74468
Less: income tax	30718
	43750
6 April 1965 - 6 April 1973	
Pre-tax profits	100000
Corporation tax @ 40%	40000
Distributable profit	60000
Less: Schedule F income tax @ 41.25%	24750
Net dividend	35250
6 April 1973 to date	
Pre-tax profits	100000
Corporation tax @ 50%	50000
Net dividend	50000
	as paid
Plus: ACT at 3/7	21428
	71428
	gross

Finance Act 1981. This shows, retrospectively at least, the extremely conservative nature of the treatment of these items in the statutory accounts prepared before then.

More than a few share valuations will have been underestimates because of the accountancy practice in the earlier periods.

OTHER MATTERS FOR CONSIDERATION

Preliminary enquiries must be undertaken before the share valuation can be made. These include the following:

- The restrictions on the transfer of shares and other rights attaching to the shares in the company's articles and memorandum of association.
- The company's management structure, personnel and succession at both board and middle management levels.

- The history of the industry, its present state and its future prospects.
- The company's history, progress and prospects.
- The profitability of the company and its growth-potential.
- Sector yields of comparable quoted companies.
- The risks and returns in the business.
- Investment requirements of contemporary prospective purchasers in the open market.
- The company's capital structure and the class rights of different shares.
- The liquidity of the company.
- The dividend history of the company.
- The basis of valuation of the various categories of assets.
- The company's gearing and its actual and contingent liabilities.
- The effects of inflation on the company's growth and shareholders' returns.
- The market value of intangibles — notably goodwill.
- The actual distribution of the shares in the company so that the holding can be placed in its proper context.
- The state of the national economy, in both its macro-economic and micro-economic aspects.
- The trend of prevailing interest rates.
- Socio-political events and trends that may have a bearing on business confidence or particular industrial or commercial activity.
- Technological innovations with a bearing — direct or indirect — on the sector or the company where either may experience a technological breakthrough benefiting the company or its competitors.
- Changes in fashion, taste and lifestyle that may alter consumer demand and affect the company's turnover (whether positively or adversely).
- News of potential takeovers or mergers or flotations or liquidations that may affect the share price.
- Local developments that may affect the company in some way.
- Government legislation that impinges on the company's business affairs.
- Details of actual arm's length transactions in the company's shares at or around the date of valuation.
- Information as to prospective purchasers — either the existing

shareholders or such other purchasers as may be known to be in the market.

- The precise size of holding to be valued in a particular case.
- The exact fiscal or other purpose of the valuation.

Each of the above merits some comment, some detailed, some cursory.

Articles and memorandum of association

The articles state the conditions, privileges and duties governing membership of the company. Table A of the Companies Act 1948 may be adopted wholesale, though often it is wholly or partially excluded. In so far as not expressly excluded, its provisions apply. The one essential clause imposed by Section 28, Companies Act 1948 is a directors' veto on transfer, normally an overriding clause giving an absolute and uncontrolled discretionary refusal to register any transfer of shares. (This is not, however, essential since the Companies Act 1980.) The legality of such clauses was upheld by the Court of Appeal in the case of *Re Smith & Fawcett* (1942) 1 All ER 542 where the directors' refusal to register the appellant's 4001 shares (as his father's executor) unless he sold 2000 of them to a named director at a fixed price was, the court decided, a bona fide exercise of the board's discretion.

The articles may provide for all manner of class rights. There may be £100 founder shares, £25 management shares, £1 A, B, C, D and E ordinary shares, shares with weighted voting rights (for example, those numbered 1–99), voteless shares, deferred and deferred ordinary shares, with no rights of any description save a low ranking right to repayment of nominal capital in the event of a winding-up, cumulative redeemable convertible and participating preference shares, to name some of the commoner kinds of unusual shares. The articles are, of course, subject to regulation by the courts and must be interpreted by the share valuer before the framework and subject matter of the valuation can be regarded as properly defined. Once the class rights of the different shares and securities have been established, then the valuation process proper can begin. The same applies of course to debentures and unsecured loan stock which may also be the subject of a share valuation. Apart from specific provisions in the articles, Table A, Companies Act 1948 may apply to give preference shares votes by default because they are not expressly excluded from voting or because their dividends are in arrear. The same may apply to other classes of shares that are normally non-voting (for example, A and B shares). Quite often the only reason why shares are designated in alphabetical order is to distinguish between different blocks held by various shareholders (possibly institutional). It is therefore unsafe to act on assumptions as to class rights. The articles must be critically examined. Interpretation of the clauses can be difficult and in the author's experience recourse may in the last resort be had to counsel to resolve conflicting opinions.

While articles may carry the minimum restrictions on transfer, or may be extremely restrictive, the clauses may be two-edged. Thus the fairly common clause providing for the other shareholders (or even the directors) to acquire the shares of a deceased member automatically on payment of the auditors certified fair value has two sides to it:

- Depreciatory in that the fair value may be on a defined basis (as in the *Crossman* case) which gives a low figure. As the celebrated case of *Dean* v *Prince* (1954) 1 All ER 749 showed, an auditor's valuation on this basis —even where he showed his workings — may be difficult to challenge. This will apply with greater force where the other shareholders are either relatively young, but well-established, or there is a monolithic block of such shares, either held by husband and wife or by a family group. The purchaser, as the 'detested intruder' (according to the celebrated dictum of Rowlatt, J. in *Re Thornley*) therefore faces a solid front.
- Appreciatory. The fact that the prospective purchaser can acquire the shares of other shareholders in the course of time at bargain basement prices is clearly an appreciatory factor in the valuation.

There may also be numerous classes of ordinary shares (most probably, though not necessarily, non-voting). These are valued according to the class rights again. In general, though, such non-voting ordinary shares are valued as ordinary shares but with some discount for non-voting status. This discount may be very low indeed — as little as 2.5 per cent (2.5p per share on a £1 nominal share) since all small minorities, even with votes, are pretty much equally uninfluential in terms of control over the company's affairs. But where special situations develop, where voting rights become crucial, the differential will increase — as happens in the actual open market.

One difficult kind of valuation arises when the shares in question have extensive voting rights but no rights to dividend, or on a winding-up, so the sole interest of a prospective purchaser is in acquiring control of the company. If the valuation is for CTT on a death, then the shares held by the deceased can all be aggregated as part of his beneficial estate and any other shares held by him can be valued together as a package. For other fiscal purposes, however, such a holding must be valued in isolation. The question is then the premium for control attributable to such shares. This will be in addition to their nominal value. Of course if the holding in question carries full control then the power to alter class rights is implicit. In that case the shares can be given their full value of a holding equivalent to ordinary shares with voting control. Otherwise the shares must be ascribed to premium for control only. The level of this will depend very much on the circumstances and, in particular, the class rights of the other class shares and the balance between the company's asset backing and earning power.

Example

Company XYZ has 100 000 £1 ordinary shares and also the following holdings of preference shares:

10 000 £1 A 4% preference shares with votes
5 000 £1 B 5% preference shares without votes
5 000 £1 C 6% preference shares without votes
5 000 £1 D 7% preference shares without votes
5 000 £1 E 8% preference shares without votes

Dividends have been paid regularly to date and there is substantial asset and income backing. The required yield is 20 per cent (16 per cent gross quoted sector yield adjusted by 25 per cent for non-marketability). Valuations of these shares might be appropriate as follows:

A preference shares @ 4/20	=	20p per share
+ 10% voting premium	=	22 per share.
B preference shares @ 5/20	=	25p per share.
C preference shares @ 6/20	=	30p per share.
D preference shares @ 7/20	=	35p per share.
E preference shares @ 8/20	=	40p per share.

As there is ample dividend cover, a history of regularly-paid dividends and substantial assets cover, the basic required yields do not require further adjustment for these factors. Thus, the priority percentages used by investment analysts need not be worked out (although there are successive increases in the coupon rate to compensate for descending priority claims on the company's income and capital).

The company's management structure

Firstly, this can be examined by its performance as seen in:

- ratio analysis;
- historic profits performance;
- use of retained profits;
- research and development;
- directors' and chairman's reports;
- its technical literature;
- its relative results within the industrial and commercial sector context.

Secondly, it can be examined by its composition and succession as seen in:

- the family context;

- the board and its qualifications and experience;
- technical support;
- age distribution;
- keyman cover;
- dependents on individuals.

This history of the industry

This can be researched through industry textbooks, newspapers, magazines, pamphlets, studies, directories, official publications and reported cases. The history is relevant only to see the context of the company's origins and as a guide to the future. A brief industry history is a good preface to the valuer's survey of industry prospects. As regards evaluation at any given period, the *Financial Times, Stock Exchange Gazette* and *Investors Chronicle* will give a reasonable idea of the general financial and possibly particular sector prospects.

The company's history

The company's history, progress and prospects can be discerned from its respective reports and any other available literature published by it or (exceptionally) by a third party on it. The valuer will read between the lines and see what inferences he can draw.

Profitability and growth-potential

This can be seen from various aspects of the company as follows.

Profitability

- The gross profit percentage, that is sales less purchases divided by sales expressed by a percentage.
- The pre-tax profits as a measure of the working capital or the capital employed.
- The pre-tax profits as a proportion of the issued ordinary share capital.
- The pre-tax profits adjusted by a commercial rate of directors' remuneration.
- Pre-tax profits before interest charges.
- The earnings per share, that is, the gross aftertax earnings divided by the issued ordinary shares after prior charges, including preference dividends and debenture interest.

Growth potential

This can be derived from:

- the rate of profits increase from the profits base at the start of the relevant period;
- the rate of profits increase in relation to the issued share capital;
- management profits projections;
- extrapolations from the existing profits trends;
- the current and projected expansion of the market.

Sector yields of quoted companies

These can be found in the *Financial Times* Actuaries Share Indices and the share information service, or researched through Extel cards that cover practically all quoted companies. Comparability is a different matter. The size, structure, products, markets and diversification of the quoted companies must be examined and the non-comparable companies eliminated. As a preliminary exercise, the extremes of yields and ratios will suggest candidates for elimination since the idea is to achieve relevant industry averages. If a full-scale comparability study is justified by the amount at stake, for example in fiscal terms, then the valuer will require detailed financial statistics, chairman's reports, technical literature and so on, expressed in tabular form for analysis in respect of half-a-dozen or so quoted companies. This research will itself give a good idea of relevant developments affecting reasonably comparable sector companies and the requirements of investors in them.

Risks and returns

These can best be considered as reflected in the yields and ratios required by investors in the open market. Specific risks peculiar to the business in question may entail refinements in adjusting such yields and ratios.

Investment requirements in the open market

These, at any time, are adequately reflected in the stock market yields and ratios of individual companies and group indices. This does, of course, rest on the implicit assumption that the stock market operates on the basis of market forces in a relatively perfect market where the share price, at any given time, reflects all the available information accessible to prospective investors. As a corollary, it is taken that relevant information in the market on the national economy has been taken into account in the determination of stock market yields and ratios reflected in contemporary share prices. This is the so-called efficient market hypothesis known to investment analysts. It has at least the virtue of extensive practice by stock market investors.

The company's capital structure and class rights

These determine:

- the relative legal powers of different classes of shares;
- the corresponding potential influence of any given size of holding;
- the company's gearing, that is the ratio of fixed to variable capital, (e.g. preference shares to ordinary shares, or long-term debt to the equity);
- the company's borrowing capacity;
- the degree of capitalisation or under-capitalisation;
- the market potential of the holding in question.

The liquidity of the company

The liquidity reflects the company's financial preparedness for eventualities and use of its resources. If over-liquid it is making insufficient use of its cash. If illiquid, it may be in danger of over-trading and liable to liquidation in a cash crisis. The critical factor is then cash flow. This is defined in investment terms as retained profits plus depreciation. If the company generates sufficient cash flow the illiquidity is a temporary phenomenon and can be overcome. If not, then the share valuer must note this as a further risk factor in assessing the required return. Liquidity itself has two meanings:

- the current ratio or current assets/current liabilities; and
- the quick ratio (sometimes called the acid test in the financial media) or current assets less stock/current liabilities.

Both tests should be satisfied by the company, but subject to a further test to examine the turnover of debtors and creditors (i.e. the settlement period for each).

The dividend history

This will show the board's practice in this respect. In particular, careful scrutiny will disclose;

- the regularity of dividend payments in good and bad years respectively;

- the proportion of earnings normally paid out as dividends;
- the willingness to pay dividends, if necessary out of reserves;
- the reasons for dividend payments (possibly only made because of family commitments or circumstances which may not continue after the share transfer in question);
- the dividend trend, for example the level of increase over the past three to five years.

The point of all this is, of course, to project the likely level of future dividends since it is only these that will benefit a prospective purchaser. Once again, past events are useful only as pointers to the future. If those factors no longer apply, in the extreme case it is possible to disregard them altogether and a different approach to the valuation based on the wholly novel situation must be undertaken. Certainly in three of the leading cases (*Salvesen, Crossman* and *Holt*) the expert witnesses in the courts scrutinised the company's dividend history in considerable detail and over prolonged periods.

The basis of valuation of assets

The various categories of assets and their basis of valuation requires examination even if minority holdings are involved since a well-rounded valuation approach will cross-check the assets basis of valuation as well as the other relevant valuation techniques. The scrutiny need only be relatively brief for minority holdings since the investor would not, for example, go to the trouble and expense of a professional valuation of the company's fixed assets. He could, however, check the value of freeholds or leaseholds by capitalising the annual rents disclosed in the company's statutory accounts, and it should be assumed he would do this as would the vendor negotiating to achieve the best possible price for his shares.

The company's gearing

This indicates the extent of the company's dependence on loan capital as opposed to equity capital. A highly geared company will do better for its ordinary shareholders when business is good than a lowly geared company but conversely when times are bad the high gearing may well wipe out most or all of the company's trading profit because of the demands of the fixed rate return on borrowings. The share valuer will examine the gearing as part of his assessment of risk in determining the required rate of return a prospective purchaser would require.

Inflation

The effect of this on the company's growth and shareholders' returns is a matter of general concern to any investor, but inflation accounting as such —still a matter of controversy within the accountancy profession — has not affected share valuation theory or practice any more than it has been introduced into the Revenue's fiscal theory and practice, although elements of it have, such as index-linked stock relief and capital gains in the Finance Act 1981 and the Finance Act 1982. It can, however, be considered in examining the company's profits-growth, over the period in relation to its share price. The same amount expressed in 1965 money and 1983 money implies rather different dimensions of value.

The market value of intangibles

This is dealt with in Chapter 9 on goodwill valuation and valuations of intellectual property in special situations. Each item has its own peculiar valuation characteristics and cannot be accepted necessarily as either the balance sheet cost figure or of nil value (written off or depreciated). However, the balance sheet figure may not be worth querying and, if a minority holding is involved, it will normally not be worth negotiating as cost would suffice. Exceptions do of course exist. The valuation of, for example, the four minority holdings of the Beatles in Apple Corporation — involving of necessity an assessment of their royalty potential — would not be acceptable at any balance sheet figure.

Distribution of shares

The actual distribution of shares in the company is a given fact crucial to the valuation even if the statutory hypothetical open market value is involved. The share valuer must note in particular whether:

- any single person has actual control;
- the family has control;
- the directors have control;
- a prospective purchaser could readily obtain control;
- any trust holdings are involved;
- any institutional shareholders are involved such as ICFC or EDITH;
- the company is a close company within Sections 282 and 283, ICTA 1970 (this will often be stated in the directors' report);
- there could be two or more shareholders bidding for control by acquiring the holding being valued;

- there is a chairman's casting vote in the articles conferring *de facto* control on any person;
- any existing shares or stocks carry conversion rights, for example to ordinary shares, and the resultant share distribution should these rights be exercised.

The national economy

The state of this must be examined as the background against which the company has operated and must operate in the future. If the country is in recession, the companies sector may be adversely affected (as with most capital and consumer goods in a state of depressed demand), or still be in a growth area that successfully rides the national trend, such as electronics, in general, and computers, in particular, at present. Moreover, a bull market may still exist while the economy as a whole and industry especially is undeniably depressed (as in the *Financial Times* All Share Index), hitting its all-time high in the current CBI slough of despond. As far as share prices go — and unquoted share prices tend to follow those in the quoted sector to a greater or lesser extent but not all the way, neither reaching the ceiling nor falling through the floor — the state of the stock market is no doubt of much more significance than the economy as a whole. The open market stands in the foreground of the investor's thinking while the economy is only the backcloth against which he makes his investment decisions.

Interest rates

The trend of prevailing interest rates affects share prices, but far less than it does gilt prices. The reverse yield gap still applies to unquoted shares, though less so than with quoted equities that may show dividend yields of, for example, 4 per cent in property and electricals, at a time when the MLR was 16 per cent. Interest rates cannot even then be said to constitute a minimum return required by equity investors in the private or the public company sectors. They do, however, determine the cost of capital and therefore the kind of gross return required when determining the multiplier in the capitalisation of profits or the interest on working capital or net tangible assets in the super-profits basis of valuing goodwill.

Socio-economic and socio-political events

These may affect business directly or indirectly. The valuer must always be aware of their potential impact. Prime examples would be EEC entry in 1973, the Arab–Israeli war in 1974, the secondary banking crisis and consequent industrial collapse in 1974/75, the general election in May 1979 and the effect of high American interest rates on the world economy in 1982. Again there is the dual aspect of the impact of such events on:

- business activity; and
- stock market investment which would feed back on to all share prices including those of unquoted companies.

Technological innovations

These can be quite crucial in changing the pattern of industrial and commercial investment and direction. Overnight existing processes may be rendered obsolete and new opportunities may arise. Invention and exploitation are, of course, not necessarily associated. A good example is the electronic calculator, invented in Britain and exploited in Japan. Computer technology has given rise to numerous spin-off companies —in both hardware (equipment) and software (programs) — and early flotations, sometimes within a few years of company formation.

Changes in fashion, taste and lifestyle

These may revolutionise consumer behaviour. The rise of supermarket giants like Tesco and Sainsbury has spawned many private company equivalents, some of them such as Caters and Northern Foods becoming ripe for takeover. The textile and furniture worlds are other prime examples — with Mary Quant and Terence Conran's Habitat changing the face of both business and lifestyles simultaneously. Fast food franchises is another current growth industry and the flotations of Horizons and Intasun showed that holidays abroad could be highly-profitable businesses even in the middle of a national recession.

Takeovers and mergers

These should be taken into account with unquoted share valuations as they affect private companies' share prices, just as bid rumours transform the share prices of sleepy public companies. Startling prices may indeed be paid, well above apparent open market values and embodying the special purchase element that marks a bidding company's determination to succeed. It should also be remembered that probably 90 per cent of bids succeed without overmuch fuss, being virtually agreed in advance after preliminary talks or feelers being put out possibly well before any formal offers. It is, of course, only the exceptional takeover or merger that makes the national headlines or reaches the scope of the Monopolies Commission.

Local developments

This may affect a factory site or a property development. So far as he can take these into account, the share valuer should do so.

Government legislation

Any legislation that impinges on the company's business may be crucial. Tax laws are notorious examples. Health and safety legislation may affect production costs just as the Equal Pay Act 1975 changed cost structures. The introduction and subsequent abolition of selective employment tax is another example. The small business legislation of the present government may be yet another. All of this may affect the share valuation in question.

Actual arm's length transactions

Details of these should be noted, including, if possible:

- the date of the transaction;
- the parties involved;
- their relationship;
- the holding in question;
- the price paid per share;
- any particular tax involved;
- any valuation agreed with the Revenue.

Such transactions are never necessarily conclusive. They are simply evidence of value. The statutory open market valuation, in particular, is never determined simply because of the existence of such transactions. The shares valuation division do, however, have detailed records of agreements and transactions over the course of many years.

Prospective purchasers

Information of these can be obtained from the auditors, the company or the shareholders themselves, or by general or specific enquiry. It should be noted that many journals — notably the *Financial Times*, *Daltons Weekly* and *Exchange and Mart* as well as all manner of trade periodicals — have information as to vendors and purchasers of businesses wanted or for sale. So do many estate agents and business transfer agents' lists.

The size of holding

The significance of this must be appreciated in every case. Different sizes of holding can command vastly different values. The authority for this proposition is in the leading case of *Ocean Coal Co. Ltd* v *Powell Duffryn Steam Coal Co. Ltd* (1932) 1 Ch 654 where Farwell, J. said

> there may be ... a considerable difference between the price at which the shareholder is willing to sell his shares if he is desirous of selling a large or small number and the price which he obtains for his shares may be only according to the number of shares he is proposing to sell. If one takes the illustration ... of an offer of shares sufficient to give control of the company it may well be that a purchaser would be prepared to pay a much higher price for a number of shares sufficient for that purpose.

In that case, the 600 000 shares of T. Co. were held equally between O. Co. and P. Co. P. Co. wished to sell their shares. The board offered them, under the articles, to O. who wished to exercise the option as to 5000. It was provided that 'if the shares or any of them are not so accepted the holder may sell or transfer them at the same or any higher price to a third party approved by the Board'. The court held that O. Co. had failed to accept the offer and P. Co. could offer them to a third party.

The significance of the size of holding depends on the legal rights it carries under the Companies Acts and the company's memorandum and articles. Thus these must be examined in the context of:

- the distribution of the other holdings in the company; and
- the class rights of the other shares in the company.

In the simplest case where all the issued shares are ordinary shares, the following categories apply:

Holdings of 10 per cent or less

These carry minimal voting influence and can be compulsorily bought out under Section 209, Companies Act 1948, by a shareholder acquiring 90 per cent of the issued voting shares.

Holdings of 10.1 to 25 per cent

These cannot be bought out so may become permanent minorities if the company is taken over. These may have to be bought out at a premium to reflect the nuisance value.

Holdings of 25.1 to 49.99 per cent

These are termed influential minorities since they may carry expectations of (though not the right to) a directorship. They can block a special or extraordinary resolution and thus have a value for their negative control in preventing a winding up, or other alterations to the company's structure or constitution. Finally they can, in certain circumstances, effectively control the company.

- In this context it should be remembered how often a winding up is the only way to unlock the company's assets and give the shareholder an actual return in a private company.
- It may be useful to list the occasions when a special or extraordinary resolution is required when this kind of holding requires a particular value:

  (a) a winding up;

  (b) increase of authorised capital;

  (c) increase in borrowing powers;

  (d) alteration of articles;

  (e) alteration of memorandum;

  (f) any other occasions specified in the articles or the memorandum.
- Consider the following distributions: (A) 48 per cent; (B) 12 per cent; (C) 12 per cent; (D) 10 per cent; (E) 12 per cent; and (F) 6 per cent. A only has to acquire the votes or the support of any one of the other five shareholders to have *de facto* control. Moreover, he has no controlling shareholder opposed to him. The value of his shares will therefore be higher than if he was facing, say, a shareholder with 52 per cent controlling interest or even a 50 per cent shareholder with *de facto* control by virtue of a chairman's casting vote under Table A, Companies Act 1948, or the articles, or even a less scattered spread of other shareholders.

A 50 per cent shareholding

Such a shareholding does not in itself carry control, though its holder may have ex-officio control as chairman of the company. Such control would not count for the statutory valuation which would not endow the vendor with the office of chairman, even if the valuation was on the chairman's death, since the parties are hypothetical. However, it is important to see if the other shareholding is a 50 per cent shareholding with a chairman's casting vote since this would definitely be a depreciatory factor. The prospective purchaser would then be accepting, effectively, a minority holding and would lower his price accordingly. The assumption is normally that both 50 per cent shareholders would exercise joint control in running the company to their mutual advantage. Indeed, such an arrangement is a quasi-partnership situation and this is important from the point of view of possible action in the courts by an agreed party (see *Lundie Bros*, v *IRC* (1965) 2 All ER 692).

50.1 to 74.9 per cent holding

This carries day-to-day control of the company and can thus control the board and dividend policy and pass any ordinary resolution. In short, such a shareholder can do anything except wind-up the company or any of the other things that require a special or extraordinary resolution. This is, of course, providing the statutory power under Section 184, Companies Act 1948 to remove directors is not defeated by a clause in the articles giving the directors weighted voting in that event, as in *Bushell* v *Faith* (1970) AC 1099.

75 to 89.9 per cent holding

This carries winding up control — full control of the company except that it does not enable a purchaser to acquire compulsorily the remaining minority interest.

90 to 100 per cent holding

Such a holding carries full control in every sense of the phrase.

In general there is little logic in distinguishing between the sizes of holdings within the broader categories stated above since there will be no difference in the legal rights attaching to such intra-categorical holdings. However, there is clearly some ground for distinguishing between, say, a 26.1 per cent holding (technically an influential minority) and 49.9 per cent (possibly only one voting share away from control of the company) if only because the prospective purchaser may be that much nearer control (or the next step up in legal rights). Again a holding of 0.1 per cent may be marginally distinguishable from one of 10 per cent. This applies particularly where the 10 per cent holding may involve a substantial number of shares and thus a significant stake in the company (e.g. 100 000 out of 1 000 000 issued ordinary shares). Moreover, as regards any minority holding, the helpless locked-in shareholder argument can be overdone. A minority action for pressure under Section 210, Companies Act 1948 (now Section 75, Companies Act 1980) can succeed and indeed this scope has been extended by the latest legislation. The likelihood of such an act of succeeding is, of course, increased if the holdings are influential minorities (see *Meyer* v *Scottish Textile & Manufacturing Co. Ltd* (1957) SC 110 where a 43 per cent shareholder obtained relief for six acts of oppression and the House of Lords approved the Court of Session's evaluation of his shares for purchase by the respondent majority shareholder as if those acts of oppression had not occurred). Minority holdings may also acquire special value over and above the market value that would otherwise have prevailed in:

- a special purchaser situation (see Chapter 5);

- on a prospective flotation, merger or takeover; and
- on the verge of, or in the process of, a liquidation where assets are being realised and the proceeds distributed.

Where action as an oppressed shareholder may fail, an action as an oppressed director may succeed in getting the company wound up by the court under the just and equitable provisions of Section 222(f), Companies Act 1948 (see *Re Lundie Bros.* where an action by a 50 per cent shareholder, excluded by a chairman's casting vote, led to such a successful action).

The fiscal purpose of the valuation

This will affect the valuer's approach in several ways. It will tell him for example what information standards apply and whether he is to value the holding in question by itself or in aggregation with other holdings. This in turn will determine whether the valuation requires a fullscale report or a brief resumé with a stated opinion of value. The exact purpose of the valuation should of course be stated at the very beginning of the valuation.

8 Valuation techniques

There is a wide variety of valuation techniques. The valuer should consider them both as instruments for assessing a share's true worth and as weapons in his armoury in presenting a client's case. Any given valuation should usually be approached using the main different valuation techniques to see the range of values suggested by each. Such a method prevents over-emphasis on one technique at the expense of others perhaps equally relevant. Each technique can also serve as a cross-check on the correctness of the valuer's calculations and concepts. Once the techniques are mastered the valuer will find it natural to examine a business or company in this way.

NET ASSETS BASIS

This may be used where the profits of the company do not imply any excess value by way of goodwill. However, even this simplistic concept conceals possible variations. It will be used only for valuing controlling interests and not minority holdings.

The simplest version is the book net asset value shown in the latest available balance sheet, so far as attributable to the ordinary shares. If the assets are such that there is prima facie no need to seek a professional market value of them, then this may give a correct result, that is one justified by actual practice. In any case, this basis will only be justified if the holding in question gives the purchaser full control (90 per cent or more).

A variation is to adjust the book net asset figure to take account of market values of assets that can be revalued, such as machinery and plant, motor vehicles, trade investments, unquoted securities and, of course, freeholds or leaseholds. This then comes up against the thorny problem of the deductibility of contingent CGT that would be incurred if the assets in question were realised at the higher market values.

If the company is a true going-concern (so it is in effect at least making a normal commercial level of profit for that sector even if no profits are being earned) there is a strong case for arguing little, if any, such CGT should be allowed. This was the former practice of the Shares Valuation Division in the statutory assets based valuation for estate duty where no sale of the assets in question was pre-supposed and the allowance would normally be small unless there was reason to suppose there would be actual sales in the foreseeable future. There was justification of this in the leading case of *Re Sutherland* (1960) [1961] 40 ATC 318 and more recently in the accountancy practice laid down in SSAP16.

Broadly, the treatment of this CGT can be determined by the nature of the company's business as the following shows:

- Companies where a high proportion of corporation tax and CGT would be allowable (say 75 to 100 per cent): investment dealing (corporation tax); property dealing (corporation tax).
- Companies where a medium proportion of contingent tax would be allowable (33.3 to 50 per cent): investment holding (CGT); property holding (CGT); property management (CGT); property owning (CGT); farming, i.e. holding freehold agricultural land (CGT);
Holding company (where category A and B companies are subsidiaries) (CGT).
- Companies where only a small proportion of contingent tax would be allowable (5 to 25 per cent): trading company (company CGT); commercial company (company CGT) — except where investments are held and regularly realised in which case the higher proportions of allowances would be available.

Of course in many cases arguments about deductibility of this contingent tax are avoidable by demonstrating that the company's profits can justify a capitalisation value at least equal to the full net asset value (as revised) without deduction of these items.

Another variation is the break-up basis where the company's profits (or losses) are such that it cannot really be realistically called a going concern. In this case the only return any purchaser can hope for is a capital return on a winding up. In this case the book assets must be revalued accordingly, although the basis of the valuation is still open market value and not therefore the basis of a panic sale or a sale by an anxious vendor. Fixed assets such as freehold factories may also be valued on a separate break-up basis by the district valuer which may be lower than the going-concern value. This is truer still, of course, of items such as machinery and plant or fixtures and fittings that may have little realisable value as separate assets. Stock-in-trade and trade debtors may also require discounting substantially for their realisable value on this basis. Some items such as investment securities and freehold properties may well hold their value irrespective of the company's trading position. On this basis too the prospective purchaser will pitch his price in relation to the net realisable value. He will therefore take into account full contingent CGT or corporation tax, all redundancy payments, expenses of sale, liquidation costs and so on. There is no reason in this case why these should not be deducted without discount.

Whichever of the above bases apply, it is arguable that a proportion of profits to the date of valuation should be added on since this is information a purchaser of a controlling interest would require and a vendor would expect him to pay for. Conversely, a proportion of a trading loss for the period would be deducted in arriving at net asset value.

DISCOUNTED ASSETS BASIS

This can be used, according to circumstances, for any kind of holding for any kind of tax and any other valuation purpose. It is not restricted to any categories such as, for example, controlling interests. Indeed the circumstances may be such that a discount for a minority holding in a prosperous property company (maybe as low as 35 per cent) is justifiably lower than the discount for a full control holding in a loss-making trading company (maybe as high as 50 per cent or even 60 per cent). The discount may be zero (or 5 per cent) for a full control holding in a property company, ranging to 99 per cent for a small holding of deferred shares in a small trading company. The flexibility of this basis is such that it is always a useful exercise as a cross-check on the valuation of the holding in question by other methods. This basis may then be used to lower or raise or maintain the basis value accordingly. This method, of course, may itself show the variations seen in the net assets basis outlined above.

A variation on this method is the 'assets floor' concept. This presupposes that the value of unquoted shares will not fall below a certain percentage or fraction of the net asset value. Below that figure it is supposed the vendor would no longer be a willing party to the transaction, such as the open market concept, for example, requires. (This rather resembles the sufficient information theory without which the purchaser would not deal.) Common percentages or favourite fractions are 20 per cent or one-quarter of net asset value (implying acceptable discounts of 80 or 75 per cent). The source of such a theory is unclear. A further variation on it applies it to property companies, only using the *Lynall* case formula of yield basis plus capital appreciation factor. If the yield basis is nil, the capital appreciation factor (one-quarter of asset value) means shares in such companies will seldom, if ever, fall below such an assets floor figure. The author has seen the argument applied to trading companies by members of both Shares Valuation Division and the accounting profession with strange results. Certainly it can give rise to theoretically-based over-valuations that cannot be justified in any way with reference to actual market arm's length transaction prices. As regards property and investment companies, the method has its merits since it reflects the investment treatment followed in the stock market. However, in a period of relatively high inflation, uneconomic rents and stagnant property values such as the period 1974–77 or 1980–82, it is arguable that dividends yield comes into its own again except that, of course, the assets backing will feed back on to the level of yield required by a prospective investor. Rigidly applied though, the assets floor concept is bound to lead to a negotiating impasse resolvable only by the rough justice of administrative discretion, cost effectiveness or pure horse trading.

The flexibility of this valuation basis is seen by its appropriateness to the following types of valuation.

- Controlling interests whether full control or day-to-day control is involved where there is no goodwill or excess capitalisation value.
- Holdings of whatever size in a property or an investment company. As regards minority holdings, a cross-check should be made in such cases on a dividend yield or price earnings ratio basis, depending on the dividend record of the company and the potential influence of the size of holding in question.
- Holdings of whatever size where the profits are erratic and no dividends are paid, so a dividend yield basis and the earnings yield basis are equally impossible (following the decision in the leading case of *A-G for Ceylon* v *Mackie* (1952) 2 All ER 775).
- Holdings in a loss-making company since presumably in the medium term all the shareholders will agree to a liquidation before the value of the capital is completely eroded.
- Holdings of whatever size in a company controlled by shareholder-directors where practically all the profits are paid out as directors' remuneration so pre-tax profits and consequently earnings are artificially lower.
- Holdings of whatever size in money-box companies where the company is simply a corporate vehicle for family savings.
- Holdings in a trading company with negative goodwill implied by relatively poor earnings or return on capital since it is presumably only a matter of time before either: the shareholders wind up the company; or there is a takeover bid.
- As a useful valuation tool to cross-check the valuations arrived at on other bases for any size of holding. This is justified since the open market value implies a spectrum of potential purchasers ('the whole world was hypothetically there making hypothetical bids' — Danckwerts, J. in *Re Holt*). At least some of these prospective purchasers, even of minority shareholdings, may be supposed to be higher-rate taxpayers to whom the attractions of a capital gain (taxable at most at 30 per cent) would be

considerably greater than income returns (taxable at effectively 75 per cent). Such purchasers would therefore, in seeking capital growth, be primarily interested in a company with assets potential and would value the holding at an appropriate rate of discount on the net asset value.

- Holdings in a comparatively new company whose profit record may justify a positive goodwill value but whose track record is too short to justify any excess capitalisation value would normally be valued on a discounted assets basis.
- Holdings in a company with vulnerable profits because the goodwill is essentially personal to the leading director or directors and would evaporate overnight should they leave (for example, advertising agencies dependent on top copywriters, account executives, service company with a highly personal service, import/export agencies dependent on personal contacts, companies with a new technology bias dependent on specialist innovators, etc.).
- Where a rough-and-ready valuation technique only is required, for example for some IHT planning where statutory exemptions are to be used, or life assurance provisions for death of a surviving spouse with aggregated estates is to be made, the discounted assets basis may serve as an approximate rule of thumb technique, obviating the need for full-scale comparability studies or recourse to a sophisticated investment criterion. The dangers of such an approach are:

  (a) different classes of companies are insufficiently distinguished:

  (b) the discount rates may not reflect drastic changes in contemproary interest rates and investment requirements; and

  (c) the particular company's unique circumstances are not necessarily appreciated.

As regards any such evaluations on this basis, questions arise as to how the assets themselves should be valued and liabilities determined. There are two mutually exclusive situations. Either the company is a going concern so the market value of the assets is at least implicitly equal to the earnings-based evaluation of the company, or it is not and in that case the break-up basis of valuation should be applied. If the former, the normal market valuation of other assets is justified. If the latter, then many assets will realise less than book value and various contingent liabilities should be deducted in full. These include:

(a) winding-up costs;

(b) legal fees;

(c) realisation costs;

(d) liquidator's fees;

(e) CGT on realisation of assets;

(f) the balancing charges of sale proceeds in excess of tax written-down values (due to capital allowances);

(g) any stock relief clawback;

(h) cross-guarantees on associated subsidiary or parent companies;

(i) actions for any consequential breaches of contract;

(j) disallowance of losses under the anti-avoidance provisions of Section 483, ICTA 1970;

(k) unavailability of business retentions arguments against short-fall assessments;

(l) redundancy payments.

Assets that generally require adjustment (usually to a lower figure but exceptionally to a higher one if depreciation has been over-generous) include the following.

Fixed assets

Freehold or leasehold property

This may have a similar value on a going concern or break-up basis if, for example, a dwelling house or investment company is concerned. However, factory premises with limited specialist use value will either have a lower break-up basis or would require substantial conversion expenditure to realise the full market value so that on either basis the going-concern value must be reduced. Leasehold property may also entail substantial expenditure for dilapidations.

Motor vehicles

These should show no reduction on the normal market value except that a forced sale could imply auction as opposed to showroom, garage or private sales prices. A measure of discount could be justified on the accounts figures if shown to be the case.

Fixtures and fittings

These may well have a negligible break-up value whatever the book or going concern value is.

Machinery and plant

These, if fixed on-site, may well have a substantially reduced break-up value.

Indeed their market value may reduce to scrap or salvage value only. A farming company, however, may well realise full value even on an auction sale of their assets if the items in question are tools and tractors of relatively recent age.

Stock-in-trade

In a farming company the herd may well realise a figure substantially in excess of book value or the valuation supplied since such sales do not depend on intrinsic profitability or performance. For high mark up, that is high profit margin stock such as textiles or hi-fi, the discount for such forced sales may be up to 50 per cent.

Debtors

The discount may again be up to 25 per cent depending on the company's bad debt record, the industry record for debtors, the spread of debtors, the debtors' solvency position, the company's own cash flow position and its debt control procedures. Factorisation of debtors is, however, theoretically available and could yield up to 80 per cent of the book value.

Loans

These depend on the borrower's solvency and could be complete write-offs if investigation showed that repayment would probably be impossible to achieve. The same applies to current accounts in other companies, for example parents or subsidiaries. Subject to this, however, the value on either a going concern or a break-up basis would be the face value of the loan or account in question.

Quoted investments

These are valued on the usual quarter-up basis.

Debentures

These are valued in the normal way with a discount taken, if appropriate, according to the terms of the debenture.

Trade investments

These are normally valued at par unless there is any indication of excess value.

Unquoted investments

These require valuation on the normal criteria appropriate to the holding in question.

Intangible assets

These are valued on the basis appropriate to the assets in question, namely copyrights, patents, trade marks, inventions, etc. On a break-up basis the value of even trade marks (closely associated with goodwill) may realise in excess of the book value (normally cost). This is still more likely as regards the other items of intellectual property.

CAPITALISATION OF PROFITS

This method values the company as a going concern at so many years purchase of pre-tax profits. The equation requires determination of: the multiplier; and the level of maintainable pre-tax profits. The multiplier can be determined by a variety of methods:

- By reference to the kind of multipliers implied in actual sales of companies, preferably unquoted comparable companies acting in a similar sector. This requires information about:

  (a) contemporary acquisitions;

  (b) the characteristics and circumstances of the companies concerned; and

  (c) knowledge of special situations (e.g. a special purchase rather than an open market purchase).

It is possible that this information is, to a greater or lesser extent, unobtainable. There may, for example, be no corporate acquisitions of similar companies since full-scale comparability studies reflect the market practice of both companies and investors before a takeover or merger. If quoted comparable corporate acquisitions are the only available information, arguably some adjustment should be made for non-listing. Subject to availability of data, this is the soundest approach to multiplier determination. It has the advantage of: sanction by long use in the market place; and traditional employment amongst professional valuers.

- By reference to the contemporary financial climate, in particular such matters as contemporary interest rates and the *Financial Times* Actuaries Share Index earnings yield and price earnings ratios. Since the shares are equities, the interest rates and yields are arguably of less significance since the latter have no inflation-proofing while equities, depending on gearing, are a natural hedge against inflation. Hence, when inflation is steady to rising there would be what is known to investment analysts as the 'reverse yield gap' whereby the shares with the higher risk (equities) have a lower yield than the preference shares which have a steady income but no prospect of capital growth. Currently, for instance, yields on quoted preference shares are around three times the yield on good quoted equities.

- By reference to the implied multipliers of companies making public issues around the date of valuation. This method is limited, however, by the comparative lack of such companies at any given time. The method has, however, been given judicial approval in the cases of *Holt* and *Lynall*. The multiplier should not, however, be confused with the price earnings ratio which is applied to the after tax profits in the form of net earnings per share.
- By reference to price earnings ratios for the index sector or a range of comparable quoted companies. Although the ratio is applied to earnings per share for minority holdings, it can be justified in multiplier determination on the grounds that:
- (a) the price earnings ratios are only for minority holdings (generally small) in public-quoted companies and the valuation of a controlling interest requires enhancing accordingly. On the other hand, there is a further countervailing downward adjustment for lack of public quoted status with its consequential comparative marketability. The ratio is additionally an indirect reflection of the earnings yield. This gives the ratio a specific relationship to other investment criteria;

  (b) the ratio indicates the number of years purchase of distributable profits available to equity shareholders required by contemporary investments, analysts, institutions and so on for that class of company; and

  (c) on balance therefore the minority nature of the quoted price earnings ratio and the controlling interest valued by the multiplier in effect cancel out so that an appropriate measure of the number of years purchase is derived.

- By reference to the quality of the profits and the nature of the business of the company from which they arise. This has special reference to a group or conglomerate where the holding company may have a variety of trading subsidiaries for each of which a separate multiplier may have to be applied to their respective pre-tax profits as distinctly analysed by the valuer.
- By extrapolation from contemporary sector earnings yields. These indicate roughly the gross rate of return investors are seeking at the time for the particular kind of company. Thus, if the sector earnings yield is 20

per cent the extrapolated multiplier is 100/20 = 5. This is justified on the grounds that the earnings yield for any given sector shows the gross investment return required for that sector.

- There is a share valuation practice to value trading companies at a standard multiplier of five years purchase of pre-tax profits. This is applied with very rare exceptions (for example if the quality of the earnings is exceptionally good or bad or the company is in an exceptionally high risk or high growth sector). This practice evidently derives from the merger-brokers' rule of thumb multiplier commonly employed in the 1950s to pre-tax profits (when inflation was 2 to 3 per cent maximum) and early 1960s (before corporation tax was introduced). There is, for example, an interesting discussion of its origins and use in Nicholas Stacey's book *Mergers in Modern Business.*
- The practice is so rough and ready it can best be justified only as a crude guide and cross-check on the discounted going-concern value when valuing smaller minority holdings. When valuing controlling interests, a much higher information standard would be required and there would, of course, be generally much more at stake so as to justify a detailed investigation and full-scale use of comparability studies.

THE LEVEL OF MAINTAINABLE PRE-TAX PROFITS

This may be determined in the following ways.

- By reference to the profits projection available from the board of directors. This follows the practice in prospectuses on a flotation for the full Stock Exchange quotation. It thus accords with the common stock market practice in an offer for sale to the public at large. There is also evidence that it is followed in private treaty sales of private companies. Indeed, such acquisitions may contain a contractual clause to the effect that part of the consideration depends on a certain profit level being maintained.
- By reference to an average of three to five years of achieved profits. This method is all very well but it understates the current price level and the profits backing it. The method can, however, be justified as a *prudent* purchaser's approach. In an inflationary period such as the present, the early results may well become almost meaninglessly low. This is partly overcome by weighting the average. The author has seen suggestions for weighting on a ten-year average profits basis — with the factors in reverse, that is giving greater weight to the early years, but the valuation was settled eventually on the basis of a seven years average in the right direction. Such averaging can also be used to overcome the problem of maintainable profits in a company with fluctuations in profits due to business cycles such as shipping, timber and textile companies. The

averaging concept can determine an average return to the investor who in the nature of things is looking for longer term returns.

- By reference to the latest year's pre-tax profits figure.
  This may well be valid if the profits position is stable or on an ascertainable trend. Such profits may, of course, mask relative decline in the company's performance and prospects. All trends should in any case be examined against the sector performance and the state of the economy. In particular the profits must be examined for extraordinary items and non-recurrent factors such as one-off orders and so on.

- By extrapolation from the known facts such as turnover figures, gross profit margins, net profit margins, current and capital expenditure and so on. This technique may be necessary where information about current trading performance is inadequate or non-existent due to the relatively poor management controlled systems of smaller companies (often referred to in qualified auditors' reports).

- The level of pre-tax profits may require adjustment for: extraordinary items such as capital profits; and directors' remuneration in excess of a commercial management rate. The former is largely self-explanatory, though, exceptionally, difficulties may occur (as in determining the income versus capital expenditure items for corporation tax purposes, or in the treatment of insurance consequential loss claims following factory fire where there may be an apportionment necessary between income and capital loss items). The question of excessive remuneration has been discussed in the case of *Smyth* v *IRC* (1931) IrR. 643 where the judge allowed, in effect, a partial adding back of such excessive remuneration, but the case is no authority for the proposition that a general adding back is allowable in principle. One stumbling block in doing this is that Section 130, ICTA 1970 could disallow excessive remuneration from the corporation tax computation. However, except in the case of investment companies (on the authority of *L.G. Berry Investments v Attwooll* (1964) 2 All ER and *Copeman* v *William Flood & Sons Ltd* (1941) 1 KB 202 where remuneration for the taxpayer's children, as part-time directors, was disallowed as excessive), the Section is invariably not invoked by the Inspector. For valuations before 1970, the stricter rules apply and challenging such remuneration excesses is easier. This can be a useful weapon in the armoury of the share valuer arguing for higher acquisition values — older valuations for CGT purposes are, of course, invariably for that reason. However, the principles are that:

  (a) controlling shareholder can dismiss the board and appoint his own nominees or run the company himself with, for instance, his spouse or a nominee director;

  (b) he can thus determine the allocation of profits including the relationship between remuneration and dividends and thus the level of retained profits; and

(c) as he can, with few limitations, divert the excess remuneration to himself as dividends or remuneration, he must be expected to have the excess taken into account in the share valuation as this is a potential benefit the vendor would otherwise enjoy.

GOODWILL PLUS NET ASSET VALUE

Goodwill as the intangible asset rarely features in company balance sheets. If it does so it will be either at the cost figure (possibly partly depreciated) originally paid or written off, or arising on consolidation in group accounts where it represents the excess of the purchase price of a subsidiary or subsidiaries over the net tangible assets required. Either way it is likely that the market value of goodwill will be either above or below the book figure. For share valuation purposes, good will represents the excess of the going-concern value or the net worth of the company over the value of its net tangible assets. Determination of the value of goodwill, as such, will often be unnecessary since it will be subsumed in the capitalisation of profits. This will emphatically be the case where the company's profitability is so high in relation to its net assets that the assets basis can safely be ignored. However, for CGT, corporation tax and stamp duty purposes the goodwill of a company or partnership or sole trader may require determination. There are three basic methods for valuing goodwill in that case:

- the capitalisation method;
- the super-profits method;
- the customary basis of valuation.

These different methods are discussed in Chapter 9. For present purposes, this method of valuation can be illustrated as follows. ABC Ltd has 100000 £1 ordinary shares and 100000 £1 preference shares. The company's net tangible assets amount to £900000 and the value of the goodwill (as determined on any of the three methods suggested) is £700000. The valuation of the ordinary shares proceeds:

Net tangible assets	900000
Value of goodwill	700000
	1600000
Less: value of preference shares at par	100000
Value attributable to ordinary shares	1500000
= £15 per share	

PRICE EARNINGS RATIO

This valuation technique was imported from the USA in the mid-1960s and first appeared in the *Financial Times* for August 1965. It was commonly used in the USA because American shares are of no par value. Essentially, the ratio expresses the market assessment of a company's shares represented in the number of years of net earnings implied in the current market price. Put simply, the price equals net earnings per share × the price earnings ratio. Thus, where the share price is £5 and the net earnings are £1 per share, the price of the earnings ratio is £5. The *Financial Times* publishes daily price earnings ratios of leading quoted stocks in its share information service and regularly in the Actuaries Share Indices for different industries and commercial sectors. This leading investment yardstick can be applied in valuing any size of holding, providing proper adjustments are made and it is used with discretion.

There are three major elements in determining the price earnings ratio:

- the size of holding;
- the quoted sector equivalent; and
- the company's performance, circumstances and state of stock.

When the company's sector is identified, the price earnings ratios can be determined for:

- a single sector based on the *Financial Times* indices which average the ratios for all the constituent companies; and
- a variety of quoted companies chosen for their comparability with the unquoted company in question.

The average price earnings ratio can be determined by eliminating extremes of high or low ratios. This is because the companies with exceptionally high or low ratios will show special characteristics such as market leadership, takeover potential, product innovation, dawn raids, brokers' reports, exceptional losses and so on, or, conversely, a profits drop, poor prospects, qualified accounts or dividend costs and will by definition be super-normal. For example, companies A–G show price earnings ratios as follows: Company A 12.7; Company B 8.0; Company C; 6.9; Company D 3.2; Company E 7.4; Company F 6.4; Company G 15.9. The *Financial Times* Actuaries Share Index sector price earnings ratio is 8.8.

Companies A, D, and G can be eliminated as either too high or too low. The remaining companies show an average of 7.17, a reduction of 20 per cent on the quoted sector ratio. This is the starting point before adjustments for B and C. Adjusting for the relative unmarketability factor of unquoted status requires a standard deduction of around 25 per cent. This can be justified as the adjustment for that factor approved by the court in the leading case of *Crossman* v *IRC* (1937) AC 26 and also referred to by the expert witnesses in the leading case of *Holt* v *IRC* (1953) 32 ATC 402. The articles in the

Table 8.1
Adjustments for size of holding

Holding (%)	Discount (%)
10 or under	60
10.1-25	50
25.1-49.9	40
50	25
50.1-74.9	10
75-89.9	5
90-100	ZERO

Crossman case were more stringent than some, but some articles will be much more restrictive so as to pre-empt any possibility of a free market in the shares. In such cases the 25 per cent should be increased to perhaps 50 per cent for really depreciatory provisions. Adjustment for size of holding may be as shown in Table 8.1. Once again the critical dividing line between different sizes of holding according to legal powers is followed. Adjusting for the company's circumstances allows substantial valuation negotiating scope.

It will be borne in mind that a preferred valuation method for controlling interests is the capitalisation of profits method. However, the price earnings ratio is sometimes used by professional valuers and with some justification. If the undiscounted quoted price earnings ratio is used the result will often come close to the results achieved by the pre-tax profit multiplier technique. Taking corporation tax at roughly 50 per cent, a price earnings ratio of 8 or 10 will equate with the results attained by multipliers of 4 or 5.

Example

Company XYZ has issued ordinary shares, £100 000 maintainable pre-tax profits and a multiplier of 4 is considered appropriate. The going-concern value is then £100 000 × 4 = £400 000 which, divided by £10 000 = £40 per share. This is the same as £100 000 pre-tax profits less corporation tax at 50% = £50 000 ÷ £10 000 = £5 earnings per share which applying a price earnings ratio of 8 = £40 per share.

For very small holdings too the multiplier may be misleading or even meaningless. Thus, realistic valuations may nevertheless imply a price earnings ratio of 0.5 or similar. The single figure is then an insufficiently discriminating device to express finer differences in value. For example, a difference between price earnings ratio of 2 and 2½ may look slight but it may be buried in the valuation difference of say £400 and £500 per share if earnings per share are unusually high at, say, £200 per share.

The ratio comes into its own in valuing influential minority interests. Such holdings may command a minimal or substantial premium over the value of a small minority. It is unlikely, however, to be a premium of under 10 per cent. On the other hand, this is, of course, within the normal expected range of values in any case. The size of premium depends on such factors as the distribution of the other shareholdings in the company, whether, for example, the holding in question faces a controlling interest or family control; the size of holding, whether only 25.1 per cent (or only just within the valuation category) or 49.99 per cent (only a fraction off being the largest possible holding); the restrictions on transfer in the articles; the significance of a potential winding-up resolution (which such a resolution could block) or of any other special or extraordinary resolution. The value of the premium is best expressed by choosing an appropriate price earnings ratio. This can be extrapolated by discounting the quoted sector ratio, preferably off a range of comparable companies, for the various relevant factors. For example, a 25 per cent discount can be applied for the unmarketability factor, following the principle in the *Crossman* case. A further 25 per cent could be applied for size of company grounds. The discounts in decided cases for such holdings, applied to the going-concern values, are also appropriate guides. For example, the discount in the *Lynall* case was around 50 per cent for a 28 per cent influential minority holding. In the case of *Re Courthope* (1928) 7 ATC 538, where the company was exceptionally liquid and was perhaps ripe for winding up, the discount was 33.33 per cent for a 48 per cent holding. In the *Salvesen* case, where a 33.33 per cent holding was involved, the discount on net asset value was as high as 70 per cent, but the articles in that case were extremely restrictive and the company's profits and dividends fluctuated drastically so the investment was highly speculative. For a medium-size holding in a medium-size company a price earnings ratio of around half the quoted ratio is perhaps appropriate. Thus if the quoted sector ratio is, say, 8, the unquoted equivalent company's ratio would be around 4 with a 10 per cent margin each side being fully negotiable to shade off any finer points of difference and to give effect to the company's peculiar circumstances. This valuation method is essentially the minority holding equivalent of the year's purchase implicit in the controlling interest multiplier.

EARNINGS YIELD

This basis is appropriate when valuing small minority holdings in non-dividend paying companies. The formula is:

$$P = E\%/EY\%$$

where P = price, $E\%$ = earnings expressed gross and $EY\%$ = earnings yield gross, in percentage terms. For example, if the earnings are 200 per cent gross and the earnings yield is 40 per cent gross, then the price is £5 per share.

Determination of the earnings, presents problems as with the price earnings ratio requirement of net earnings per share. For comparison purposes, the quoted sector indices are based on the net earnings shown in the latest available accounts. The valuation practice is to take, say, three years' average earnings as a guide to the average return. If these show a distinctive trend, then a weighted average may be used. If the earnings are really erratic, a longer period may be appropriate to take account of longer-term business cycles. If the average results are minimal or negative, the basis of valuation must be supplemented or replaced by an alternative method, even if minority holdings are involved. If there have been losses and the cause of the losses have been definitively eliminated, it may be possible to ignore them. This means substantial successive losses, not a mere hiccup in a normal business cycle which must be included in the computation of average returns. The average return concept necessarily implies past performance is in some sense a good guide to the future. Thus mechanical formulation is insufficient. The figures must be checked against the likelihood of the trend continuing or declining. This is ascertainable from chairmens' and directors' reports, industry, surveys, sector industries, technical literature and so on. Capital commitments and investment programmes are also signs of an expanding company.

In comparing earnings yields of quoted and unquoted companies to value shares in companies not paying dividends, several important differences must be borne in mind.

- Quoted companies normally do pay dividends. Only when in loss-making situations or with exceptional capital commitments do they not. Their earnings yields therefore reflect this fact. As many as 75 percent of unquoted companies do not pay dividends and in fact will never do so.
- Quoted companies are much bigger generally speaking than unquoted companies. This size factor — involving crucial differences in stability, diversification and so on — must be taken into account.
- Quoted companies have larger reserves and are therefore better placed to ride economic and business fluctuations and still pay dividends.
- Quoted companies depend much less on financing growth from internal resources and in particular have much easier access to long-term loan capital, lessening the pressure on immediate cash flow.
- Quoted companies can also expand more readily by acquisition by share exchange since the shares have a ready stock market quoted price. This is particularly the case with quoted companies who have exceptionally high price earnings ratios.
- Quoted companies are unlikely to be single customer companies or single product companies.
- Quoted companies are much more likely to experience sharp rises or falls in their share prices. The share prices of unquoted companies are likely to be more stable as regards both rises and falls.

- Quoted companies are less likely to be under-capitalised or to over-trade.
- Quoted companies do not have the close involvement of shareholders in the management of the company that characterises unquoted companies due to the common experience of control by shareholder–directors. By corollary, quoted companies are more likely to show greater sensitivity to needs of shareholders as regards allocation of profits by way of dividend rather than remuneration as is often the case with unquoted companies. There may well also be institutional pressure for dividend growth. A conservative dividend policy is also likely to be an invitation to a takeover-bid, whereas a director-controlled close company, which is the characteristic private company, has nothing to fear from such takeover bids.
- Exceptionally high earnings in relation to low issued share capital can be misleading, resulting in a top-heavy share price. Return on capital employed should always be examined as well in assessing the company's profitability.
- Unquoted companies may often show unrealistically low rates of directors' remuneration. Adjustment to take proper account of this factor by deducting a notional figure for a full commercial rate of remuneration would prevent an inflated share valuation. The same, of course, applies to artificially high directors' remuneration which must also be adjusted to a commercial rate. Finally, many unquoted companies have substantial directors' loan accounts, in effect in many cases representing first business loans from incorporation of unincorporated businesses or partnerships. Where this applies, interest is very seldom paid on such loan accounts. Adjustment should be made by a notional deduction for interest on such loan accounts to give a truer picture of the company's profitability.

It follows from the above that very substantial adjustments to sector indices or ranges of quoted yields are necessary before an appropriate yield can be determined in respect of many unquoted companies. Indeed, as regards the smaller companies an earnings yield of 3 or exceptionally even 4 × the earnings yield found in the *Financial Times* Actuaries Share Index would be necessary before an accurate market value could be determined. The adjustment depends basically on the relationship between the size of the company in question and the size of the companies contained in the sector index or used in the range of comparable companies. Certainly, the relatively low earnings yields found in the *Financial Times* Actuaries Share Indices at the present time suggest that very substantial adjustments would have to be made. For example, the electricals sector containing 12, in many cases very large, quoted companies, shows earnings yield of under 8 and this gross earnings yield would have to be adjusted probably by a 4 × multiplier to give a gross earnings yield of around 30 or 32 per cent for an unquoted company of relatively small size in this sector. The earnings yield for stores, containing 41 in many cases very large quoted companies shows an earnings yield of around 7 per cent and this again would suggest that a gross earnings yield for a small unquoted company in the stores sector would be around 28 per cent. Mechanical engineering contractors, on the other hand, contain 63 quoted companies and the earnings yield of around 9 per cent gross would perhaps be adjusted by only a multiplier of say 4 to give an earnings yield of around 36 per cent gross for a small unquoted company in this particular sector. The industrial group index contains 483 quoted companies of varying sizes and the gross earnings yield for this group is 8 per cent gross as at July 1986. This suggests that a gross earnings yield for a small unquoted company that does not fit into any of the particular specialist sectors should be around 40 per cent gross.

Some mention should be made of the relationship between the earnings yield and the price earnings ratio. The earnings yield represents the investor's return expressed as so many years' purchase. Thus a 20 per cent yield represents five years' purchase of the company's gross earnings or a pay-back period of five years. After 6 April 1965, and before the imputation system of corporation tax was introduced on 6 April 1973, the earnings yield showed a reciprocal relationship with the price earnings ratio. Thus an earnings yield of 50 per cent implied a price earnings ratio of 2. This is no longer the case since the earnings yield represents earnings grossed up at the current rate of ACT, while the price earnings ratio is applied to net earnings per share. The reciprocal relationship can be restored, however, by degrossing the earnings yield by the ACT factor (currently 7/10). Thus an earnings yield of 40 per cent represents 7/10 × 40% net = 28.5% net = a price earnings ratio of 100/28.5 = 3.5.

DIVIDEND YIELD

This is the leading valuation method for small minority holdings but has little relevance for valuations of controlling interests. It is based on the kind of income return expected by a prospective investor as at the valuation date. The equation is

$$V = D/DY$$

where V is the value, D is the dividend and DY is the required yield or rate of return. Since 6 April 1973 the yield is expressed gross as the dividends paid net carry a tax credit at the current rates of income tax and must be grossed-up to reflect this. The cost to the company is, of course, the net dividend which bears ACT set-off against the mainstream corporation tax liability. If, then, a company pays a net dividend of 70p per share on its £1 ordinary shares, this is 70 per cent net dividend which is grossed-up at 30 per cent, i.e. by multiplying the net dividend by 10/7 (equals 100/70) or dividing it by 0.7, the gross dividend is 100 per cent. If the required yield is 20 per cent gross the valuation is at £5 per share (100% ÷ 20% × £1 = £5). The questions that arise are:

- What is to be taken as the maintainable dividend?

- What determines the required yield?

Determination of maintainable dividend

- One method is to take the latest declared dividend as maintainable. This is in fact the basis followed in the investment media and in particular in the *Financial Times* Actuaries Share Index. In most cases it would probably be a reasonable estimate of the immediate future dividend level. It is obviously best applied where the company's dividend policy is well established, preferably relatively independently of earnings levels. It is not unknown for a conservative board of directors, in a company with a need for extensive plough-back of profits, to show the same dividend level for ten years or more. In such cases the next dividend can easily be anticipated, but it is arguable that the pure dividend yield is not an appropriate basis since the earnings will generate future capital growth.
- Another method is to follow the trend of dividends in a company with rapidly rising dividends linked to ex-potential earnings growth. Thus, the company in a growth industry showed the following earnings and dividend growth:

	1983	1984	1985	1986
Earnings increase level	25%	60%	150%	300%
Dividend	10%	20%	40%	80%
Cover	2.5	3	3.75	3.75

In calculating the 1987 figure, to take the latest dividend would probably represent an underestimate of the dividend potential. Extrapolation suggests a gross dividend of around 160 per cent based on earnings of around 600 per cent. A prudent purchaser would discount the trend to some extent, unless evidence of similar profits could be adduced. It will be borne in mind that a prospectus issued at the time of an offer for sale contains just such similar profits and dividends projections based on broad estimates. Such earnings growth and dividend growth will be exceptional. Where it exists, however, the share valuation must recognise it and take it fully into account.

- Another method frequently encountered is to take an average of three years (or five years in a cyclical business) dividends paid. Such a method can be justified as based on:

(a) the average rate of return;

(b) elimination of cyclical fluctuations;

(c) the requirements of a prudent purchaser;

(d) the recognition of upwards or downwards trends by a weighted average.

As opposed to this, however:

(a) the average takes full account of past dividends that are history and of less concern than future maintainable dividend levels;

(b) fluctuations may be relatively irrelevant depending on the dividend policy of the particular board, and significant earnings fluctuations may be ignored because dividends are paid out of reserves;

(c) the prudent purchaser will examine more than history;

(d) the average may itself be misleading, for example a downward trend may give the same net result as an upward trend:

Company A	Company B
100	300
200	200
300	100
600	600
Average: 200	Average: 200

Here the weighted average for Company A would be 233 (i.e. (100 × 1) + (200 × 2) + (300 × 3) = 1400 ÷ 6 = 233) or 16.66 per cent higher than the unweighted average, but this is still 22 per cent below the latest dividend declared and is unlikely to give as accurate a figure as the latest dividend level. The weighted average for B is 166 (i.e. (300 × 1) + (200 × 2) + (100 × 3) = 1000 ÷ 6 = 166) which is 16.66 per cent lower than the unweighted average, but still 66.66 per cent higher than the latest actual declared dividend and is almost certainly a significant overestimate of the future dividend level. This indicates the care and caution with which an average dividends approach must be used.

- The determination of future dividends level from projected profits performance is another method. One difficulty in applying this method (which may sometimes be the best) is that the small minority holding may not justify disclosure of the future projected profits level. This will not, however, be the case where a substantial outlay is prospectively involved. Thus a purchaser of 200000 £1 ordinary shares in a profitable company is not likely to accept an inferior information standard — especially if the more detailed statutory information standard is involved.

Determination of the required dividend yield

This will depend on:

- the sector index yield;
- the yields shown by comparable quoted companies;
- the yields shown in relevant actual transactions in the company's shares;

- the dividend cover;
- the asset backing;
- the level of contemporary interest rates;
- the size of holding in question;
- the distribution of other holdings;
- the company's liquidity position;
- the prospective rate of dividend growth;
- the quality of the company's earnings;
- the prospect of capital appreciation through takeover, merger, flotation and so on;
- the restrictive clauses in the company's articles and the extent of the market for the shares, as well as the prospect of extension of that market, for example through access to Stock Exchange Rule 163 transactions and the unlisted securities market.

Sector index yield

This can usually be seen in the *Financial Times* Actuaries Share Index. Use of such index yields is justified with reference to Sir Henry Benson's testimony in *Holt* v *IRC* (he used the All Share Index) and *Re Lynall* (where he used motors and aircraft, and engineering). With some sectors, such as building and property, the sector yields may require such substantial adjustments so as to make it difficult to justify their use at all. If the company's business does not fall into any of the given sectors, then the yield for capital or consumer goods or for industrial or commercial equities generally can be used. In any event, a very substantial adjustment must be made to the ascertained quoted dividend yield. A minimum would be an adjustment of around 50 per cent (following an expert witness, Mr Hill-Wood, in the *Lynall* case who adjusted the *Financial Times* industrial share index yield of 5.33 per cent by this factor) for a medium-size trading company and a doubling for a smaller company. Where the company is small and the sector companies are exceptionally large and in growth areas such as electricals, the yield could be trebled or even quadrupled to arrive at a meaningful market value. However, for such a valuation a better yield check would be found by examining some smaller comparable quoted companies. The minimum adjustment for unquoted private company status alone where the articles are severely restrictive is 25 per cent as in the *Crossman* case, assuming the company, as in that case, is as large as the quoted companies. If the articles are less restrictive, the adjustment might be 20 per cent or even conceivably less. For the exceptional case where a public unquoted company is involved, an adjustment as low as 10 per cent might be justified as applied by the court in the Australian case of *Federal Commissioner of Taxation* v *Sagar* 71 CLR 421.

Yields shown by comparable quoted companies

These require less adjustment than broad sector yields, although some adjustment must still be made for unquoted status (say 20 to 30 per cent) and the size factor (very much dependent on the facts, but a minimum of say 25 per cent for a medium-size company would be reasonable). If the company's profits, assets and place in the market justify it, the size factor could be minimal or even ignored altogether. What is required is a table of comparable company yields with the highs and lows eliminated so that an average required yield will emerge. The companies may be researched through such sources of information as the Extel classified list supplemented by reference to Extel cards for specific company information; the *Stock Exchange Yearbook* and the official daily list for yields at the relevant time; the *Financial Times* share information service; and, of course, financial and trade journals, annuals, directories, gazettes and so on.

Actual transaction yields

These will seldom be available and must be used with caution since, at best, they represent restricted market, not open market, prices. However, if the company has a relatively active market and comparable holdings have been transferred at a recent date, they will be relevant evidence of required yields.

Dividend cover

This feeds back on to the required yield, and higher cover normally means a lower yield. However, this effect is subject to diminishing returns. Thus if the yield at a cover of 2 is 10 per cent, a cover of 18 will not justify a yield of only 1.11 per cent. There will be cases where the cover is as high as 40 or 50 in private companies and this indicates that the company is possibly under-capitalised and the basis of valuation should not be dividend yield at all but an earnings-based valuation. On the other hand, high cover does not necessarily mean dividend growth in the short-term since the profits may be almost indefinitely ploughed back. Since the Finance Act 1980, there has also been no shortfall pressure on trading profits while even investment income may be retained if business requirements can justify it.

There is a formula used to determine the relationship between dividend yield and cover. This is the so-called rule of $2\frac{1}{2}$ suggested by the table produced by Sir Henry Benson in the *Lynall* case. If the yield is Y and the cover is C, then $Y(C + 2\frac{1}{2})$ stays constant. Thus, if the twice cover dividend yield for a company paying a dividend is 10 per cent, then $Y(C + 2\frac{1}{2}) = 10(2 + 2\frac{1}{2}) = 45$. Comparable companies with dividends of, say, 3, 4 and 5 × covered would show yields of:

$45/(3 + 2\frac{1}{2}) = 8.18\%$;
$45/(4 + 2\frac{1}{2}) = 6.92\%$; and
$45/(5 + 2\frac{1}{2}) = 6.00\%$, respectively.

The Berliner method (see p. 99) of averaging different valuation bases is another way of allowing for dividend cover. Exceptionally, the cover may preclude the dividend yield basis altogether. The other point is that the required cover, like company liquidity and depreciation rates, will vary fantastically from industry to industry. Some heavy industries with high capital investment and long-term development programmes may require exceptional plough-back profits. Examples would be oil (with front-end loaded expenditure), road haulage (with perennial replacement of vehicles), shipping (with vessel replacement) and engineering (with large-scale investment in factories, machinery and plant). Subject to this, however, the words of Lord Fleming in *Salvesen's Trustees* v *IRC* are relevant:

> I cannot think it is right to ignore the very large sums which the company had actually earned but had not distributed as dividend, but I do not subscribe to the view that the shareholders acted irrationally in not distributing the profits which they had earned.
>
> The shareholders' confidence in this speculative industry had been such that they were not content merely to reap the harvest invested, say, in less speculative securities, but they reinvested it in the industry in the expectation that they would earn still greater prizes.
>
> Assuming that the future of the company has its ups and downs as it had in the past, its reserves must ultimately, according to all reasonable probabilities, inure to the benefit of the shareholders ... it could not go on indefinitely piling up its reserves.

The yield determination method by comparison with quoted companies is much favoured by the shares valuation division with its vast resources of industry, commercial and company information, but it was criticised by Ploughman, J. in the *Lynall* case on three counts:

- the different dividend policies of public and private companies;
- the different transfer procedures of the two kinds of company; and
- the fact that an investor is looking at the company and its management rather than the industry as such.

However, the comparative approach can be justified as follows:

- The first two above points of criticism are resolved by the compensatory better dividend cover generally found in most private companies.
- The last point of criticism affects not the required yield, but rather the assessment of dividend and growth prospects by the investor.
- The experts in the *Lynall* case generally agreed on the required yield, although they differed considerably on the overall valuation: the yield range among the four experts in question was only 7 to 8 per cent.
- The comparative method is factually based and not wholly arbitrary as are some alternative suggested methods.

- The quoted sector yields reflect the requirements of equity investors in the only available open market for stocks and shares (the Stock Exchange) and thus satisfy the open market element in the statutory valuation.
- This way the specific industry risk factors can be taken into account on a reasonably rational basis.
- This is the only way the investment impact of such matters as government policy, economic events, political crises and so on are given effect.
- Such a comparability study is the practical approach used by investment experts such as investment analysts and merger brokers as well as institutional managers and professional advisers. It therefore accords with actual market practice.
- All valuation is a relativistic exercise and presupposes judgement based on the economic concept of alternative use of funds. An investor must be supposed to compare the probable returns, short-term and long-term, from different investment media. In particular, he will compare equities with gilts and other fixed-interest investments. Logically he will compare like with like and thus unquoted shares with quoted shares, setting the prospectively greater income or capital gains of the former against the immediate marketability of the latter.
- Specific justification for comparison with yields on newly issued quoted shares is found in Lord Simon's statement, in the case of *Gold Coast Selection Trust Ltd* v *Humphrey* (1948) 27 AC 459, that a valuation of unquoted shares will take into account an offer for sale of similar shares in a contemporary prospectus. Information as to any such prospectuses can be obtained from Singer and Friedlander's new issue statistics. Prospectuses are, of course, published in full in the *Financial Times* accompanying the offer for sale.
- Maguire, J. in *McNamee* v *Revenue Commissioners* (1954) IrR. 214 directly attacked the yield comparison method in the following terms:

> Mr Cave, Mr Scanlon and Mr Abrahamson have gone to great trouble to prepare comparative tables of other companies carrying on similar business having Stock Exchange quotations for their shares. Those have been examined and explained. I am satisfied, without going into details and having considered all the evidence, that the analogies which they have drawn from other companies are far from complete and that they are misleading. I am satisfied too that the inferences they asked me to draw cannot fairly be drawn in the case of those shares in the Convoy Woollen Co. The affairs of each company must be considered in relation to its own position, its own difficulties and its own domestic control.

However, the evidence of Lord Plander in the *Crossman* case, founded on a comparative basis to give a valuation approaching 60 per cent higher than the articles price based on fair value, was fully accepted by the courts right up to the House of Lords and, as *Crossman* was fully approved in the leading modern case of *Lynall* it constitutes considerably greater authority than the *obiter* remarks of the Irish judge at first instance.

Asset backing

If the asset backing is substantial, lower yield may be justified than would otherwise prevail since it means greater security for the investor and, if the assets are appreciatory ones such as freeholds or blue chips, there may be inbuilt capital growth. The implied lowered risk will reduce the yield. How far this goes in the valuation in question is a moot point. It would normally be marginal, however, and thus only a negotiating point or a small yield adjustment factor. Excessive asset backing compared with dividends and earnings would make the company a prime takeover target and the appropriate valuation basis would then probably be discounted assets.

Contemporary interest rates

These normally reflect inflation rates (and, as monetarists would suggest, the state of the money supply) and should be taken into account in arriving at the required yield. However, it cannot be said that the Base Rate represents a minimum yield. The reverse yield gap shows clearly that equities as growth stocks can outpace inflation and may require a substantially lower yield than fixed-interest stock. Interest rates should, in effect, form a check merely on share valuations based on unusually and unrealistically low quoted sector yields.

Size of the holding

This determines the extent to which a pure dividend yield basis can apply. For holdings larger than 25 per cent, such a basis is not in any case adequate. A 1 per cent holding, say, in a small company paying dividends will on the other hand be valued almost exclusively on a pure dividend yield basis. A way of differentiating the valuations of different sizes of holdings is to decrease the yield for the larger ones. If appropriate, differentials between holdings of say 10.1 per cent (with a Section 209, Companies Act 1948, right not to be bought out), 15 per cent (with a power to demand an extraordinary general meeting) and 25 per cent (only one share away from the power to block a special resolution) can be maintained.

Distribution of other shareholdings

This distribution, and in particular whether or not there is a controlling interest, or the company is director-controlled, may be crucial in determining the pay-out ratio for future dividends. This necessarily affects the purchaser's perception of the required yield.

Company's liquidity position

This determines the maintainability, or even the likelihood, of future dividends whatever the profits position may be.

Rate of dividend growth

This growth affects the yield, and if there is none the yield will be higher since low yields represent, in effect, expectation of further dividend growth or capital appreciation through ploughed-back profits.

Quality of company's earnings

This determines the company's future prospects and therefore the probability of further profits and consequential dividends. The composition, as well as the amount of profits, is important, particularly in a conglomerate enterprise since the global figure may conceal significant subsidiary trends.

Prospect of capital appreciation

If this prospect is remote it will have a negligible effect. If likely, the yield will be reduced to equate with the comparable quoted yield, subject to a deduction solely for contingencies. Even if a flotation, winding up, or sale of the company, as a whole, as a going concern is imminent, a deduction of anything between 20 and 33 per cent from the prospective offer or bid price is suggested as appropriate.

Restrictive articles

These will partly determine the required yield as the decided cases plainly show. Characteristic adjustments have been as follows:

- *Crossman* v *IRC* (a 10 per cent holding in a company with severely restrictive articles). A 25 per cent adjustment (Lord Plander).
- *Holt* v *IRC* (a holding of under 7 per cent in a company with highly restrictive articles). A 30 to 33 per cent adjustment was required by four different expert witnesses.
- *Lynall* v *IRC* (a 28 per cent holding in a company with extremely restrictive articles). An adjustment of 30 per cent was required (Sir Henry Benson).

Finally, it should be added that the state of the company's reserves may also be critical in determining the yield since the existence of substantial reserves means that, even in a bad year, the company's dividend level may be maintained. The existence of such reserves may also suggest that the benefit of bonus shares may accrue in the future to a prospective purchaser out of such reserves.

THE BERLINER METHOD

This method values shares by combining different bases of valuation into an average figure. The weighting of the different bases is a matter of judgement as is the choice of the valuation bases themselves. The method has particular application where the holdings in question are minorities. For a very small minority holding in a company paying low dividends with high dividend cover and strong assets backing, an example of this valuation method would show a weighting of, say, 3:2:1 to the dividend yield basis, the earnings yield basis and the discounted assets basis, respectively. Thus:

Valuation of a 20 per cent holding in XYZ Ltd:
Valuation on pure dividend yield,
£2 per share × 3 = £6 per share.
Valuation on pure earnings yield,
£3 per share × 2 = £6 per share.
Valuation on net assets basis,
£4 per share × 1 = £4 per share.
Average value = £16 ÷ 6 = £2.66 per share.

This has the merit of taking all three main valuation bases into account, although the method is a little arbitrary. It can, however, be recommended as an alternative valuation approach in actual negotiations where both parties are getting bogged down in dogmatic stances since it may add the crucial element of flexibility that can result in a satisfactory settlement by compromise.

THE HAMILTON BAYNES METHOD

The late Hamilton Baynes was a professional share valuer and expert witness in the leading cases of *Holt* and *Lynall*. His valuation method for minority holdings is hedged around, as he said, with a series of 'ifs' and, assuming all 12 stated conditions are satisfied, the valuation would be based on a specified dividend yield of, say, 12 per cent in the depressed early 1960s, 10 per cent in the equity-boom early 1970s and, presumably, at least 12 per cent again in the recessionary early 1980s. The method only applies for, say, a 10 per cent holding on a sale in the restricted market for private company shares, not the open market required by statute, and then if:

- there is not then a political or financial crisis;

- the industry is not declining;
- the articles have no unusual clauses;
- the company has level profits;
- the management is satisfactory and reasonably well-paid;
- the profits shown have fluctuations;
- dividends have been regularly paid with adequate but not excessive cover;
- the company does not depend on a single customer or supplier;
- gearing is adequate;
- the company is reasonably liquid and has no overdraft or temporary loans;
- the fixed assets are adequately maintained; and
- no shareholder has control or will obtain control by buying the holding in question.

Criticisms of the method (which may still be met in practice) are that:

- it is not stated to apply in the statutory open market for which many, if not the majority of, valuations are professionally made;
- it is not a method usually applicable since the conditions are such that the basis of valuation cannot apply in the case of the majority of private companies since one or more of the conditions will not be satisfied;
- the method takes no account of specific company circumstances or fiscal requirements; and
- although half-heartedly advocated by the originator, in the tribunals in which he appeared, as an alternative to the more orthodox valuation methods and, in particular, the method of valuation by comparison with quoted sector equity yields, his method was not judicially approved.

Assuming the method was applicable and the company in question paid a gross dividend of 24 per cent, the valuation would, of course, in the given example be 24/12 × £1 = £2 per share.

THE INTRINSIC VALUE METHOD

This is based on the theory that a shareholding or a company may have an intrinsic or true value which may differ from the actual transaction price at any given time. This is something known to investment analysts who determine whether quoted share prices on the Stock Exchange fall above or below such an intrinsic value so as to constitute dear or cheap buys. The concept is also sometimes called the bid value since the value of the shares to a takeover bidder will approach the intrinsic value, but many takeover bids are, of course, made on the basis of a special purchase and this will generally exceed what could be called the market value (open or restricted) of the shares. In effect this method operates by:

- valuing the company by one of the appropriate normal valuation techniques; and
- adding to this value, arrived at in such a way, a premium to reflect the special purchase element, but without incorporating the full special purchase price.

This is justifiable on the basis that it accords with the actual open market practice for takeover bids. The initial valuation is, after all, normally a negotiating starting point for the serious bidder. A negotiated compromise figure would make the intrinsic value mid-point, say, between the normal market value and the special purchaser's price.

Example

The normal market valuation of shares in XYZ Computers Ltd, a company specialising in business software programs, is £2m or £20 for each of its 100000 issued ordinary shares. However, the special purchaser's price would be £4m or £40 per share as the company's products, management, order book, export potential, cash flow and profits prospects have a special appeal to ABC Computers Ltd, a multinational turn-key systems conglomerate. The intrinsic value equation suggests a market valuation at £2m + (£4m – £2m/2) = £3m or £30 per share.

THE *LYNALL* FORMULA

This is justified as the basis of valuation approved by the court in the leading modern *Lynall* case in unquoted share valuation. The formula is to determine the value of a £1 ordinary share as £$D/Y + P$ where D/Y is the dividend yield base valuation (dividend/yield) and P is a premium for prospective capital appreciation. The formula is adaptable to a variety of circumstances. However, the majority of unquoted companies are relatively small, do not pay dividends and will never achieve flotation (in each case unlike the company in *Lynall*) so that the scope for applying the formula is somewhat limited. Moreover, the kind of holding in *Lynall* (an influential minority) is arguably best valued on a price earnings ratio basis rather than a method that starts from a dividend yield basis. The formula as applied in *Lynall* proceeded by a dividend yield based valuation at £3 per share (where D/Y was 22½/7½) and applied a capital appreciation factor of £1.50 (or 50 per cent) on the information standard, which now applies. This resulted in a valuation at £4.50 per share or a discount of 40 per cent on the prospective flotation price of £6.50 per share at the date of valuation.

Example

Valuation of a 25 per cent holding in XYZ Ltd which has 200000 issued ordinary shares, pays a steadily rising dividend (currently 30 per cent net or 42.86 per cent gross) with a cover of 4 or £1.20 earnings per share and a net asset value of £10 per share. It operates in the electrical sector (a growth area) where there is much takeover activity, and flotation prospects are at least reasonable in view of its pre-tax profits level (£450000) and its assets base of £2m.

Applying the *Lynall* formula, a valuation could be:

$D/Y + P$ = £42.85/£10 + 25% = £4.285 + £1.071 = £5.356 say, £5.35 per share or a valuation in the range of £4.80 to £5.90 per share. This represents a price earnings ratio of 4.46 (5.35/1.20) at the base price, or gross earnings yield of 32 per cent (120/0.7 = 171.43%/5.35), both of which would be prima facie acceptable having regard to the sector ratios and yields currently prevalent.

DISCOUNTED CASH FLOW/NET PRESENT VALUE METHOD

This is a mathematically-based method, much used in company capital budgeting or project evaluation. As such it is perhaps a spuriously precise tool for share valuation. It may have more justification in valuing copyrights or patents where the likely cashflows over a reasonably long-term period of, say, up to five or even ten years may be adequately projected. The technique is to equate the share value with the net present value of the projected future cash flow. Whether these are dividends or earnings must be first determined.

Table 8.2
Net present value calculation

	Projected dividend discount	Discount factor @ 10%	Discounted dividend
Year 1	10p	0.909	9p
Year 2	20p	0.826	16½p
Year 3	30p	0.751	22½p
Year 4	40p	0.683	27p
Year 5	50p	0.621	31p
		Net present value	£1.06

The valuation procedure is then to determine a required rate of return (normally equated with the contemporary bank base rate plus a risk factor addition of, say, 25 to 50 per cent). Thus assuming a dividend-based cash flow evaluation for a five-year period, depreciating at 10 per cent per annum, the method could be applied as shown in Table 8.2. On this basis, the net valuation would be around par for a £1 ordinary share on an immediate dividend yield of around 15.42 per cent gross.

9 The valuation of goodwill

The concept of commercial goodwill evidently dates back to a late Tudor will of 1571, but the most famous judicial definition was Lord Eldon's in the case of *Curtwell* v *Lye* (1810):

> Nothing more than the probability that the old customers will resort to the old place even though the old trader or shopkeeper has gone.

A variation on this definition was attempted by the Research Committee of the Professional Institute of Accountants which stated:

> Goodwill consists of those elements in business relationships which make a continuance of such relationships probable notwithstanding a change in the ownership of the business.

That is, however, both rather cumbersome and also inadequate as lacking in any reference to profits.

The profit element was stressed by P.D. Leake in his book on *Commercial Goodwill:*

> Without the reasonable probability of the earning of future super-profit, no present value in the form of goodwill can exist.

The Revenue concept of goodwill is apparently the excess of the going-concern value of a business over the value of its net tangible assets. This does not necessarily imply any particular mode of goodwill valuation. This particular definition is, however, inadequate in that it implies that the existence of such profits will necessarily entail the existence of goodwill and conversely that the lack of such profits would mean that there is no possible value in the goodwill. In fact, as will be seen, neither of these propositions is necessarily correct.

A particularly common accountancy concept is 'goodwill arising on consolidation' which occurs in a group balance sheet to indicate the excess market value of an acquired subsidiary or subsidiaries over the net tangible assets taken over. This is clearly, in such cases, similar to the Revenue concept referred to above.

An alternative concept of special use in the smaller business concept is that goodwill is the value of an ongoing business to a newcomer to the trade or profession. Such an entrant, by acquiring a going concern rather than starting from scratch, should to that extent find it easier to build up a profitable business (including further self-generated goodwill) of his own. That is why he is prepared to pay a price in excess of the net tangible assets acquired.

Such goodwill sales can be seen advertised regularly in trade journals, business periodicals and professional magazines. It will be clear that many small businesses are not sold for their profitability so much as for their entry into a particular business lifestyle. This is why goodwill cannot necessarily be related, in every case, purely to profits and super-profits.

Conversely, the fact that substantial profits are being made does not necessarily imply that goodwill exists as a marketable asset. The goodwill, such as it is, may attach essentially to the owner of the business rather than to the business itself. This means that, were the owner to leave the business, his successor could not hope to benefit from continuing goodwill. This might well be the case where the business is of a personal service so that the goodwill is highly personal to the proprietor. Another instance might be where the proprietor was a technological innovator so that his loss might leave the company highly vulnerable to loss of profits and goodwill. Further examples might be the advertising agency crucially dependent on creative personnel and the import/export agency dependent on a given director's contacts and connections. In all such cases, the goodwill could be said to have no market value unless the purchase of the business could have some guarantee of retention of the proprietor's services or connections, for example by a written service agreement. The personal nature of such goodwill is, however, a moot point. It is therefore arguable that, even in such cases, the goodwill has some value and its potential vulnerability merely calls for a lower than average number of years purchase of super-profits, or capitalisation of pre-tax profits by discount on any value arrived at on a customary trade basis. This is because:

- The vendor's services may be retained by service agreement — indeed the prospective purchaser may not be a willing party to the transaction in the absence of such an agreement.
- Of course, if the valuation is on the death of the proprietor in question, such as to preclude such an agreement, full effect must then be given to the impact of such a death on the value of the goodwill.
- Nevertheless, the dependence of the value of the goodwill must vary from business to business. Only in the most extreme case (for example a business set up to exploit the discoveries of a particular inventor, or a

literal one-man band with no management succession in sight and a highly-specialised personal service, for example a fashion house) could the goodwill be effectively written off.

- The prospective purchaser could himself have the necessary skills, personality, flair, creativity and so on to match the potential of the proprietor so as to possess the capacity to achieve a similar level of profitable growth embodied in the goodwill concept.
- Even were none of these positive points applied, the company's profit record might be such as to suggest that, at least for a limited period, some benefit could be derived from ongoing goodwill after the departure of its original creator. The proprietor's co-directors or partners might be shown to possess comparable ability so that they shared in the goodwill and could continue to generate further goodwill after the loss of the person in question.

Valuations of goodwill can be made on one of three bases.

CUSTOMARY OR TRADE BASIS

There may be a customary or trade basis of valuation. A share valuer should always be alerted to the possibility of this. The following is a fairly comprehensive list of such businesses.

- Bookmakers — the goodwill in such cases is commonly valued at so many weeks betting receipts (currently three to four weeks' purchase is used).
- Dairies — in such cases the average daily retail gallonage is multiplied by £*x* per retail gallon (this figure is currently around £80–£100 per daily retail gallon). It may also be possible to use a figure for average daily semi-retail gallonage with a reduced figure for the £ per semi-retail gallon. This particular figure would currently stand at around £25–£30 per semi-retail gallon.
- Pharmaceutical chemists — the goodwill in this case is calculated on two to three years' purchase of so-called absolute net profit (i.e. net profit after allowing for the salary of a fully-qualified manager for each shop).
- Garages — the goodwill figure in such cases is derived from the average net profit margin per gallon, multiplied by the daily throughput.
- Hotels — a common customary basis for large hotels (100 beds or more) is the average annual turnover regardless of profits achieved. It should be borne in mind that all hotels have some inherent goodwill value deriving from the location, and smaller ones may have no more than this.
- Licensed premises — again the goodwill is either inherent in the site or

personally attached to the owner. There is no customary valuation based on average daily pints drunk or spirits consumed.

- TV rental companies — goodwill is based on £*x* for each black-and-white rental agreement (for example £10 for each agreement) of £*y* for each colour rental agreement (for example £40). The value of goodwill in a TV rental business with 1000 black-and-white sets and 2000 colour sets will therefore be: 1000 × £10 = £10 000 + 2000 × £40 = £80 000, which makes a total of £90 000.
- Accountants and other similar professional practices with a more or less regular clientele can be said to value goodwill as a multiple of blocks of gross recurring fees such as are regularly advertised in such journals as *Accountancy* and *The Accountant*. This multiple will generally be 2 to 3 but may go higher in London or other metropolitan areas and may well be slightly less in the provinces.
- NHS doctors and dentists do not generate any goodwill in their practices. The goodwill of consultants in private practice can again be determined on the basis of *x* years' purchase of gross recurring fees.
- Gambling casinos have goodwill valued on a similar basis to betting shops. The argument is that it is essentially turnover that matters since this shows the amount of client participation at the roulette or blackjack tables. It is up to the house then to maximise profits from the available clientele.
- Butchers, bakers, greengrocers and other similar small businesses can often be valued at around two years' purchase of the average of the last three years net profits without deduction for proprietor's remuneration or interest on capital. Such businesses are essentially valued as a kind of living rather than a highly-profitable going concern and the valuation of the goodwill follows accordingly. Substantial sums of money may nevertheless change hands for such businesses. The market value is therefore real enough and should not be ignored. Indeed it has been suggested that the best guide to the goodwill value in such instances is records of actual sales. The multiplier and basis in this case can be derived from the figures used in decided cases, many of them concerning rating or compensation.
- Newspapers and magazines — the value of the goodwill in such cases derives from: the business name; and the subscription lists, if any. A history of loss-making in this instance is not necessarily any bar to a positive market value for the goodwill, as the acquisition of *The Times* newspaper over the years has shown. In view of the nature of the goodwill it cannot be determined with reference to any mathematical or other formula. Even more than with other valuations the actual circumstances would clearly be crucial. The only factual basis for a valuation is actual acquisition

prices paid in the trade for pure goodwill. Where, however, the enterprise is at least reasonably profitable, the valuation can be made by adding a premium for goodwill on to the going-concern value of the company. Thus, in the only leading case on goodwill (*Findlay's Trustees* v *IRC* (1937) 80C 438) a valuation of the goodwill was arrived at as eight years' purchase of maintainable profits of £135 000 less the value of the net tangible assets. In other words, the valuation of the goodwill in that instance was arrived at pretty well on normal valuation principles.

SUPER-PROFITS BASIS

An alternative method of valuing goodwill is the superprofits basis. Superprofit is essentially profit earned by the business in excess of the normal commercial rate for that particular kind of business. It is determined by deducting from the net profit:

- proprietors' or managers' or directors' remuneration; and
- interest on the working capital.

The value of the goodwill is then x years purchase of the super-profit in question. Depending on the trading sector in question the factor x may be anything from 1 to 5. The common factor will, however, be 2 to 3. Only exceptionally will the factor fall outside this range of years' purchase. Once again this method of valuing goodwill is mainly applicable to sole traders and partnerships, or small companies that may be quasi-partnerships anyway. It is not normally a valid valuation method for larger companies.

The number of years purchase can be fairly objectively determined in several ways.

Firstly, by examining records of actual goodwill sales.

Secondly, by applying a broad criterion of the approximate gross return required for a small business in the given sector. For this the contemporaneous earnings yields shown in the *Financial Times* Actuaries Share Index is as good a rough-and-ready guide as any. Granted where small businesses are concerned the quoted earnings yield must, of course, be at least doubled. The year's purchase factor is then derived from the reciprocal $100/Y$ of the earnings yield, so where the required adjusted earnings yield is 40 per cent the factor x will be $100/40 = 2\frac{1}{2}$. Conversely, the use of a factor of three years' purchase implies a yield of $100/3 = 33$ per cent.

Examples

- Fred is a sole trader with part-time assistance from his wife behind the counter selling fruit and vegetables in a small shop in rented premises in a local shopping parade. For 1981/82 they make £40 000 profit on a turnover of £400000 on working capital of £30000. In this case the earnings yield should be at least trebled because this is such a small business compared with, for example, Sainsburys or Tesco as food retailing operations. The factor x is therefore 3. The super-profit is derived as follows:

	£
Net profit	40000
Less: proprietor's remuneration	20000
	20000
Less: interest on working capital @10% on £30000	3000
Super-profit =	17000
× 3	51000
Rounded down to say	50000

Goodwill is conventionally rounded down in such exercises because its calculation is inevitably lacking in precision and the purchaser is therefore in a strong bargaining position to achieve this.

- John and Jill run an antiques emporium set up as a limited company. Their turnover for 1981/82 is £750000 and their net profit before tax is £90000 after paying themselves directors' remuneration of £20000 each. Their working capital is £100000. Assuming the directors' remuneration is at a reasonable commercial rate, a super-profit is derived as follows:

	£
Net profit	90000
Less: Interest on working capital @ 10%	10000
	£80000

The goodwill in this case is based on a factor of four years' purchase, or a gross return of 25 per cent. This gives a goodwill valuation at £32000 and the value of the business as a whole as a going concern is therefore £42000 or a multiplier of 4.66 applied to the £90000 pre-tax profits.

In every goodwill valuation the question of *maintainable* net profit will arise. This can be based on a profits projection for the current year if a reasonably-based management figure is available. Failing this it is common practice to average the net profit for the three previous years. If a distinct rising or declining trend is discerned, then a weighted average is used.

Examples

- The profits of Ken's car rental business are:

	£
1980	25000
1981	27000
1982	23000
Unweighted average =	75000
÷ 3 =	£25000

If a reasonable proprietor's salary is £15 000 and he has working capital of £30 000 on which interest should be charged at 10 per cent, the position is:

	£
Average net profit	25 000
Less: salary	15 000
	10 000
Less: interest @ 10%	3000
Adjusted net profit	7000
Super-profit	£7000

The car hire quoted sector earnings yield is around 20 per cent which should be doubled to arrive at the figure of 100/40 = 2½ years' purchase of £7000 super-profit. This gives a figure of £17500 for goodwill in this case.

- Weighted average

	£
Net profits – 1980 £20 000 × 1=	20 000
1981 £30 000 × 2 =	60 000
1982 £40 000 × 3 =	120 000
	200 000
£200 000 ÷ 6 = £33 333 net profit	33 33
Deduct interest on, say, £100 000 working capital @ 10%	10 000
	23 333

£23333 super-profit × 2 = £46 666 rounded to, say, £45 000 goodwill.

CAPITALISATION METHOD

This values the goodwill as the excess of the going-concern value over the net tangible assets. It is the method most suitable for valuing corporate goodwill.

- Any investment income is excluded.
- Trading income is adjusted for directors' remuneration at a commercial rate, notional interest on any directors' loan accounts, notional rent on rent-free premises and realistic depreciation rates. An appropriate multiplier is then applied to the pre-tax profits level to determine the going-concern value. This is discussed in detail in Chapter 8.

The net tangible assets are then deducted to arrive at the value for goodwill.

Example

ABC Ltd has £100 000 pre-tax profits of which 10 000 is investment income. It pays four directors only £30 000 whereas £60 000 would be a realistic commercial rate. Net tangible assets are £200 000. Assuming a multiplier of 5 is appropriate, the goodwill is determined as follows.

	£
Pre-tax profits	100 000
Less: remuneration adjustment and investment income	40 000
	60 000
£60 000 × 5 = £300 000	300 000
Deduct: net tangible assets	200 000
Value of goodwill	100 000

10 Valuations of particular types of companies

In deciding the correct valuation approach the share valuer must see in which economic sector the company falls and what kind of business operations the company carries on within that sector. This decision will show which valuation factors are relevant and the appropriate weightings attributable to each factor. This preliminary investigation will also disclose what industry studies and trade or professional journals will contain up to date information on sector and company performance as well as the investment criteria a prospective purchaser would be likely to apply.

The basic valuation divide is between trading companies and non-trading companies.

TRADING COMPANIES

These divide in turn into:

- mining and extracting
- manufacturing
- construction
- distribution
- service
- farming.

Mining and extracting

These are companies engaged in mining, quarrying, oil prospecting and so on. They are capital-intensive and cyclical industries with highly-specific financial structures. They are also closely linked to their quoted sector counterparts. Valuation by comparability study will often be appropriate if, as is likely, the company is of a relatively significant size, where more than an insignificant minority holding is involved.

Manufacturing

This includes the broadest spectrum of companies in primary industries. They share a common emphasis on substantial fixed-asset investment and stock inventories as well as often comparatively high gearing. As a sector it is consistently declining — an economic phenomenon generally.

There are, however, notable exceptions, such as electronics hardware, notably video systems and computer equipment. The size of company will vary enormously from a large multinational private corporation to the new business formed from a local tailors.

Construction

This sector has the highest failure rate of any. It is notoriously cyclical, subject to waves of booms and slumps. Occasionally a company may buck the trend, but generally the overall market will play a significant role in the profits performance of the unquoted company. The sector also divides into pure construction and quasi-development companies. The former will have stocks of unsold properties and the latter stocks of undeveloped land in a land bank. As regards both, the key ratios are the gross profit margins and the stock/turnover ratio since high gearing is also a common feature of companies in this sector. The majority of jobbing builders and small-scale developers will be one or two man businesses or family concerns. Comparison with the leading quoted companies must be heavily qualified, as must the use of sector indices. There is, however, a plethora of small to medium quoted companies which can be used for comparison purposes. The basis of valuation will follow that for other companies in the primary sector.

Distribution

These include road haulers, corner shops, supermarket chains, market stalls and auction rooms. The longer-term trend is for the market leadership of the massive retail consortia to be crucial. Argylle Foods, Sainsbury and Tesco for instance tend to swallow the local stores. The latter fight back through trade associations like Mace, VG and Spar, but the trend is apparently irresistible, particularly with the advent of the freezer and the rise of the motorised consumer. It is possible for the small shop owner to set up the chain in a growth area — like the Dodge City shops in DIY — and then sell out at a hugely-inflated price to a diversifying retailer such as Woolworth or

Debenhams. The share valuer should be on the lookout for a company or groups that fall into this takeover category, as otherwise a serious undervaluation will result. The use of sector indices and comparable company studies is of special value as regards these companies since there is a wealth of available information. Conversely, the wheat must be sifted from the chaff and the recognition of the market leadership of the huge quoted companies taken proper account of.

Service

These include an enormous range of trading companies. Many of the smaller ones are quasi-partnerships and should be valued accordingly. The common features here are a relative lack of fixed capital assets, a low level of stocks, a high proportion of investment in personnel and a substantial element of goodwill in the value of the business. These are essentially people-based businesses and it is the talents of entrepreneurs and skills of creative personalities that contribute to their continuing success. Conversely, relatively little is needed to start a new business and the value of goodwill is subject to the qualification that it is often personal to the business owners and subject to erosion by fresh competition. Good examples are advertising, publishing, pop music, radio, TV, films and videos. There are many nationally-known names in this sector and market leadership must be discounted in valuing unquoted counterparts. On the other hand, this is a sector in which fortunes can be made almost overnight and the share valuer must be on the lookout for any such companies he may encounter.

The basis of valuation of companies in this primary sector will be as follows:

- small minorities: dividend yield or earnings yield;
- influential minorities: price earnings ratio or discounted capitalisation basis; and
- controlling interests: discounted assets or net assets or capitalisation of profits.

Farming

These companies traditionally show low yields and represent a way of life as much as trading operations. They also stand somewhere between a pure trading entity and a property-holding company. The appropriate basis of valuation therefore reflects their hybrid nature.

Companies owning their own freehold property

These are arguably quasi-property companies and should be valued as such. The reasons are many.

- Earnings yields (even with relatively low directors' remuneration) are traditionally low so a purchaser is not going to buy shares with a view to obtaining an income or to accumulate profits. This precludes a meaningful valuation on an earnings yield basis. Of course a dividend yield basis is completely out of the question.
- Such companies, even if making profits, do not normally pay dividends. This pre-empts even a notional dividend yield basis of valuation.
- The company's main asset — its freehold land — has an intrinsic value apart from its earning power (differentiating it from a freehold factory for example) and is likely to appreciate significantly over the years. It is also saleable apart from the business itself.
- The prospective purchaser is therefore likely to be a personal institution able to take a longer term view of its investment and enjoy the capital appreciation that will accrue to the company's property until a realisation of the assets in due course.
- The most meaningful method of valuation for all sizes of holdings in such farming companies is therefore a discounted assets basis. Applicable discounts will be higher than for property companies although the basis of valuation may be similar. This is because investors in such property companies enjoy the following advantages:

  (a) interim dividend income reinforced periodically by the shortfall distribution standard;

  (b) reversionary increases in rental income which will in turn feed back into high dividends;

  (c) capital appreciation arising from (a) and (b) apart from normal property capital growth;

  (d) greater likelihood of earlier realisations.

Suggested rule of thumb discounts are therefore as follows:

Size of holding (%)	Discount on net asset value (%)
90–100	0–5
75–89.9	5–10
50.1–74.9	15–25
50	30–35
25.1–49.9	40–50
10.1–25	60–70
10 and under	75–80

This may be compared profitably with the discount table used for the valuation of property company shares.

Companies not owning their freehold, but with an agricultural tenancy

Although it is still a somewhat contentious point, it is presently considered by the Inland Revenue valuation office that an agricultural tenancy protected under the Agricultural Holdings Act 1948 has a substantial market value. Of course the prices of agricultural land are ascertainable by a prospective purchaser since prices of such land are published information in trade journals such as *Farmers Weekly* and economic periodicals such as *Estates Gazette*. However, the market value of the tenancy itself depends much more on such imponderables as the terms of the tenancy, rental levels, rent reviews, any onerous or restrictive clauses, provisions for dilapidations and so on. A further difference is that the farmland itself represents the greatest security for the company and the investor in its shares since it represents acceptable collateral and also can be sold off in convenient parcels. The discount levels used in valuing shares in such companies should be increased at each significance of holding size by, say, 5 to 10 per cent to take account of these differences. The basis of valuation, however, will normally be a discounted assets basis, similar to that used in valuing companies owning their own freeholds. The agricultural tenancy which will not, of course, appear in the company's balance sheet is to be included at its market value, and the net assets value of the company revised accordingly. The above applies of course on a going-concern basis. Should the company be lossmaking or, for any other reason, not a going concern and the only basis of valuation is a break-up basis, it is arguable that the basis of valuation then will be analogous with that of companies owning neither a freehold nor a tenancy, since the tenancy itself on a winding up would have no market value.

Companies with no freehold or tenancy

These should be valued like other trading companies except that:

- there will be no dividend yield basis of valuation — actual or notional;
- the earnings yields required will be lower since the sector traditionally requires lower yields than are generally prevalent in the industrial sector;
- discount levels will be marginally lower than for trading companies valued on the same basis, but the discounted assets basis will, in this case, not normally be used unless it would be used even if a normal trading company was concerned (for example if losses are being made or if earnings are totally erratic so no meaningful average or maintainable profits figure is deducible).

Farming accounts have numerous peculiar features. The valuer may have to grapple with unfamiliar items such as unexhausted manures, rough grazing and NFU trade investments. They often appear somewhat in arrears — 18 months or two years in arrears not being particularly unusual. Of course up-to-date information may be required under certain statutory information standards. In particular, the livestock may require revaluation if a controlling interest is involved. The valuation of livestock is very much a specialist activity and the Shares Valuation Division have their own specialist valuers in this field. The same applies to bloodstock such as racehorses. If an undervaluation at book value is suspected, the share valuer will have to call in a specialist professional valuer in this context.

The other significant point about items in farm accounts is that farm machinery and vehicles, such as implements and tractors, may well fetch a price on sale significantly in excess of the depreciated book values. This contrasts with the position regarding machinery and plant and motor vehicles in the accounts of ordinary trading companies.

As regards agricultural tenancies, it should also be noted that such an asset now attracts agricultural relief under the Finance Act 1981 which is a factor enhancing its market value.

Examples

Company A: Net asset value — £25 per ordinary share; average earnings per share — £1; average gross earnings — 142.84%; issued shares — 10000 £1 ord.

Financial Times Actuaries Share Index: food manufacturing sector — earnings yield 10%, price earnings ratio 8; property sector — earnings yield 4%, price earnings ratio 32.

25 per cent holding

Valuation basis (i): earnings yield Required yield: average 10% (food manufacturing yield) plus 4% (property sector yield)/2 = 7. This should be at least doubled for unquoted company status. Valuation 142/14 = £10 per share.

Valuation basis (ii): price earnings ratio Average food manufacturing sector and property sector price earnings ratios = 4 + 20/2 = 20. Valuation after halving the required price earnings ratio to take account of unquoted company status = 10 × £1 = £10 per share.

Valuation basis (iii): discounted assets Net asset value (£25) less 60% discount for size of holding (£15) = £10 per share. The coincidences of the cross-checks on different valuation bases suggests that the valuation at £10 per share is reasonably right within a valuation range of say £10 to £11 per share.

49.9 per cent holding

Valuation basis (i): price earnings ratio Average quoted ratio (as above) = 20. Discount 25% for unquoted company status (*Crossman* case). Applicable price earnings ratio = 15. Valuation 15 × £1 = £15 per share.

Valuation basis (ii): discounted assets Net asset value (£25) less 40% discount (*Lynall* case) (£10) = £15 per share.

Controlling interest of 60 per cent Net asset value (£25) less 20% discount (£5). = £20 per share. This possibly over-simplifies the situation since the full net asset value based on market values is unlikely to be determined for a small minority holding (though a 25 per cent holding may not come in that category as the stake in the company is sizeable and the prospective outlay is significant). Moreover, the purchaser of the larger holdings and certainly the controlling interest may well require further information regarding current profits that may revise the net asset value (by apportioning anticipated post-tax profits if significant). Providing it is realised that the rule of thumb necessarily yield to prevailing circumstances, the valuation principles and techniques remain. Morever, before the share valuer gets down to the basic valuation data, he must go through the statutory and any other available accounts or statistics with a fine toothcomb to ensure that the crucial figures are correct.

NON-TRADING COMPANIES

Investment trusts and companies

Quoted investment trusts will be authorised under the Taxes Act and enjoy special privileges, notably taxation of capital gains at 10 per cent instead of 30 per cent. The investment trust sector suffered in the 1970s under the impact of rapid growth from unit trusts and has still not fully recovered. Indeed in 1982 the sector as a whole enjoyed a relatively poor year in spite of the equity revival.

Valuation of such companies is traditionally by way of a discount on net asset value. The rate of discount varies from period to period and company to company. At any given time, however, the prevailing discount rates are readily ascertainable since they are published in the *Financial Times* and *The Daily Telegraph* on the last Saturday of the month. The discount reflects contemporary interest charges, inflation rates and other financial and investment criteria. Primarily, however, it reflects the investment world's assessment of investment trusts management and its portfolio performance, fulfilling a similar function to the price earnings ratio in the case of a trading company. Unquoted investment companies can be valued therefore on a discounted assets basis. The discount in this case will take into account:

- the company's results over five years, in short its portfolio performance;
- the company's rating, measured by comparison with:

  (a) the *Financial Times* Investment Trust Index; and

(b) the performance of similarly constituted trusts and companies in the quoted sector;

- the company's size as measured by its net asset value;
- the discount rates on net asset values of comparable quoted companies;
- the taxation position of the unquoted company as compared with, for example, an authorised investment trust (which a close company can never be);
- the size of holding in question.

What this means in general terms is that the discount appropriate to the unquoted investment company will be that prevalent in the quoted sector plus further increments to take into account its unquoted status and its specific circumstances. The effect of such adjustments is that the discount for a small minority holding in an unquoted investment trust is not going to fall below 60 per cent, and indeed up to 70 to 75 per cent may be justified. Because of the volatility of the equity market and the lack of reversionary yield performance such as applies to property companies, the general level of discount will be higher, holding for holding, than is normally applied to holdings of shares in unquoted property companies. On the other hand, given the readily realisable nature of the investment company's portfolio, the level of discount will be significantly lower than applicable to, for example, farming companies.

Investment holding companies

These should be valued like investment trusts.

The valuation of even minority holdings in such trusts and companies is normally made on a discounted assets basis and, before discounting, the book values of the assets must be revised to reflect full market values. Depending on the realisation record of the company in question, allowances for contingent CGT can be taken. Quoted securities are valued on the usual quarter-up basis, while mortgages, debentures and unquoted securities must be valued like other unquoted investments in the notional open market. Unlike authorised investment trusts, unquoted investment trusts and companies do not receive preferential CGT treatment.

Investment dealing companies

These may be either pure investment companies dealing in a variety of quoted and unquoted securities, or even commodities, or else share dealing companies. These turn over stocks and shares according to market opportunities and range from highly speculative commodity dealers to well-secured dealers in gilts and bonds. As portfolio management is paramount, these are valued best on a mixed basis to take full account of both earnings, prospects and assets potential. Such companies will still be subject to shortfall pressures to distribute, and both dividends and capital growth should accrue to shareholders. Again a Berliner averaging of earnings and assets bases should result in a reasonably satisfactory valuation. Fortunately, information as to yields and assets is easily accessible from the sources already indicated earlier.

Property companies

These fall into four main classes:

- property holding companies
- property dealing companies
- property development companies
- property investment companies.

Property holding companies

These are the purest kind of property company. They hold properties as medium-to long-term investments to generate:

- rising rental income; and
- capital growth from reinvested rental income and appreciation in property prices.

Realisations will be relatively rare. Valuations of even small minority holdings can justifiably be made on a discounted assets basis. This is because a prospective investor is likely to be buying with a view to the longer-term capital position, and interim income (if any) is a secondary consideration for him. Such a purchaser may even prefer to have no interim income because of higher-rate tax which could be incurred at 60 per cent instead of CGT at 30 per cent (the corporation tax treatment is analogous with investment companies, for example as regards management expenses).

This valuation method also reflects the quoted sector market practice for such companies and thus satisfies the open market requirements. It should be added, however, that at a time of rampant inflation or collapse in property values, such as occurred in 1974/75, the income position of the company may require more careful consideration. In such circumstances a valuation on a dividend yield or earnings yield basis may be appropriate, if only as a cross-check or as part of an averaged valuation. The variable emphasis on income or capital returns differs indeed at different periods. When capital values fall, or there is investment uncertainty, the valuation criteria may shift towards the shorter-term income return and yields will rise accordingly. When capital values mirror a buoyant property market, this will reduce yields to low or even minimal levels.

Property dealing companies

Such companies deal in properties the way trading companies deal in goods or services. Property does form part of their current assets as stock-in-trade, although some properties may form part of the fixed assets (for example offices or other business premises) and they may also hold properties as investments. Directors' remuneration may be as high as for executives in other trading companies. The unique nature of their business must be taken into account. Minority holdings would not normally be valued on a discounted assets basis, but the involvement in the property sector means that the yields required will be usually significantly lower than for other trading sectors (unless like contemporary electricals they are market favourites and show very low yields), but not as low as for property holding companies. The asset backing (which itself feeds back on the yield) is taken into account to a greater extent. The asset value is, even on a break-up basis, more readily realisable than in the ordinary trading company since there is no specialised use attaching to the properties which can be sold without additional conversion expenditure and in the wide investment market, not the narrower market for industrial and commercial premises.

Property development companies

Such companies may well be part of a construction group. Their land banks and property stocks will be current assets, as with dealing companies, and there will be both work-in-progress and not necessarily comparatively frequent turnover of properties, since some companies have development programmes that may take two years or more from start to finish. The sector is a high-risk one since the developer incurs substantial cost before any positive cash flow is generated, but also correspondingly enormous profits potential (the vast majority of the 110 post-war millionaires up to 1968 made their money in this trading sector). There will be valuation difficulties as regards the assets since a purchaser may get little information on the values of properties in varying stages of development, if a minority shareholder, and, since it is unlikely that rental income is generated before completion, approximate capitalisation of rentals cannot be made. Moreover, unlike the property dealing company, there may be little enough guide to the profits potential until the first realisation. CGT may also bite into a company's profits.

Property investment companies

These lie between property dealing and property holding companies. They are best regarded, however, as investment companies holding properties as investments. The analogy is then close to investment trusts whose shares may be valued on a yield basis somewhat around mid-point between the yields of property holding companies (the majority of the *Financial Times* property sector indices) and such trusts. They may not, however, be valued on an earnings yield or price earnings ratio basis. The important valuation factor here is the frequency of disposals and the quantum of profits on realisations since substantial reserves may be built up.

11 Special situations

This book is largely concerned with the valuation of ordinary shares in profitable unquoted companies. Special situations, however, require exceptional treatment. These include preference shares and other special classes of shares, loss-making companies and companies in liquidation, companies dealing in or deriving income from intellectual property such as copyrights and patents, quasi-partnerships. This chapter examines the particular valuation approaches required in such cases and suggests practical solutions to valuation problems and pitfalls commonly encountered in such valuations.

SPECIAL CLASSES OF SHARES

Preference shares

The articles must be examined to determine their precise rights. Where the articles are silent as to voting rights, Table A, Companies Act 1948, will apply and the preference shares will have voting rights (as will any other class of shares unless expressly excluded). The essential characteristics of the preference shares are as follows:

- the fixed dividend;
- non-participation in surplus dividends and any surplus on winding up;
- priority to repayment of nominal capital on a liquidation;
- usually no voting rights.

Exceptionally, there may be cumulative participating preference shares. These enjoy:

- the right to a fixed dividend with priority over the ordinary dividend;
- cumulation rights so that any year's dividends arrears must be made up the following year or at the earliest opportunity;
- additional dividends after a minimum ordinary dividend has been paid, usually of a fixed amount or percentage;
- priority to repayment of capital on a winding up;
- participation in any surplus on a winding up (again often of a fixed amount or proportion);
- frequently, voting rights though these may be restricted, for example, to winding up or other special occasions.

Other preference shares may be divided into A, B, C, D or E or first, second, third, fourth or fifth preference shares with varying rates of fixed dividend. These will enjoy income and capital rights in the stated order of priorities. The lower-ranking preference shares may get a slightly higher coupon rate to compensate for the greater income and capital risks. Given good cover which can be determined on a priority percentage basis, sound reserves and adequate liquidity, the yield differential between these classes of preference shares need only be marginal or effectively non-existent.

Examples

Company A
Earnings after tax £100000
Preference shares:

	Cover	Net dividend (£)	Gross dividend (%)
A 5% net £2000	1000	100	7.14
B 6% net £5000	250	300	8.57
C 7% net £10000	99	700	10.00
D 8% net £10000	50	800	11.42

As the cover is substantial even at the lowest priority, no practical valuation differential need be made between the different classes of preference shares. If therefore the quoted sector yield (as shown by the appropriate index, for example *Financial Times* industrial and commercial preference shares index) is 15 per cent gross, an adjustment on the lines of the *Crossman* case unmarketability factor adjustment of 20 per cent will suggest a yield of 18 per cent gross. Valuations will then be as follows:

A prefs 5% net = 7.14% gross
  Price 7.14/18 × £1 = 39.66p rounded to 40p.
B prefs 6% net = 8.57% gross
  Price 8.57/18 × £1 = 47.61p rounded to 48p.
C prefs 7% net = 10.00% gross
  Price 10.00/18 × £1 = 55.55p rounded to 56p.
D prefs 8% net = 11.42% gross
  Price 11.42/18 × £1 = 63.44p rounded to 63p.

Company B
Earnings after tax: £20000
Preference shares:

		Cover	Net dividend (£)	Gross dividend (%)
First	4% net £20000	25	800	5.71
Second	5% net £40000	7.14	2800	7.14
Third	6% net £50000	3.45	5800	8.57
Fourth	7% net £60000	2	10000	10.00

The cover for the fourth and, arguably, the third preference shares is not really adequate. The yield should therefore be increased. One way would be to increase the required yield, say, by 25 per cent adjustment to the quoted yield instead of 20 per cent. For the fourth preference shares an adjustment at 30 per cent might well be appropriate as the cover for them is approaching the cover for ordinary shares. Consequential valuations are then as follows:

First prefs — 5.71/18
  Valuation = 31.72p rounded to 32p.
Second prefs — 7.14/18
  Valuation = 39.66p rounded to 40p.
Third prefs — 8.57/18
  Valuation = 47.6p rounded to 48p.
Fourth prefs — 10/19.5
  Valuation = 51.28p rounded to 51p.

Preference shares as a breed are becoming rarer since the introduction of corporation tax (which made the tax-deductible debenture and loan stock interest a more tax-efficient way of raising capital than non-deductible preference dividends), still more so with the coming of the invitation system with ACT payable on dividends. There is, however, the pref-trick stamp duty saving device which involves converting auditor preference shares with minimal rights and the allotment of new ordinary shares transferred to a purchaser for the bulk of the consideration, but these are by definition hardly going to bother the share valuer. The valuation of participating preference shares or voting preference shares does, however, present valuation problems. It is after all possible for preference shares to control the company, although in the author's experience this is likely to follow from accident rather than from design (for example the articles draftsman may have overlooked the implications of Table A).

Valuation of participating preference shares

These must be valued after careful scrutiny of their rights under the articles. They may be voting shares that may even carry control of the company on some or all occasions, apart from the usually limited participation in dividends and in any surplus of capital on a winding up. Or they may be non-voting and get only a restricted share of extra income and capital surplus. If the former class, they may be valued pretty well as controlling ordinary shares since they will then carry all the essential features of an equity (apart from the name). The equities themselves will then be minorities and valued accordingly. The much more common kind are those that are, however, restricted in their class rights. These must be valued as quasi-equities. They carry preferential income rights and capital rights on a winding up and also enjoy a measure of the company's distributable profits with the equities. An example of dividend treatment of such shares could be:

ABC Ltd

	£
Distributable profits	20000
Fixed (5%) dividend to £20000 divided by participating preference shares	700
	19300
Further dividend (10% of surplus)	1900
	17400
The total preference dividend is then or £2600/£20000 = 13% net = 18.57% gross	2600

The surplus on a winding up could be:	
Net assets	200000
20000 £1 participating preference shares	20000
	180000
10000 £1 ordinary shares	10000
Surplus	170000
Attributable as to 10% to participating preference shares	17000
Attributable to ordinary shares	153000

Net asset value of participating preference shares = £20000 + £17000/£20000 = £1.85 per share.

The gross dividend level and the net asset backing would suggest a valuation at around £1 per share or par. Ranging would still be applied and a valuation in the range of £1.20 to 90p per share would be applicable.

Valuation of controlling preference shares

This relatively rare event may be illustrated as follows. Company XYZ Ltd has 100000 £1 preference shares and 100 £1 ordinary shares. The assets are £750000 and the pre-tax profits £100000. Two possible valuation problems exist.

Valuation of a controlling interest in the preference shares The shareholder could convert the preference shares to participating preference shares. The valuation is therefore on a net assets basis. This proceeds:

	£
Net assets	750000
Less: preference shares at par (priority capital)	100000
Balance (surplus)	650000
Divided by 100100 (preference shares and ordinary shares) = £6.49 net asset value per share	
Add: priority capital	£1.00
	£7.49 per share

Evaluation of the ordinary shares This would not be £6.49 per share but on a discounted assets value (on a minority basis) or a dividend yield basis or earnings yield basis.

Management shares and founder's shares

These often have high nominal values such as £5 or £25 or even £100 and £1000 per share. They usually carry abnormal class rights under the articles, sometimes even retaining voting control because of weighted voting in their favour. The valuation must take full account of their class rights and other peculiar clauses in the articles such as directors or founder's vetoes. If the shares do carry control, they may be valued on a controlling interest basis. This means in this case the value attributable to the share on either a going concern or a winding-up basis should constitute the market value. Even a controlling interest cannot, however, alter class rights. Valuations of minorities, on the other hand, are made on the usual basis. The greater capital values should cause no trouble. Of course asset backing or earnings cover can lower the required yield in the usual fashion.

Controlling interest

ABC Ltd

Net assets (no higher going-concern value in this case)		£ 800 000
	£	
100 £1000 founder's shares	100 000	
5000 £1 ordinary shares	5000	
	105 000	105 000
Surplus		695 000

= £136.27 per share

100 000 ÷ 105 000 × 695 000 =	£661 905 (share of surplus)
+ £100 000 nominal	£100 000
	£761 905

= £7619.05 per founder's share

Minority holding (say 25)

ABC Ltd

Dividend yield (cover of 5) with 28.57% gross dividend required yield, say, 14.28%.

Valuation at 28.57/14.28 × £1000 = £2000 per share for the founder's shares.

Deferred shares

These are often created as part of the usual stamp duty avoidance device. This converts the existing ordinary shares to deferred shares and creates the ordinary shares with full normal rights for equities. The nominal value is usually £1, but the minimal rights attributable to the deferred shares means that they can have only minimal market value based on the remote possibility of a winding up and consequential repayment at par. A common special resolution class rights clause would give these deferred shares:

- no voting rights;
- no dividend rights or dividend only after £1m dividend to the ordinary shares;
- no share in any surplus in a winding up; and
- only at best the right to repayment at par on a winding up and then, in many cases, only after £10m priority to the ordinary shares on capital repayment.

If the absolutely minimal dividend and winding up rights apply, the value is nil or 1p per share. If there is at least a right to a repayment at par in the normal course of a winding up and without multi-million pound priority to the equities then a valuation at, say, 5p per share could apply. This is based on a 95 per cent discount on the par asset backing — in effect a discounted assets basis for a vote for a small minority in a non-dividend paying company.

Such shares also have their use as an IHT planning device. They may be convertible only in, say, 10 years time so that, while their immediate market value at the time of a transfer is loaded to extremely restricted class rights, their value after conversion in the hands of the donees will be very much higher. The Revenue have not, however, given official approval or clearance so that it is not clear at this stage that the wide-ranging statutory associated operations provisions (CTTA 1984 s. 268) would not be successfully invoked against such schemes.

Non-voting shares

These enfranchised shares are a disappearing class that may still be found in many companies. Their valuation depends on their class rights, but in the normal case they will rank *pari passu* with the ordinary shares in all respects except voting rights. The valuation will then follow the value of the ordinary shares with a differential discount for non-voting status. The size of this differential is determined by several factors. These are primarily:

- the differential maintained in past transactions if there has been an actual market for the shares;
- the differential prevalent amongst quoted non-voting shares;
- the shareholder distribution of the voting shares;
- the takeover prospects, or other possibilities of capital appreciation;
- any internal or external developments that may facilitate enfranchisement.

The less voting influence attributable to the ordinary shares the lower the differential can be. In practice, the differential can often be taken at the standard 10 per cent, but in individual cases the spread could be between 5 per cent or even zero (if justified by market practice and wide distribution of shares amongst a variety of shareholders) or up to 50 per cent (if, exceptionally, the voting shares are large holdings and there are control or takeover prospects). The significance of takeover prospects is of course that voting shares will then command a premium and non-voting shares may be both comparatively and absolutely devalued.

Examples

- There are three classes of shares in ABC Ltd: A — voting; B and C —non-voting. The value of the ordinary shares is £2 per share. The value of the ordinary shares should be discounted by 10 per cent to arrive at a valuation at £1.80 per share for the B and C non-voting shares. This assumes that the shares are equal in all respects save for voting rights.

- As above, but say one year later a takeover bid has been disclosed by the press with no details known at present. The differential should be increased depending on the strength of the takeover rumour and projected terms. A valuation could be, however (remembering that the ordinary shares themselves will increase in value following the successful bid apart from changes due to later achieved results): ordinary shares at £3 per share; non-voting shares at £2 per share. The implied discount is 33 per cent.
- The ordinary shares and B and C shares are traded normally at the same price and the distribution of the voting shares is such that no holding is greater than 5 per cent. The differential can be zero and all classes of shares command the same market price. Any valuation differential would run against market trends, be swallowed up in a valuation range, and lack specific justification.

Shares with voting rights on a weighted basis

Such rights may be attributed under the articles to any class of shares. The valuation will take into account the legal power given to the holding in question, but also take into account all other relevant factors, including the critical ones such as distribution of the other holdings in the company (in their particular class and otherwise) and the likelihood of a successful sale or takeover of the company as a going concern. Whilst the voting rights are crucial as a matter of elementary share valuation principle, other factors such as the total company context and the potential influence on the company's affairs on the part of a prospective purchaser are also of prime importance. Even if the holding carries greater importance because of weighted voting rights, a discount may be required to take account of, for example, the vulnerability of the attributable class rights.

Example

X holds 250 ordinary shares (25 per cent) in ABC Ltd, a private trading company. He is a managing director. His shares carry 33.33 per cent of the votes in the company because the articles have a peculiar clause giving director-held shares three votes for every two shares held. The other shareholders in the company — A, B and C — are all non-directors, of whom one is the company secretary, and they each hold 250 shares. The going-concern value of the company is £50 per share. If the holding was a straight 33.33 per cent, the discount appropriate would, say, be 40 per cent. However, a further discount is required since:

- X's holding is only of greater value (as an influential minority) if sold to a director, and there is therefore no immediate market at that greater value;

- X's holding is also vulnerable because A, B and C could vote him off the board and agree to elect themselves as directors;
- A, B and C could also collectively wind up the company; and
- A, B and C could also offset the articles, depriving X's holding of the special voting rights.

A further discount of 20 per cent is therefore suggested (making the total discount at 60 per cent mid-point between the value attributable to a 33.33 per cent holding and a 25 per cent uninfluential minority holding). X's shares would, of course, only obtain the share in a surplus on winding up attributable to a 25 per cent holding. The increased valuation is therefore effectively only a fairly marginal premium for the weighted voting rights. The consequential valuation at the suggested 60 per cent discount would therefore be £20 per share.

LOSS-MAKING COMPANIES

If a company has a history of losses, the valuation of any size of holding must be on a discounted assets basis. The size of the discount will relate to:

- the assets backing;
- the size of holding;
- the extent of the losses;
- the level of contemporary interest rates.

If the trading loss follows a history of trading profits, the commercial reasons for the loss must be ascertained. These may be:

- the national economic situation;
- the sector position;
- the normal trading cycle;
- the management of the company;
- the company's product or service decline.

The first three factors should be temporary and the future can be predicted from macro-economic business and industry information. The last two factors, on the other hand, may indicate more long-term difficulties that can ultimately result in a liquidation, winding up or takeover. Bad management can be seen by examining the trading and profits and loss account in detail.

The normal investment analytical ratios such as stock/turnover or pre-tax profit/capital employed will show where the business is failing, as will the growth in overheads compared with turnover growth and, of course, gross profit and net profit margins. Product appeal can be judged from the sales history and any available product literature if this is indeed the problem. The chairman's and directors' reports may reveal what is being done in this respect.

Evaluation of the assets is on a break-up not going-concern basis in this case. This presupposes a relatively early realisation of assets on a liquidation or winding up. In this event the assets themselves may well realise amounts considerably less than the book values though some, notably freehold or leasehold property, may realise substantially more. Generous discounts may be applied to current assets such as stock — particularly in high profit margin areas such as textiles. However, debtors can be factored and up to 80 per cent recovered in this way, so a maximum discount would be 20 per cent or perhaps 25 per cent. Machinery and plant may have only a scrap or residual value, but motor vehicles may well realise reasonable market values which can be checked from *Glass's Motorists' Guide*. Loans to subsidiaries or other companies can be checked against the relevant accounts. The overriding principal is that market value should be applied to each and every item in the balance sheets. Intangible items such as goodwill and research and development, copyrights, patents, trade marks, inventions and so on will then normally be written off. Exceptionally they may, however, command substantial value. This can even be the case with an intangible asset such as goodwill which would not normally be expected to command any market value in a loss-making company, but may have a substantial independent market value on a conventional trade basis. If this is apparently the case (see Chapter 9 on valuing such assets) the value will be determined on normal market lines. Deductions should then be made. These will be balance sheet items such as current liabilities, long-term loans and debentures and so on. Significantly, however, deductions may also be taken for contingent corporation tax that would arise in respect of realised assets in excess of book values (for example company property) and all deferred taxation for disposal values greater than written-down tax values since these will also crystallise. Realisation costs must also be deducted and liquidation costs and contingency costs as well as legal and professional fees and redundancy payments. A revised balance sheet can then be drawn up reflecting full market values.

If the losses are cyclical, as they may well be in some industries, notably construction, property development, timber, textiles, builders' merchants, commodities, chemicals and consumer durables, for example, then average dividend and earnings figures can be calculated, possibly over a five-year or even longer cycle. If the losses are exceptional, a similar averaging may be applied to perhaps three years' results. If the explanation for the loss is satisfactory, it may be minimised. It is notorious that a loss may not only affect quoted shares only minimally, but they may actually result in a price rise if already discounted in advance by the stock market. Two possible kinds of share valuations in loss-making companies follow.

Examples

A cyclical loss-making company XYZ Ltd are a trading company dealing in timber and associated products. Their trading results for 1974/75 to 1982/83 are set out below. The company has 100000 £1 issued ordinary shares. The net asset value is £30 per share. The valuation is of 25000 £1 ordinary shares or a 25 per cent uninfluential minority holding. The appropriate price earnings ratio is 4.

Pre-tax profits	
1974/75	(£150000)
1975/76	£200000
1976/77	£300000
1977/78	£250000
1978/79	(£150000)
1979/80	£200000
1980/81	£400000
1981/82	£300000

In this case there may well be a four-year natural business cycle. This corresponds approximately to the industry cycle which operates around 18 months to two years in arrear and may also be geared to the building industry cycle if the company specialises in building materials. The average pre-tax profits figure for 1978 to 1982 is £250000. After corporation tax at, say, 50 per cent (if the losses would give rise to corporation tax refunds under section 177(2), ICTA 1970) the earnings per share are £1.25 and, applying the price earnings ratio of 4, a valuation at £6 per share results. This represents a discount of 80 per cent on the net asset value of £30 per share which would be roughly the value appropriate to a full controlled holding.

A continuous loss-making company ABC Ltd is a loss-making textile company. Its main asset is its freehold factory. The losses are as follows: 1980 £30000; 1981 40000; 1982 60000. The net asset value is £900000 represented by:

	£
Freehold factory (as revalued on a break-up basis)	800000
Other fixed assets (mainly vehicles)	200000
Stock-in-trade and work-in-progress	250000
Debtors	150000
	1400000
Loans and current liabilities	500000
	900000

The issued shares are 100000 £1 ordinary shares. The net asset value is therefore £9 per share. Discounting the stock by 50 per cent and debtors by 20 per cent reduces the net assets by around £150 000 to, say, £750 000 or £7.50 per share. In view of the recurrent and increasing history of losses, a full control holding would be valued at perhaps not more than £6.50 per share representing a discount in excess of 16 per cent. A small minority holding of 25 per cent or under, on the other hand, could be valued at a more subsidial discount than usual, say 90 per cent on the revised net asset value and the valuation of such a holding would be, say, 75p per share representing at most a hope value of an ultimate capital return on a winding up.

MONEY-BOX COMPANIES

These are companies that hoard family wealth in a corporate guise but do no active trading. They may well retain substantial cash on deposit, generating interest, or equities, generating franked investment income, or alternatively non-interest bearing directors' loan accounts. Their valuation will be analogous to investment holding companies, despite their nominal trading functions. Particular attention must be paid to the terms of the articles restricting transfer of shares and the distribution of their shareholdings. Even minority holdings should be valued on a discounted assets basis unless significant dividends have been paid due to family reasons or shortfall pressures from the Inspector. Both latter factors, of course, are likely to continue.

COMPANIES HOLDING INTELLECTUAL PROPERTY

Royalty-recipient companies

These can be valued on the basis of net assets value plus the additional market value of the right to receive future royalties. This latter right will depend on the outstanding term and the projected future cash flow on a discounted basis.

Minority holdings, of course, are valued on a discounted net assets basis.

Example

XYZ Ltd is a royalty-recipient company. Its net asset value is £50000. A 10 per cent rate of return is required. The royalty term is six years and the royalties on a rising scale will be:

Year 1	£10 000 × 0.909 = £ 9090
Year 2	£12 000 × 0.826 = £ 9912
Year 3	£14 000 × 0.751 = £10 514
Year 4	£16 000 × 0.683 = £10 928
Year 5	£18 000 × 0.621 = £11 178

Year 6 £20 000 × 0.565 = £11 300
Net present value £62 922

The net present value of the £90 000 projected gross receipts is £62 922, say rounded to £63 000 and increases the company's net assets on a market value basis of £113 000.

Copyrights

These subsist in literary, artistic, musical or dramatic works for 50 years after the death of the author under the Copyright Act 1956. Certain literary agents such as Curtis Brown Ltd and musical agencies such as Novellos specialise in such valuations. The trade rule of thumb most frequently applied is three years purchase of the average of the last three years' royalties. However, there are many variations on this. In particular:

- If an author's popularity is likely to continue even after death (for example J.R.R. Tolkien or Georgette Heyer), the year's purchase may be justifiably as high as 6 to 7 (implying a 14 to 16 per cent gross return).
- If the likely royalties are covered by a substantial advance, on the other hand, the copyright value may be low or nil.
- Rising or declining trends may require a weighted average.
- The method deals in gross receipts, and tax, which is peculiar to the purchaser's personal situation, is usually ignored.
- If the author engages in much personal publicity in his lifetime, the death will be a depreciatory factor. On the other hand, a much publicised death may in fact promote sales for a considerable period.

Example

X, the author of historical novels with a lasting appeal, died on 14 January 1983. The copyrights are owned by a company, ABC Ltd, and royalties received were: 1980 £40 000; 1981 £30 000; 1982 £50 000. The three years average is £40 000 and three years purchase will suggest £120 000 as the value of the copyrights or the capital value of the right to receive future royalties from the deceased author's books. Assuming that the company in question has no other assets, apart from the copyright, this will also, of course, be the market value of the company.

Patents

These are often valued at cost. If there is no actual or projected licence income, then cost is at a reasonable basis. If there is licence income, this can be capitalised at *x* years purchase depending on:

- the outstanding term of the patent (initially seven years and renewable for a further 14 years);
- the amounts and trends of the licence income; and
- contemporary interest rates and rates of return. As with pure royalties, a discounted cash flow basis may well be appropriate. Otherwise a rule of thumb application of three to five years purchase (implying gross rates of return of 20 to 33 per cent) can be applied.

Example

A patent has five years unexpired. Licence income has been 10000 a year and will continue at this level. A required rate of return is 10 per cent, having regard to contemporary interest rates and alternative rates of return on relatively risk-free investments. The valuation proceeds:

Year 1	£10000 × 0.909 =	£ 9090
Year 2	£10000 × 0.826 =	£ 8260
Year 3	£10000 × 0.751 =	£ 7510
Year 4	£10000 × 0.683 =	£ 6830
Year 5	£10000 × 0.621 =	£ 6210
	Net present value	£37900

Trademarks

These seldom have a value apart from related goodwill. Assigned apart from goodwill, the acquisition cost is therefore usually applied. With goodwill, the question is the valued assigned with the trade mark and the related goodwill, in other words one pre-supposes a purchaser with a business with the net tangible assets and a vendor possessing solely the trademarks and goodwill. The value is then the price a purchaser in that situation would pay to acquire the trademarks and goodwill. Statistics to project additional revenue and associated profits may be available. If not the valuation can again only be nominal.

Example

Business goodwill is valued at £100000 and a well-established trade mark is to be assigned. This can best be expressed as a special premium over the market value of the goodwill of, say, 10 per cent, in other words a value for the trade mark at £10000.

Know-how

This has arguably little or no market value apart from the related business goodwill. Nonetheless, as a matter of experience, substantial sums may be paid for know-how. Theoretical formulation is difficult, if not impossible, however, and there is no customary or trade basis of valuation. The question is again simply what additional profits can be generated by acquisition of the know-how and then to capitalise this on the basis of contemporary interest rates and rates of return.

Example

It is anticipated that acquisition of certain know-how will increase profits by £25 000 per annum. Contemporary rates of return suggest a capitalisation factor of 4 (implying a gross rate of return of 25 per cent). On this basis the market value of the know-how is £100 000.

QUASI-PARTNERSHIPS

These are companies where all the directors are equal shareholders, often after incorporation of a partnership. The purchaser buying in is much more likely to get a directorship, assuming his holding is at least 25 per cent. Moreover, the courts are much more likely to apply the stricter partnership tests for, for example, treatment of members and grounds for dissolution if the shareholder–directors cannot agree. This is illustrated by the case of *Re Lundie Bros Ltd* (1965) 2 All ER 692. The Lundie brothers and Mr Blackmore had equal financial stakes and shared joint control under the company's articles. A chairman's casting vote was used to exclude Mr Blackmore from the company and he obtained a winding-up order under Section 222(f), Companies Act 1948 as an excluded working director, although his claim under Section 210 as an oppressed minority shareholder failed.

Another important case in this context of equal situations showing the presumption that the shareholder–directors will work in co-operation was *Ebrahimi* v *Westbourne Galleries* (1972) where a 50 per cent shareholder obtained a winding-up order on the grounds of his treatment by the controlling shareholder. The crucial point is that such shareholdings are much less likely to become locked in, longer-term, helpless minorities and therefore have enhanced value. Minority holdings can also therefore be valued on a discounted assets basis assuming that the company has substantial assets value and less than substantial earning power.

Bonus issues

Where a valuation is after a bonus issue, the effect will be to reduce the share price proportionately.

Example

Shares in XYZ Ltd have a market value of £4 per share and there is a one-for-one bonus issue. The effect is to half the market value of the company's shares from £4 to £2 per share.

Existing historic data may require adjustment accordingly, for example earnings per share and the gross dividend in the above example would also be reduced by 50 per cent. The bonus issue does, however, have positive advantages. Thus it increases the company's capital and enhances the shareholder's portfolio flexibility.

RIGHTS ISSUES

These have a similar effect to bonus issues except that the company receives cash instead of capitalising reserves gratuitously.

NEW COMPANIES

Valuation depends on the availability of profits-projections or other financial data to determine the company's maintainable pre-tax profits or earnings per share. If management estimates are not available, then examination of turnover levels, profit margins and likely markets may produce an extrapolated figure. In any case the net asset value will invariably be the starting point until a realistic capitalisation of profits can be applied.

Example

ABC Limited, a computer software company, was incorporated on 31st October 1984. The pre-tax profits projection for 1985/86 is £50 000 after paying 3 full-time working directors £75 000. The net asset value is £30 000. Pre-tax profits for 1984/85 were £30 000 after £60 000 directors' remuneration. As this is a growth sector profits capitalisation can be applied. However, both the lack of an assets base and normal commercial caution would suggest that a multiplier of around 5 would be the maximum a prudent purchaser would accept (a multiplier for an established company in this sector would be around 7–8) giving a value of £25 000 for the company as a going concern).

PARTLY-PAID SHARES

Valuations must adjust for the circumstances in which the company may call for more cash. The probability of future calls — whether for expansion purposes or otherwise — must also be estimated. A prosperous company's shares may, however, entail only nominal adjustment because of the consequential benefits of ploughed back call money. A loss-making company on the other hand will probably require adjustment for contingent losses to be made up, quite apart from erosion of the company's capital by trading losses.

LIQUIDATIONS

General

In 1982, Dun and Bradstreet reported record liquidations of 11 131, 35 per cent up on 1981 and 63 per cent up on 1980. These broke down into 7403 voluntary liquidations and 3728 compulsory windings up. The retail sector with 2779 reported one-quarter of all liquidations, followed by the building trade (1574 or 14.1 per cent), motor trade (1496 or 13 per cent), engineering (1237 or 11 per cent), and the textile sector (1151 or 10.3 per cent).

Petitions for winding up

These may come from:

- any creditor owed £200;
- a contributory;
- the DTI;
- the Attorney-General if the company is a charity;
- the company itself by special or ordinary resolution according to its articles and memorandum;
- the official receiver.

Consequences of a winding-up order

These are:

- the dismissal of all employees;
- circumscribed acts of directors;
- actions by the company are stayed;
- dispositions of the company's property or shares are void;
- the official receiver, if any, becomes provisional liquidator.

The order of payment on a winding up

All creditors within a given category rank equally and none may be preferred. The order of payment is:

- secured creditors;
- the liquidator's expenses and remuneration;
- preferred unsecured creditors, for example rates, VAT, national insurance, corporation tax and other assessed taxes, employees' remuneration and holiday pay;
- ordinary unsecured creditors;
- members with preference shares having priority and ordinary shares ranking the last.

Valuation consequences

- Valuation is exclusively on a break-up basis.
- Liquidator's accounts should be requisitioned.
- The realisable residue of net assets must be estimated.
- The period of the winding up must be established.
- An appropriate discount must then be applied. The discount relates to:
  (a) the realisation period;
  (b) contemporary interest rates;
  (c) the purchaser's prospective profit;
  (d) the relative risk involved which is assessed on the sector's performance and the company's record.

***Re W.F. Courthope* (1928)**

The leading case on the subject is *Re W.F. Courthope* (1928) 7 ATC 538 where the company had sold off its business and lost its trading function and held cash or near cash (directors' loans). The valuations offered for a 48 per cent holding were:

- £10 per share from the executors; and
- £19 per share from the Commissioners.

This compared with £20.91 per share book net asset value and £19.50 per share estimated realisation proceeds. The judicial determination by Rowlatt, J. at £13 per share represented exactly 33.33 per cent discount or 50 per cent prospective profit based on the likely liquidation proceeds and a realisation period of three to four years.

Example

XYZ Ltd is a textile company in liquidation. Proceeds of £5 per share are likely to be realised, according to the liquidator's accounts, within two years. The MLR equivalent is 10 per cent. A discount of 30 per cent is suggested, being bank rate adjusted for the company's status and a purchaser's consequential return of 30 per cent over two years. Valuation at £3.50 per share results.

FOOTBALL CLUBS

These offer a good example of shares that stand on their own and are difficult to value on normal commercial criteria, partly because they are not run on such lines. Minority holdings cannot be valued easily on an earnings basis since so often the clubs run at a loss and receive assistance from directors, businessmen, supporters, or the community at large. The share transaction prices may give an indication of market value if sufficient in frequency and number to justify the idea of a market in them. The open market value will still then stand higher, say by a 10 per cent premium — on the lines of *McNamee* v *Revenue Commissioners* (1954) IrR 214 where the premium at the adjudged value of £1.62½ was 12½p over the £1.50 per share transaction price. Controlling interests may show some reference to the asset value — and even the transfer value of the players who constitute current assets. But though the idea of selling-off freeholds to achieve financial viability and leasing, or sharing grounds even, has occured occasionally of late the clubs do not constitute a ready-made hunting ground for budding property developers as the Football Association have a power of veto and may override the articles which are themselves likely to be very restrictive on rights of transfer. There is, moreover, a Football Association provision that ordinary shareholders receive only the nominal value of their shares in the event of a liquidator being called in.

Division Four clubs are, of course, vulnerable to loss of league status and each spring the struggle to avoid relegation to a lower league develops. On the other hand, participation in extra-league competitions, particularly in Europe, can be very lucrative. The clubs seldom pay dividends and normally only capital profits can be made. The market values of the shares reflects the club's sporting prowess and financial performance, but only to a haphazard extent. In the last three years, clubs have used sponsorships, executive boxes, shared facilities and diversification into leisure, travel and marketing.

Financial survival is still, however, very much the name of the game. Features of the shares of the 92 league clubs are characterised by the following:

- Lack of any ready market — perhaps a turnover of 4000 shares a year under Stock Exchange rule 163.
- Lack of dividend income — with a Football Association maximum of 10 per cent.
- Extreme restrictions on transfer — refusal to register is comparatively common.
- Virtual irrelevance of asset backing — due to the Football Association's stipulation.
- A premium for popularity — for example a Manchester United rights issue at £1 nominal per share traded immediately at a £4 premium.
- Misleading market capitalisation — Liverpool at £1.8m (£1.50 per share) in 1980 capitalised at a lower value than the reserve team.

On the other hand, equity capitalisation is not the market value of the club as a whole — simply the sum total of its constituent individual share values. To buy control would cost vastly more — much nearer the total assets value with a substantial discount of say 20 to 25 per cent for any potential losses and other liabilities and the Football Association restrictions. Small parcels can then be valued on:

- a dividend yield basis, assuming dividends are paid;
- on the basis of transaction price plus open market premium if there are transactions; or failing this
- a discounted net worth basis — the discount being 50 to 60 per cent for influential minorities and 70 to 85 per cent for still smaller minorities.

The yield will be that for the leisure sector as adjusted for unquoted status.

There is now, of course, the first quoted football Club — Tottenham Hotspur. Unfortunately, the share price has never really taken off and is currently around a 33 per cent discount on the initial flotation price of par (£1). Interestingly enough, by way of contrast, the published figures for Manchester United for 1983/84 disclose that the captain, Bryan Robson, earned £105 000, or more than twice his manager's earnings level. This was, moreover, in a year when the club only came fourth in the First Division and lost in the semi-final of the European Cup Winners' Cup. In fact, Robson topped the earnings of Liverpool's superstars Kenny Dalglish and Ian Rush by around £20 000. The club, on the other hand, did enjoy a record-breaking year financially with profits of £1 731 200 and the debts following the £2 million loss in 1981/82 have been eliminated, despite lavish expenditure on the Old Trafford ground and on the team. The club's successes are clearly, however, totally exceptional amongst League clubs generally.

FLOTATIONS

Flotation is one of three occasions when capital appreciation can be realised from an unquoted share-holding — the others are takeover and winding up. The flotation value depends on the stage the flotation has reached. These stages are:

Stage 1

The flotation is anticipated within 2 to 3 years. This was the position in Lynall apart from the category B documents. The discount on the flotation price should be around 50 per cent.

Stage 2

The flotation is anticipated within 1 year. This was the position in Lynall revealed by the category B documents. The discount should be around 33 to 40 per cent.

Stage 3

The flotation is commenced. The discount should be around 25 per cent.

Stage 4

The flotation is in progress. The discount should be around 20 per cent.

Stage 5

The flotation will be effective within 4 weeks. The discount should be around 15 per cent.

Stage 6

The flotation is imminent. The discount should be around 10 per cent.

Stage 7

The flotation occurs. The discount should be around 5 per cent.

At each stage, of course, a flotation price must also be calculated. It should be remembered that the flotation team must be assembled comprising:

- the investigating accountants who must have time to prepare a report;

- the issuing house — normally a merchant bank;
- underwriters to write the issue;
- a firm of solicitors;
- public relations consultant;
- any sponsoring brokers.

The flotation price will moreover be determined perhaps a month before public issue. This will be unlikely to reflect perhaps the intrinsic worth of the shares owing to what is known as 'market discount' comprising the following:

- A minimum 35 per cent shares must be sold to the public.
- Stags need an incentive to create an initial market.
- The issue price helps create a successful record of future share price rises to assist in raising further capital and facilitate future sales of privately held shares.
- Underwriting is difficult if the price is at its probable peak.
- The investor must have an incentive to put his money into a new company as opposed to a comparable existing company.

Having said that, new issues are frequently fantastically over-subscribed — Lynall 22x and 185x has been recorded.

The discount levels must also take into account that almost up to the last minute the flotation could go wrong and be postponed or even indefinitely shelved. In particular, economic or political events could prove suddenly unfavourable. Nevertheless even the necessarily adverse recessionary period has seen some extremely successful flotations — such as Intasun, Business Computers, Habitat, and the first quoted estate agency Bairstow Eves.

Determining the flotation price should involve investigation of the company so as to disclose the kind of information found in a prospectus for an offer for sale. This will require details on the company's affairs going back at least 5 years. Oddly enough no profits forecast or dividend projection is necessary, nor, contrary to myth, need dividends have ever been paid. The procedure would be to project the price the public would pay to realise the surplus capital and subscription level the directors require. In a ball market such as 1971/72, the Singer and Friedlander index of new issues doubled in just over a year, easily out-performing the FT index. In a bearish market, the new issue index may even, however, fail to match the Financial Times index and could register a fall. The latest bull market 1982/87 suggests a similar flotation price trend with such successes as Amersham's International and Oriflamme.

The flotation price will therefore be determined after examination of:

- comparable company acquisitions;
- comparable company dividend yields and price earnings ratios;
- comparable new issues;
- comparable alternative investment returns;
- pre-existing share price levels;
- projected profits levels (if any);
- premium for the fact of flotation;
- cash and asset resources;
- any element of goodwill;
- the appropriate market discount: one study showed this ranged from 5 to 20 per cent;
- adjustments for profits taken as bonuses or remuneration or even as reinvestments for capital allowance purposes;
- capital expenditure programme;
- gearing and borrowing levels;
- technical research and developments;
- management capacity and succession; and
- the company's tabulated statistics as a real unit's statutory accounts, the board reports, its product literature, stockbrokers' reports, sector studies and trade reports, interim results and last but not least the prospectus itself including investigation accountants' reports and other expert reports.

It is also arguable that the flotation price reflects the newly quoted status of the company and should be there for further discount by 20 to 30 per cent for the unquoted status of the pre-flotation state of the company so that even if the company is an unlisted public company it is possible to argue for a minimal discount for non-listed status, but no further market discount then applies.

12 Valuation for specific fiscal purposes

INHERITANCE TAX (formerly capital transfer tax)

The statutory open market valuation is prescribed by Section 160, IHT Act 1984. The holding to be valued may, however, be with reference to a larger holding by virtue of the 'estate' concept applied for lifetime transfers by Section 3 (2) and death cases by Section 4 (1) and the related property provisions in Section 161 (part VI, IHT Act 1984) applicable to both lifetime transfers and transfers on death. These various provisions may have the effect of aggregating the transferor's other beneficial holdings including settled property, his spouse's holdings pre 27 March 1974, discretionary trust holdings made by either spouse (for transfers before 10 March 1981 only) and transfers to charities after 15 April 1976. The holdings in his estate are valued together with the appropriate fraction of their value with related property before and after the transfer in a lifetime case. In a death case there is no after transfer valuation to be made.

Example one - lifetime transfer

Transferor X holds 600 shares and transfers 400 to his son on 29 October 1980. His spouse holds 300 shares. A pre-27 March 1974 discretionary trust made by the transferor holds 50 shares. He had transferred 50 shares to charity on 28 June 1979.

Values agreed are as follows: a 100 per cent holding — £25 per share; a 60 per cent holding — £20 per share.

The spouse's trust and charity holdings are all related property, though not comprised in the estate. The position for IHT is as follows:

Transferor's estate before the transfer:

600 shares at £25 per share	£15000

(strictly, the appropriate fraction
is 600/1000 × 1000 × £25)

Transferor's estate after the transfer:	
200 shares at £20	£ 4000
Value transferred (loss to estate)	£11000

Example two – transfer on death

If transferor X above dies on 17 July 1985, the trust holding is no longer related property.

The valuation at 17 July 1985 is of 200 shares as the appropriate fraction 200/1000 of

$$\frac{200 + 300 \text{ (spouse)} + 50 \text{ (charity)}}{1000 \text{ issued shares}}$$

or 200/1000 of a 55 per cent controlling interest. Valuation of such a holding at, say, £40 per share would give a value transferred of 200 × £40 = £8000 on the death, subject to any available exemptions and reliefs.

Before any valuation for IHT is investigated in any detail, the available exemptions and reliefs must be considered, if only from a cost-effective viewpoint, since there is no point in expensively undertaking the valuation of an exempt or wholly-relieved holding. In particular potentially exempt transfers may not require extensive investigation of any share-holding involved. However there is still a lifetime charge on transfers into trusts which may be desirable for family reasons. Privileged trusts such as maintenance and accumulation trusts are likely to become more popular as they avoid any exit charge. Moreover for tax planning purposes and to calculate sums assured for life policies used in providing for contingent or unavoidable IHT normal valuations will have to be made.

On the other hand, the fact that no IHT is presently payable because, for example, the zero rate band applies does not mean that nothing is at stake since any value agreed will still form part of the cumulative total. Even valuations falling apparently within the annual exemption may still require formal agreement since the amount agreed will pro tanto reduce or exhaust the exemption and affect future transfers.

Specific valuations for IHT

Where the arm's length exemption is in point (IHT Act 1984, s.3(4))
This contains four elements.

- Absence of gratuitious intent on the part of the transferor which is best demonstrated by free negotiation with both parties fully advised by professional advisers.

- The full arm's length nature of the transaction since IHT was evidently not framed to catch mere bad bargains.
- The price must be one such as would be likely to be realised in a hard bargain between strangers.
- The price must be either freely negotiated or else at such a price as might have been expected to be realised in a transaction between strangers in free negotiation.

These exemption requirements depend on some of the statutory open market concepts such as the willing buyer and willing seller. It remains clear, however, that the exemption price is not the statutory open market value of the holding, still less the value transferred for IHT determined as the loss to the transferor's estate, but lies in the extremely wide range in between. Indeed, the price reflects the actual circumstances of the particular parties to that specific transaction and not the hypothetical elements of the statutory valuation. It will therefore take into account any special purchase element and such non-monetary consideration as applied in the leading case of *A G* v *Boden* (1912) 1 **KB** 539 where goodwill passed between father and sons for the latter's undertaking to play the major role in the partnership, and estate duty was thus avoided. It is also clear that the exemption price is determined without reference to any related property, but solely with regard to the particular holding in isolation. This one rule of thumb suggests that the exemption price will generally fall at the bottom of the spectrum of possible open market values. This must be heavily qualified since, in this situation, the possibly extremely restrictive articles will be given full prominence. The notionally negotiated value must reflect the loss to the transferor and the gain by the transferee, however. On the other hand, these are merely incidents in the valuation process in this case.

Example

Shares in XYZ Ltd, a trading company, are agreed at the following values:

a 60% holding at £25 per share
a 50% holding at £18 per share
a 40% holding at £15 per share
a 30% holding at £12 per share
a 20% holding at £8 per share
a 10% holding at £7 per share.

If the transfer of, say, 100 shares is a gift, the value transferred would be:

600 shares	@	£25 (estate pre-transfer)	=	£15 000
500 shares	@	£18 (post-transfer estate)	=	£ 9000
				£ 6000

This can, however, be avoided by the transferee paying the statutory exemption price. The exemption price would not be as high as the value transferred price (effectively £6000 ÷ 100 = £60 per share), the controlling interest price (£25 per share), or even the 50 per cent holding price (£18 per share) since the transferor is losing control and the transferee, while not gaining control, is at least acquiring control in the negative sense. That is, he has the power to block a special resolution, and could hope possibly for a directorship in a situation where no single person will control the company where, for example, B held a 20 per cent holding before the transfer, though A may still have the chairman's casting vote and therefore *de facto* control. The exemption price would also not lie as low as the open market value of the 100 shares transferred (say £7 per share agreed for adjudication purposes) or (arguably) the 20 per cent holding price. It should fall in the range £8 to £10 per share and quite probably any value in that range, if paid in a transaction otherwise satisfying the statutory exemption, would qualify. The matter would, of course, have to be disclosed to the Capital Taxes Office who would then refer it to the Shares Valuation Division with whom the question of the exemption would have to be negotiated. The loss to the transferor and the gain to the transferee are both reflected in this valuation exercise. Sufficient compensation to the transferor can perhaps be achieved by the transferee paying a price mid-point between the value of the holding held and the holding acquired. This would suggest a statutory exemption price in the present case of £10 per share. A second value transferred of a further 100 shares would show:

500 shares	@	£18	=	£9000
400 shares	@	£15	=	£6000
				£3000

Again the effective value transferred price is £30 per share which is higher than the full going-concern price (say £27.50 per share). The exemption price would, however, be lower than in the first transfer and would be, say, £7.50 per share (mid-point between £7 per share and £8 per share).

Attempts have been made to require the Shares Valuation Division to express an opinion on share values before proposed transactions, or in respect of purely hypothetical transactions. The Revenue are not, in such cases, in a position to maintain the standard of care required of a professional valuer —see *Arenson* v *Casson* (1975) All ER 901. More significantly, the Revenue do not wish, and have no statutory obligation, to undertake non-productive work because the transaction in point may be exempt, or may not proceed in the light of its advice. Nor is the Department in business to provide gratuitous assistance for advisers to tax avoidance schemes. One contractual formula used is that the consideration for the acquisition of the shares should be the open market price as agreed by the shares valuation division and, of course, could be held void for uncertainty. It could also, however, be considered to come within the statutory provision to IHT Act 1984 s.2(4), that is the price as agreed with the Revenue could arguably be a price such as might have been expected to have been freely negotiated at the time of sale. A suitable compromise figure is appropriate in all such cases.

Where close company provisions are in point (IHT Act 1984, ss.94–101)

These apportion the value transferred by a close company (or an alteration of rights deemed to constitute a transfer of value such as including omissions and extinguishments by virtue of Sections 3 (7) and 94 (6), IHT Act 1984 amongst the participators, defined as members with 5 per cent or greater holdings. The close company follows the Taxes Act definition (s. 282), namely:

- control by five or fewer participators;
- control by any number of directors; or
- the apportioning of income results in either of the two above.

However, the one difference is that for IHT purposes an overseas-situated company can be treated as a close company, which is never the case for corporation tax purposes.

The valuations are determined on normal open market lines. However, any value included in his estate is deducted and IHT is charged (since some or all of the transfer value by the company may fall into his estate) only on the net decrease, but the whole apportioned amount forms part of his future chargeable estate. Sub-apportionment of a subsidiary's transfer is made to the ultimate parent company.

Example

A close company C Ltd sells property worth £200 000 to B Ltd for 100 000. C Ltd is 80 per cent owned by A Ltd which also owns 100 per cent of B Ltd. There is a transfer of value of £100 000 by C Ltd and this is apportionable amongst the participators of C Ltd, including A Ltd as well as subapportionable as to 80 per cent amongst the individual participators in A Ltd. This latter sub-apportionable £80 000 is matched by an equivalent increase in the assets of B Ltd. Therefore the majority participators in A Ltd will, in effect, incur no IHT. However, the balance of £20 000 can be apportioned amongst the minority participators in C Ltd, subject to the small effect provisions. If they can show that the transfer has only a small effect on the values of their interests in C Ltd, as opposed to the interests of the other majority participators, then again no IHT will be incurred.

CAPITAL GAINS TAX

Open market value applies in this case. As with IHT, however, there are distinctive features of valuations for this tax. Valuations of unquoted shares on an open market basis must be made when the transaction in question is any of the following:

- not at arm's length;
- a gift;
- a transfer into a settlement;
- a company capital distribution;
- for a consideration that cannot be valued;
- in connection with loss of office or past services;
- between connected persons;
- an appropriation of stock.

This will, of course, be subject to the numerous CGT reliefs and exemptions available which may pre-empt the need for a negotiated valuation if it can be readily agreed that these are in point. Specific CGT valuation provisions, however, require special consideration.

The Budget day election under para. 5, s. 12, CGTA 1979.

The taxpayer must make an irrevocable election for valuation at 6 April 1965 (to determine the notional acquisition cost) instead of a time-apportionment basis before the Revenue will advise as to its applicability. This is, of course, a classic catch-22 situation. The only safe approach is to take the valuation bull by the horns and produce an answer well within any valuation safety margins. This is, of course, after ascertaining the time-apportioned acquisition cost-based liability. There is potentially a difficulty with the latter if the acquisition cost is unknown (because of lack of records) or it depends on market value (because acquired by gift or not at arm's length).

The Budget day valuation is determined on normal open market lines. In particular, certainly apparently fairly popular misconceptions should be removed. Thus valuation at a higher value based on husband and wife's joint holdings or family control is inapplicable. Nor are the taxpayer's other holdings at that time (if any) to be taken into account since the valuation is only of the holding in question in respect of which the Budget day election was made. Similarly, the fact that the disposal proceeds at a much later date reflect a takeover price for the company does not mean that the earlier valuation will reflect any such premium. There are three possible instances, however, when an enhanced valuation may apply as at 6 April 1965.

- There may, as a matter of fact (provable by contemporaneous evidence and not by *expost facto* statement), have been a takeover situation existing as at the valuation date.

- The articles of association may be such that a sale of shares is only possible on a group basis. If this is the position at both 6 April 1965 and at the disposal date, the majority basis of valuation may be applied for a minority holding.
- If evidence is adduced that all the shareholders had, as at 6 April 1965, decided collectively to sell their combined holdings.

Apart from the election, a valuation at 6 April 1965 is mandatory if there has been a reorganisation of the company's share capital since the acquisition date (CGTA 1979, para. 14 (1), s. 5). However, under paragraph 14(3) this will not apply where the new holding is simply a different number of shares of the same class. On the other hand, paragraph 14(3) is not considered by the Revenue to apply where the shares in the new holding are in a different company — following the decision in *CIR* v *Beveridge* (1979) STC 592 and the Revenue *Statement of Practice SP14/79* effective after 19 July 1979.

Valuation for acquisition purposes

This will arise where the original acquisition was by gift or not at arm's length or between connected persons. A common feature of such valuations is their antiquity: going back in some cases 60 or 70 years. The valuation may be avoided if the acquisition was by will and an estate duty valuation (on open market lines under Section 7(5), Finance Act 1894, not the statutory assets basis under Section 55, Finance Act 1940, as amended, unless a controlling interest was acquired so the two bases more or less coincide) was agreed, or an old stamp duty adjudication of value is available. Otherwise, the valuer must do some time travelling into the industrial, commercial, economic and investment climates at the relevant date. The quickest way to do this is to examine the prevalent quoted sector yields of the leading blue chip securities and gilt edged stocks. The reading of the case reports of the court decisions on the subject may also assist to get back into the state of mind of contemporaneous share valuers, for example *Jameson* (1905), *Courthope* (1927), *Salvesen* (1931), *Crossman* (1937), *Holt* (1953) and *Lynall* (1972). Finally, the different company tax positions as at those early dates should be borne in mind. This will affect determination of both dividends and earnings and respective yields. In valuing controlling interests some ideas should be gleaned from contemporary financial literature as at the commercial rate for directors' remuneration so as to see whether any excess can be added back to justify a high capitalisation value on the lines of *Smyth* v *IRC* (1931) IrR 643.

Valuation under s. 151, CGTA 1979 — aggregation of holdings

This will necessitate a series of valuations and revaluations. It applies where a donee receives more than one gift of shares from the same, or different, but connected donors. The principle is applied only of course where the aggregation of holdings will produce a higher market value, essentially because a greater legal power attaches to the larger holding because, for example, the aggregate holding exceeds 25 per cent (power to block a special resolution) or 50 per cent (giving day-to-day control). The stages might be as follows where Company X has 2000 issued ordinary shares and the donors to A are B and C:

Gifts of shares by:	B	C	
30 June 1977	50	50	Not yet a s. 151 case.
30 June 1978	100	100	Still not a s. 151 case.
30 June 1979	200	200	s. 151 applies, therefore value 500 shares (50 × 2 + 100 × 2 as at 30 June 1977, 1978 and 1979.
30 June 1980	100	100	Not yet a s. 151 further application (40 and 30 per cent holdings show no differential of significance).
30 June 1981	100	100	S. 151 applies. Value 1000 (50 per cent) shares as at 30 June 1977, 1978, 1979, 1980 and 1981.
30 June 1982	100	100	S. 151 applies. Value 1200 (60 per cent) controlling interest as at 30 June 1977, 1978, 1979, 1980, 1981 and 1982.

The aggregation of holdings applies for both acquisition and disposal purposes. Assessments and reassessments can be raised by the Revenue within the normal six-year time limits. The larger holdings have their values apportioned to the actual holdings transferred at each relevant date. Thus after the latest transfers on 30 June 1982 the revaluation of the original transfers of 50 (× 2) shares means an assessment on strictly 50/1200 of the value of a 60 per cent controlling interest, or, in effect, 50 shares valued at the price level of a 60 per cent holding. This demonstrates graphically the dangers of cumulative transfers falling within this statutory aggregation principle.

Valuation where value passes out (CGTA 1979, s. 25(2))

Valuations for this purpose arise where a person (or persons) having control so exercise it that value passes out into the holding of another person. The case of *Davis* v *Floor* (1979) where the Revenue in the House of Lords won the case shows that :

- the term 'person' in the legislation includes 'persons' (applying s. 1,

Interpretation Act 1889); and

- passive exercise of control (by an omission to act for instance) is sufficient to come within the charging provision.

Valuations must be made of the transferor's and transferee's positions before and after the transfer but (in sharp distinction to the IHT position) the CGT charge is restricted to the value accruing to the transferee, not the loss to the transferor. Thus, in the following situation Mr A and Mr B are father and son. Mr A holds 750 shares and Mr B the remaining 250 shares in the company. Mr A renounces a one-for-one bonus issue. Valuations are:

- 750 shares (75 per cent) at £50 per share;
- 250 shares (25 per cent) at £12 per share.
- 1250 shares (62.5 per cent) at £22.50 per share;
- 750 shares (37.5 per cent) at £10 per share.

In the first two cases, before the bonus issue, in the latter two, after the bonus. Their respective positions are then:

- Mr A — transferor (by renunciation):
  Before the transfer: 750 shares at £50 = £37 500; After the transfer: 750 shares at £10 = £7500. Loss = £30 000.
- Mr B — transferee:
  After the transfer: 1250 shares at £22.50 = £28125; Before the transfer: 250 shares at £12 per share = £3000. Gain = £25 125.

The chargeable gain on this notional disposal is restricted to the £25125 gain by the transferee. No losses on such deemed disposals are allowable after 17 June 1975.

Valuation where negligible value is claimed (CGTA 1979, s. 22(2))

Where the Inspector agrees, a valuation for this purpose will support a loss claim. The shares in question will be deemed to have been sold and reacquired at the agreed negligible value. A Revenue concession provides that a claim at a particular date may be made up to two years after the end of an accounting period or tax year in which that date falls as long as the shares in question had a negligible value at that date (whether or not they had such value before then — see Revenue press release dated 4 August 1985). In this context, negligible value evidently entails considerably less than nominal value.

Valuations for a part disposal

These will most commonly arise when there is a liquidation and a series of capital distributions are made by the liquidator in realising the company's assets. The usual Revenue formula for such part disposals applies to determine the apportionment of original cost to the particular disposal proceeds: $A/A + B$ where A is the market value of the part disposal and B is the value of the part remaining. Valuations on liquidation follow the usual discounted assets basis with the discount relating to the liquidator's estimated time for distributing the company's assets and contemporary interest rates. Depending on the valuation date, the liquidator's accounts may have to be supplemented by a statement from the liquidator personally. Valuations may also have to be made where part of a holding is disposed of since there is no pooling for unquoted shares. If a part disposal consideration is small (5 per cent of market value), the Inspector may dispense with a formally-negotiated valuation and may simply deduct the appropriate fraction of original cost on a purely numerical basis. If, for example, only 2 per cent of a holding of 100 shares (100 per cent) were disposed of, the Inspector might deduct 2/100 × original cost and forego the valuation. It will be borne in mind that, where the transaction is at arm's length and not between connected persons, no market valuation to determine disposal value will be needed. The Inspector has only to enquire about market value of the part remaining to determine the proportion of the original cost to apportion to the proceeds in determining the chargeable gain. A protracted negotiated valuation will therefore seldom be required in such cases unless a very substantial amount of cash flow is at stake.

Where there is a part disposal (by a capital dividend or other non-income distribution) before 6 April 1965, time-apportionment is calculated on the market value at the date of the part disposal (CGTA 1979, s. 35 and sch. 5, para. 11 (7)).

Valuation after a share reorganisation (CGTA 1979, ss. 78/79 and sch. 13, para. 5)

The reorganisation itself is not a disposal since the old and new holdings are treated as the same asset. Any further consideration is added to the original cost in determining the gross gain. Any consideration other than the new holding results in a part disposal. Where the new holding comprises more than one class of share of security or debenture the notional acquisition cost is determined with reference to their market value as at the date of the disposal (in whole or in part) of the new holding. If, for instance, a share reorganisation takes place in 1984 and the new holding comprises 20 000 ordinary shares (consolidated) costing par and 5000 preference shares (a rights issue at par), the disposal of 2000 preference shares at £2 per share in 1986 will also involve valuation of the ordinary shares (say at £4 per share) to determine the apportionment of original cost as follows:

Preference shares — 5000 × £2 = £10 000
Ordinary shares — 20 000 × £4 = £80 000

Proportion of original cost attributable to preference share disposal is: 10 000/90 000 × (£20 000 + £5000) = £2778

Valuation where there are connected persons (CGTA 1979, s. 63)

This provision simply imposes a mandatory open market valuation where such transactions are involved. There is open an element of inequity involved since similar transactions, one between connected persons and the other between unconnected persons at arm's length, both at the same price, may result in different values to CGT since the open market valuation may be higher than the restricted market price (prima facie this should always be the case). If the transaction price lay at the bottom of the range of market values anyway, it may be impossible to avoid some increase in valuation by the Revenue. This may also be the case where the articles are exceptionally restricted or there is, for whatever reason, virtually no actual market or none at all. In such a case, the differential between the actual market value and the notional statutory value may start to look significant. The Revenue will then emphasise the open market and hypothetical elements while the professional adviser will have no doubt that it must be pointed out what a greater number of depreciatory incidents there are. Assuming the transaction price might not be an unreasonable one, in the normal case (with a reasonably active market and no severely depressive articles), then a parallel transaction at arm's length between unconnected parties would be a useful pointer. So is the arm's length nature of the transaction if such is the case (hard bargaining between professionally advised parties and so on).

STAMP DUTY

Stamp duty is charged *ad valorem* on a variety of share transfers and on incorporation of businesses and partnerships. Unless a specific stamp duty exemption is involved, such as a company reorganisation within s. 55, FA 1927, these transactions will involve share valuations.

There is no *statutory* open market value for stamp duty purposes, but ever since the decision in *Stanyforth* v *IRC* 1930 AC 339 that value under s. 6, Stamp Act 1891 meant *market* value, the Revenue have applied similar valuation priciples. The statutory hypothetical valuation exercise must therefore be undertaken. On the other hand, there is no specific statutory information standard for stamp duty. Thus, the information standard is the lower one applied by the House of Lords in the leading case of *Lynall* v *IRC* (1972) AC 680. This is of special significance in the context of the valuation of *influential* minority holdings since, for very small holdings, all taxes will have the same minimal information standard, and for control holdings a very full information standard will again invariably be required.

All stamp duty valuations fall into three different categories:

- sale of shares by individuals or companies;
- share exchanges on takeovers or mergers,
- incorporation of unincorporated businesses.

The tax treatment of these different transactions affects the valuation approach.

Sale of shares by individuals or companies

If these are arm's length transactions, a full-scale valuation may not be justified since initial screening may reveal that the bargaining price is a reasonable measure of the market value. There should also be no IHT implications unless the transfer is by a close company or out of a controlling interest. A valuation for CGT will not arise unless the Inspector suspects the transaction was not genuinely at arm's length or if the partners are connected persons.

Share exchanges as takeovers or mergers

Share exchanges may require a radically different treatment. It is arguable that the share value should reflect the going-concern value for all the shares since this is the basis of the takeover price. In practice, however, there may be a different Revenue treatment. The essential thing is that the valuation takes into account the takeover situation.

Two possibilities then exist. One is that the enhanced capital appreciation element implied in the takeover is reflected in the valuation of different sizes of holding, but the differential between them is still maintained. Alternatively, the going-concern value is reflected in the valuation of all sizes of holding taken over at an appropriate takeover price. It is submitted that the latter approach reflects commercial reality though the former may be justified on the grounds that a purchase would not pay as high a price on a controlling interest as for a 1 per cent holding. These apparently contradictory propositions can be reconciled as follows. Firstly, it is accepted valuation practice that in a liquidation situation the net asset value, less a discount for realisation costs, delays, uncertainties and so on of, say, 10 per cent is acceptable for all sizes of holding. Thus, the differential between different classes of holdings is in that case at least effectively abolished. Now there is a difference, in that on a winding up the full net asset value is realised so the valuation of all holdings approaches the full net asset value for a greater differential. While a takeover price may merely reflect only a premium for control, the full going concern, or even the full break-up value, may not be applied. However, bearing in mind (a) the enhanced value of even small minority holdings and the 10 per cent valuation margin shown in a normal valuation range, there are good grounds for supposing that in a given case the range of acceptable valuation differentials may well be small. The appropriate practice can be seen from the following illustrations:

- ABC Ltd (a quoted company) takes over XYZ Ltd offering two new shares (value £2) in the acquired company. The valuation of shares in XYZ Ltd shows the following holdings acquired:

  10000 + 20000 + 30000 + 60000 + 1 ordinary shares representing the whole issued share capital.

  The shareholders in this case have driven a hard bargain. It is evident that the maximum market value of the shares in XYZ Ltd will not exceed the value of the consideration shares so no precise valuation is required. This is often the case in a takeover — the stamp duty treatment is then relatively simple.
- The going-concern value of the whole company is £300000. If allocated to the different holdings in XYZ Ltd, this reflects a valuation at £2.50 per share which makes £25000, £50000, £75000 and £150000 for the respective holdings. No valuation will be necessary for CGT as this will be charged on the actual disposal proceeds, namely: £2 per share. This assumes, of course, that the acquiring company is not controlled by shareholders of the acquired company which would bring in a market valuation under the connected persons legislation.
- A variation on this process is in a company reorganisation *or* a takeover of several companies by a new holding company. In this event Company X must be valued as the sum of:

  (a) its inherent value;

  (b) the value of the acquired companies; and

  (c) the additional value (if any) generated by the larger concern (the so-called synergistic value originating from the go-go growth consortia in the early 1970s).

Incorporation of unincorporated businesses

Valuation on incorporation of a business or partnership into a limited company, or the acquisition of a business or partnership in exchange for shares are similar situations.

Incorporation into a limited company

In effect, this valuation is required only if there is goodwill acquired by the company. If the value of the share does not exceed the value of the business assets acquired, then no formal valuation is necessary. Goodwill exists for two reasons in this instance. Either there is positive value for goodwill founded on a customary or trade basis, or the profitability of the business generates super-profits so that the capitalisation of the company as a going concern would demonstrably exceed its net asset value. In this context it is likely that the matter is only worth pursuit if the valuation difference exceeds the 10 per cent valuation margin. If, therefore, the net tangible assets are £100 000 and the capitalisation value is £1100 000, it is unlikely the matter would be worth pursuit. The valuation will invariably involve the whole issued share capital so that full information standards are required. Thus, the business accounts should be supplemented by a profits projection based on the estimates of the directors.

Moreover, so far as based on actual past profits, these should be adjusted for a reasonable level of directors' remuneration at a commercial rate.

Finally, if a valuation is necessary because of excess capitalisation on other goodwill value, the share values must bear in mind that, in such valuations, the valuation margin is perhaps broader than in other cases because of:

- the comparative novelty of the corporate structure;
- the associated greater proportion of imponderables such as management;
- the possibly different infrastructure such as gearing and borrowing potential;
- the stamp duty at stake may justify, without prejudice, a compromise settlement with the Revenue.

Examples

- customary goodwill:
  John and James have traded in partnership as dairymen for several years and have decided to incorporate their successful business on 31 March 1983 and 100 000 shares are issued to them for this purpose.
  The customary basis of valuing their partnership goodwill is as follows:

  Daily gallonage:

	£
Retail 10000 gallons at £80 pg	800 000
Semi-retail 2500 gallons at £20 pg	50 000
Value of goodwill	850 000
Net tangible assets	150 000
	1000 000

  Therefore issued shares 100 000 = £10 per share

- Capitalised goodwill:
  Ted and Thomas have decided to incorporate their highly-successful

engineering concern on 30 April 1983 and 50000 shares were issued to do this. The net profits of the business as at 30 January were: 1980 £30000, 1981 £40000, 1982 £60000. Projected pre-tax profits were disclosed as £60000. Net tangible assets were £100000. The net profits must first be adjusted for the directors' remuneration that would be incurred by the company. Deducting this at levels in accordance with managerial salary levels revealed in *Financial Times* surveys shows pre-tax profit levels as follows:

	1980	1981	1982	1983 (projected)
Net profit	30000	40000	60000	90000
Directors' remuneration	20000	22000	25000	30000
	10000	18000	35000	60000

In view of the consistent upward trend a maintainable pre-tax profits level of say £50000 is reasonable. A capitalisation factor derived by either extrapolation from the contemporary earnings yield of $14\frac{1}{4}$ per cent = $100/14.25 = 7$ or a figure of $\frac{1}{2} \times$ the quoted sector price earnings ratio to take account of corporation tax at, say, 50 per cent = $\frac{1}{2} \times 14 = 7$ based on a multiplier of 7 gives a valuation of £350000 for the incorporated business represented by £100000 net tangible assets and £250000 goodwill.

CAPITAL DUTY

These valuations usually involve substantial or majority holdings since a takeover or regrouping is frequently the occasion of the valuation. The charge to tax arises under Section 47 to 49 and Schedule 19, Finance Act 1973. The rate is 1 per cent under Section 47(5) on chargeable transactions (defined in part 1, sch. 19, paras 1–3) made by capital companies (a term which includes all UK incorporated limited companies). Capital duty resembles stamp duty and the main exemption for company reorganisations with paragraph 10, Schedule 19, is analogous to the exemption from stamp duty under Section 55, Finance Act 1927. The common transaction falls within category 1(b) of Schedule 19, namely an increase in the capital of a company by the contribution of assets. Capital duty (by virtue of paras 4(1) and 7(1) (a), sch. 19) is chargeable on the market value of the assets contributed (the share capital of the acquired company) *or* the nominal value of the increase in the share capital of the acquiring company (*not* its market value), whichever is higher. The valuation is of the entire shareholding acquired *en bloc* and not of the separate minority holdings that may have been acquired from the individual shareholders in the acquired company.

In view of the relatively low tax rate, prolonged negotiation will seldom be justified and the Revenue will no doubt appreciate this. Complications may arise, however, when the statutory exemption is in point. There may also be disputes over the subject matter of the valuation. The crucial factor is the alternative basis of charge. In the normal case, the valuation would be of the whole issued share capital of the acquired company forming the subject of the takeover bid. Exceptionally, part only will be acquired because, for example, the acquiring company already has an existing stake. Once the subject matter has been clarified the valuation can then proceed on normal open market lines.

Examples

- Company A (a quoted company) issues 100 000 £1 ordinary shares (market value £75 000, i.e. 75p per share) to acquire the entire issued share capital of Company B (100 000 £1 ordinary shares). Company B has £45 000 net assets and a maintainable pre-tax profit figure of £10 000. As it is clear, on a preliminary examination, that the market value of Company B ('the contribution of assets') will not exceed the *nominal* value of the newly-issued shares in Company A (£100 000), no precise valuation of the shares in Company B is necessary. Capital duty will then be chargeable on £100 000.
- Company A (an unquoted company) issues 200 000 £1 ordinary shares (market value £3 per share) in exchange for 10 000 £1 ordinary shares in Company B (also unquoted). Company B is a precision engineering company and has £100 000 maintainable pre-tax proft and £350 000 net assets. The valuation proceeds on normal valuation lines for a full control holding and a multiplier of 5½ is appropriate as at the date of valuation. The valuation of Company B is therefore 5½ × £100 000 = £550 000 (not the £200 000 nominal value of the acquiring company's newly-issued shares or the latter's market value of £600 000 which shows that an element of special purchase or an additional premium for control was paid).
- Company A already possesses 45 per cent of Company B and now issues 250 000 25p ordinary shares (market value £2.50 per share) to acquire the other 55 per cent. Company B has an issued share capital of 100 000 £1 ordinary shares, pre-tax profits of £200 000 and net assets of £750 000. In this particular case, the valuation is of 55 per cent × 100 000 = £55 000 £1 ordinary shares in Company B. The company is in the leisure sector and a multiplier of 7 is appropriate. The company is therefore valued at £1.4m or £14 per share. This should, however, be discounted for lack of winding up control. A discount of 10 per cent is evidently appropriate in this case and the valuation is consequently £12.60 per share or £693 000. This will be the value for capital duty purposes since it exceeds both the nominal value £62 500) of the newly-issued shares in the acquiring company and the market value of the acquiring company's newly-issued shares (£625 000) which, in any case, is strictly irrelevant for capital duty purposes.

It will also be evident, however, that, in capital duty cases, the market value of the acquiring company's shares, which in many cases will easily be determined as the acquiring company will be a quoted public company (assuming the transaction is a strictly commercial venture fully at arm's length between unconnected parties), will be at least an approximate guide to the market value of the acquired company's shares. This will then be a rough and ready cross-check on the valuer's determination of the open market value of the acquired company's shares.

13 Valuation examples

The share valuer should draw up a preliminary picture of the company by abstracting, in tabular form, basic data from accounts and reports for at least three years, if available, as follows:

- accounts year
- auditors' certificate
- turnover or rents
- gross profit (%)
- trading profit
- directors' remuneration
- pre-tax profit
- taxation
- post-tax profit
- preference dividend
- earnings for ordinary shares (%)
- dividends
- cover
- fixed assets
- land
- machinery and plant
- motor vehicles
- current assets
- stock
- debtors
- trading investments
- loans and accounts
- interest in subsidiaries
- current liabilities
- creditors

- bank overdrafts
- loans
- directors' accounts
- mortgages
- net assets
- significant points from directors' and chairman's reports.

SPECIMEN PROFESSIONAL VALUATIONS

These follow in ascending order of complexity.

Valuation note for minority holding in a small trading company

A Smith deceased — died 7 January 1983. Valuation for IHT purposes of 150 shares (12.5 or 25 per cent with widow's shares which are related property) in A. Smith & Sons Ltd (a textile company). Total issued shares 1200 £1 ords held as follows:

Discretionary trust created by settlor in 1973	400
Mrs A. Smith (widow)	150
J. Smith (son)	500
Deceased	150
	1200

Control of company

This was not held individually or jointly with widow at his death.

Recent share transfers

None since 1973.

Dividends paid

None.

Accounts to 31 October 1982

These were available as at the date of death. Results:

	Directors remuneration charged	Pre-tax profits	Earnings
October			
1979	£25000	£100000	£60000
1980	£30000	£ 80000	£48000

1981	£40000	£ 70000	£42000
1982	£50000	£ 40000	£24000

Net asset value — £160 per share

Basis of valuation

The profits for 1979 to 1981 reflected a low rent charge for premises owned by the deceased. The rental value was increased by £20000 on a third party determination and this was reflected in the 1982 accounts. The quoted sector price earnings ratio was 9.09 and the earnings level is £20 per share. The quoted sector price earning ratio should be discounted by 75 per cent to, say, 2.25 to give a valuation at £45/£50 per share, representing also a discount of around 75 per cent on the net asset value.

Valuation of controlling interest in an investment holding company

Valuation of 50000 50p ordinary shares as at 18 January 1983 of XYZ Investment Co. Ltd.

General

The company was incorporated on 31 March 1969 and has carried on business as an investment holding company with investments in freehold ground rents and Stock Exchange securities.

Share capital

The company has an issued share capital of 60000 ordinary shares. The shares originally had a nominal value of £1 but were reduced to 75p by capital repayment of 25p per share on 28 June 1973 and were later reduced to 50p by a second capital repayment of 25p per share on 18 January 1983.

Shares to be valued

The holding to be valued is 50000 50p ordinary shares on 18 January 1983 immediately following the second capital repayment of 25p per share.

Basis of valuation

The holding under consideration represents 83.33 per cent of the total company. Valuation will therefore be made primarily by reference to net asset value, either on a going concern or break-up basis.

Valuation as a going concern

The company's profits available for distribution during the three years immediately prior to the valuation have been very small, £500 for year ending 31 March 1980, £1000 for year ending 31 March 1981 and £2000 for year ending 31 March 1982. However, the company has realised substantial capital profits which it is prohibited from distributing under the terms of its articles. The holder of shares representing 83 per cent of the share capital could, however, change the articles to make the profits distributable. In those circumstances the distributable profits of 1980 to 1982 would become:

Year ending	Revenue	Capital	Total
31 March 1980	£ 500	£ 4500	£ 5000
31 March 1981	£1000	£ 9000	£10000
31 March 1982	£2000	£13000	£15000

The capital profits realised were from sales of property, and as properties were sold off and not replaced the scope for making such profits in the future was becoming progressively more limited. A reasonable man might therefore have considered the future maintainable post-tax earnings of the company to be £6000 per annum. This represents 10p earnings per share. Applying a price earnings ratio of 20 to such earnings (the quoted sector ratio less 20 per cent adjustment for unquoted status) would value the shares at £2 per share or £100000 for the holding.

Valuation on net assets basis

The net assets of the company at 31 March 1982 were £100000 as disclosed by the balance sheet of the company at that date plus an adjustment for the market value of the company's investments. Allowing, say, £10000 to cover the cost of liquidation and realisation of assets would give a value of £90000 as the break-up value of the company or £1.75 per 50p share.

Suggested valuation

A potential purchaser of 83 per cent of the share capital might value the shareholding at £100000 as a long-term investment prospect, but at approximately £75000 if he were intending to realise a short-term gain from disposal of the company's assets in a liquidation. Accordingly a valuation is suggested at, say, £1.75 per share of £87500 for the holding of 50000 50p ordinary shares.

Valuation of shares in ABC Ltd — a catering company

The valuation to be made on the date of death of A. Brown deceased on 18 January 1983.

Holding to be valued

18000 £1 ordinary shares. There is no related property within the statutory definition for CTT purposes.

Issued capital

£1 ordinary shares	30000
£1 A ordinary shares	40000

The A shares are non-voting but otherwise rank *pari passu* with the ordinary shares.

Basis of valuation

The holding has voting control and should be valued on an assets basis.

Profit and loss account

The accounts to 31 December 1982 were not completed as at the date of valuation but were available in draft form and should constitute the basis for an asset based valuation. The profit and loss account discloses a trading loss for the period of £21 100.

	£
Freehold properties at cost	100000
Leasehold property at cost	21000
Fixed plant at cost less depreciation	3000
Equipment at cost less depreciation	65000
Motor vehicles at cost less depreciation	14000
Goodwill at cost	2000
Fixed assets	205000
Current assets	60000
Current liabilities	100000
Shareholders' interest	165000

Adjustments

	Book value £	Market value £
Freehold property	100000	500000
Leasehold property	21000	60000
Fixed plant	3000	nil
Goodwill	2000	nil
	126000	560000
Difference £434000		434000

Add shareholders' interest	165000
	599000
Deduct:	
CGT inherent in foregoing adoption of values:	
£434000 at 30% =	130200
Trading loss for the period	21100
Redundancy pay and closing down costs implied	48700
	200000
	399000

Value per share (70000) = £5.70

But greater value attaches to the voting shares which suggests a premium of at least 10 per cent. The value of the voting shares is therefore £5.70 plus 10% = £6.27 per share. The value of the 40000 A ordinary shares on this basis will be £399000 – £188100 (i.e. 30000 × £6.27) = £210900 = £5.27 per share.

Valuation

The value of the deceased's 18000 shares at £4.70 is therefore £84600. This is the value for IHT purposes, subject to 50 per cent business relief for a controlling interest.

JUDGMENTS ON VALUATION.

Findlay's Trustees v IRC (1930) ATC 438

The conclusion of Lord Fleming's opinion in this celebrated case, involving the value of the goodwill in *The Scotsman* newspaper, is reproduced below.

> The decision of this case must accordingly depend upon the figure which is to be adopted for expected profits. I do not doubt that, when one is seeking to ascertain the profits which will probably be earned by business in the future, it is quite usual to do so by taking an average of the profits actually earned for the three preceding years. This probably operates quite equitably when one is dealing with a well-established business which has normal ups and downs, and has no violent fluctuations in either direction. If there is definite trend upward or downwards it may be different. If, for example, profits are increasing year by year by large figures, an average of three years may be unfair to the seller. In a similar movement downwards it may be unfair to the purchaser. The relevant figures as regards this business are to be found in no. 14 of Process and the figures of adjusted net profit are in column 7. In order to find the figures actually used by Mr Geoghegan and Mr Robson it is necessary to add to each of the figures in that column a sum

of £16500 representing debenture interest. But the actual figures in the column sufficiently indicate the movements of the business upwards and downwards so far as profits are concerned and the remarkable fact is that you have in 1930 a drop in profits of not less than £36000, which is greater than any other increase or decrease in the column. There are large increases in the years 1922 and 1923, but it is apparent that these increases are explained by the reduction on the amount of one item of expense, namely the cost of the newsprint. *Prima facie* the drop in profits in 1930 was such a large amount as to suggest that it cannot properly be dealt with by the application of what is at best merely a rule of thumb.

This *prima facie* view is I think confirmed by a consideration of the newspaper industry in the year 1930. That year was a period of general depression, which had begun in 1929, and it was certainly not a time at which sellers could expect to get good prices. Traders had to go in cycles, and booms follow slumps, but there were a number of factors which, apart from the slump, were not favourable to this business in 1930. The competition by what are called the national newspapers with their headquarters in London was in an increasing degree affecting the prospects of the morning newspapers published in the provinces of England and Scotland. According to the evidence of Sir Bertram Ford and Mr Scott, the 'structure' of the Scotland business was not well-suited to withstand such competition. In their view the morning newspapers are much more amenable to competition from London than the evening paper associated with it, and this business was criticised on the grounds that *The Scotsman* was the permanent partner in the group. Though the evening despatch was increasing its circulation at this time, their view was that it was not a sufficiently strong evening paper to counteract any retrograde movement on the part of *The Scotsman*, especially as it had to face competition from a well-established rival newspaper. Another factor which they regarded as unfavourable was that *The Scotsman* newspapers circulated mainly in a non-industrial area, in which the population was not increasing, or increasing slowly; and that there was little scope for expansion or development. It was maintained by the appellants that the figures in the other columns in no. 14 of Process indicated that the business was declining and reference was made in particular to the figures with regard to newspaper sales, advertising revenue and expenses. The decrease in the volume of newspaper sales, though not great, is certainly not a favourable feature, especially as a reduction in circulation may tend to diminish the advertising revenue. The figures in relation to advertising revenue were the subject of a good deal of discussion. There is a drop of £27000 for the year 1930, which might give a buyer some uneasiness, but otherwise the tendency is rather upwards, and I do not think the figures relating to this matter give much assistance to either side. Admittedly, however, a disquietening feature as regards the future is the increase in the expenses other than the cost of newsprint. The expenses show an increase year after year, without a single exception, for a period of 10 years. I do not think the respondents were able to show that this was due to a factor that was likely to be eliminated in the future.

The question however remains: what effects as regards the question of the price to be given to the considerations to which I have been referring? I reject as being altogether exaggerated the idea that this business falls to be regarded as moribund in 1930. The Solicitor-General criticised with much force the evidence produced by the appellants, because no witness had been brought from *The Scotsman* office to speak direct with the effect which the alleged adverse circumstances had upon the business. I am certainly not surprised to find that no one has come from *The Scotsman* office to say that this was a moribund business. I think, however, it is impossible to avoid coming to the conclusion that the outlook in 1930 could not be regarded as favourable for the newspaper industry or for *The Scotsman* business, in particular, and I think it is unreasonable to suppose that a buyer would expect to earn profits from this business amounting to the figure of £147 000, or anything approximating to that figure, in the immediate future. A prudent buyer would, I think, proceed upon the view that the business would not recover from the serious set-back which it had sustained in 1930 for some years. Respondents, however, argued that ample allowance had been made for this as they were willing to accept a valuation over £45 000 less than Mr Robson had brought out; and they pointed out quite correctly that this was equivalent to diminishing the average annual profit which they had taken by a sum of over £5000. I am not satisfied, however, that this is a sufficient allowance. There is still left a wide gap amounting to about £15 000 between their reduced figures and the actual profits earned in 1930, and I suggest to your Lordships that we should take, as the figure of expected profits, the sum of £135 000 which exceeds by more than £10 000 the actual profits in 1930. If the figure of £135 000 is multiplied by eight and the value of the tangible assets, namely £707 680, be deducted as left to represent the value of the goodwill of £372 320.

The other two judges delivered concurring judgements.

***Dean* v *Prince* (1954) Ch 409**

Lord Denning's judgment in the Court of Appeal in this case is extracted below. The Court of Appeal reversed the judgment, at first instance, that the auditors' valuation had been made under a mistake. The most decisive factor in the valuation was an agreement most unfavourable to the company. Under this, Mrs Dean had contracted to sell and the company had contracted to buy the premises in question for £5000. This was payable by annual instalments of £200. It was dubious if the premises were worth the balance of the purchase money. On a winding up, or failure to observe the covenants or to pay any instalment the vendor could terminate the contract. The company's tenure of the premises was therefore extremely precarious. Lord Denning's judgment considered in essence the critical valuation factors.

The right to control the company

The auditor was not bound to take this into account. The deceased held 140 shares and the other two directors 30 each. The other directors were bound by the articles to purchase the shares of the deceased director. The fair thing to do would be to take the whole 200 shares and see what they were worth, and then pay the widow of whichever director had died the amount appropriate to her husband's holding.

Valuation of the business as a going concern

It was not necessary that the auditor should have valued the business as a going concern. It was a losing concern and once Mrs Dean has sold her shares to the other two directors, as she is bound to do, there is nothing to prevent her calling in the monies owing to herself and her husband, amounting to over £2000, against which there was only £1200 in the bank. The company might have been forced into liquidation.

Valuation of the assets of the business

Since the going-concern basis was rejected, the only possible way of valuing the business was to find out the value of the tangible assets. No one would buy the assets *in situ* unless he could also buy the premises, and the company had no saleable interest in the premises. It had no right even to assign the contract for the purchase of the premises. If the assets were sold it would probably be forced into liquidation and hence lose the premises.

Valuation on a 'break-up basis'

The trial judge had thought that the break-up value was wrong. He would have been right if the business had been a profitable concern; but it was a losing concern, and it was a well-known fact that a losing concern could not realise the book value of the assets. This element is 'negative goodwill'. A purchaser could buy only on a piecemeal basis and it was obvious the vendor would make heavy losses compared with the book figures.

The special purchaser

The fact that there were 140 shares out of 200 to be sold had suggested to the judge that the shares would have a special attraction for some persons — namely the next-door neighbour. It was not fair that the directors purchasing the shares should pay a price based on the assumption that they would be turned out. They were buying the shares, compulsorily, on the basis that they would continue as working directors.

For all these reasons the appeal should be allowed and the auditors valuation upheld.

As tailpieces to these extracts from expert witnesses and judicial opinions, three further cases concerning professional valuations should be mentioned.

- The old case of *Collier* v *Mason* (1858) Vol 119 RR 394 is notable for the proposition stated by the then Master of the Rolls:

  > This court must act on that valuation unless there be proof of some mistake or some improper motive, I do not say fraudulent one; as if the valuer had valued something not included or had valued it on a wholly erroneous principle, or had desire to injure one of the parties to the contract.

- In the case of *Jones (M.)* v *Jones (R.R.)* (1971) 2 All ER 676, it was agreed on express valuation terms that a valuation arising out of a petition for compulsory winding up, dismissed by consent on a going concern basis, was made by Mr D. who did not, however, employ an expert valuer for the stock or machinery and had additionally instructed a valuer to value the premises at break-up values. Ungoed-Thomas, J. held that the valuation had been made on an erroneous principle.

- Significant, in the case of *Arenson* v *Casson* [1977] AC 405, was the proposition that an auditor owes a duty of care to a shareholder when valuing the shares of the company. The auditors valued the shares at their fair value in their capacity as experts and not as arbitrators.

  However, a few months later the company went public and it was evident that the shares were worth six times the auditors' valuation. The auditors were consequently found to have been negligent in making their valuation.

14 Valuation experts and case histories

Leading open market case histories show the following results in order of size of holding.

Re Holt (1953)

A holding of 43698/697680 or 6.26 per cent in a West African trading and shipping company was valued at 95p per share as at 11 March 1948, or just under mid-point between the respective Revenue and executors' valuations at £1.25 per share and 86p per share. The implied dividend yield on the 5 per cent gross dividend paid from 1938 to 1947 (with cover varying from negative to around 3) was only 5.26 per cent compared with 5.09 per cent for the actuaries investment index for industrials and 4.89 per cent for a range of quoted companies. The discount on the £3.50 book net asset value was 72.85 per cent. Other features of this case included the company's extremely speculative business, poorer liquidity, long trade cycles, the company's large size for one with private status and, not surprisingly, the wide discrepancy between both the valuations and the techniques. Thus the experts ranged as follows:

For the executors

- An accountant's valuation at 86p per share based on a dividend yield basis at 76p per share plus a 10 per cent premium (7½p) for flotation potential plus 2½p addition for net expected dividend.
- The chairman of the United Africa Company used a dividend yield of 6.14 per cent plus further 2.05 per cent (33 per cent adjustment) for unmarketability to give a valuation at 61p per share with nothing for capital appreciation.

- A merchant banker valued the shares at 75p per share based on a yield of 7½ per cent (a quoted 5 per cent plus 50 per cent addition) plus a 10 per cent premium to give a rounded figure.
- A new issues specialist stockbroker valued the shares at 80p per share, namely par value (based on a 5 per cent dividend yield) less 20 per cent deduction for non-listing and relative unmarketability.

For the Crown

- An accountant (past president of ICA) valued the shares at initially £1.70 per share (based on a yield of only 3 per cent giving £1.66½ plus 3½p for capital appreciation). This was the Crown's initial submission, but later was reduced by the statements in court to £1.25 per share.
- Another accountant valued the shares on a fixed element giving 81p per share (5 per cent dividend based on £1.05 per share agreed for the 6½ per cent preference shares) and a contingent further dividend of 5 per cent suggesting a further 81p per share discounted by 25 per cent for uncertainty giving a final figure of £1.415 per share.
- A third accountant valued the shares at £1.50 per share based on a prospective flotation price of £2.05 per share founded on a 17½ per cent dividend and 8½ per cent yield discounted by one-third for uncertainty.
- A stockbroker valued the shares at £1.40 - £1.45 per share by some mysterious intuitive process reduced to £1.25 per share by comparison with the not altogether comparable Brooke Bond & Co.

***Crossman* v *IRC* (1937)**

A 10 per cent holding in a large brewing company with extremely restrictive articles and a pre-emption price at a fixed fair value was valued at £351 (3½ × £100 par value). The court effectively followed Lord Plender's valuation (after an initial Revenue valuation at £475 per share and the executors' valuation at £221 per share, namely the articles price) — based on:

- a 7 per cent quoted sector yield;
- 8½ per cent adjusted dividend yield;
- prospective 45 per cent dividend;
- 19½ per cent dividend required to give the £221 per share fair value; and
- the balance of 26 per cent of dividend was capitalised at five years' purchase showing a valuation at £221 plus 5 × £26 = £351 per share.

***Lynall* v *IRC* (1972)**

A 28 per cent influential minority holding in a large fastener manufacturing company was valued at £3.50 per share as at 19 May 1962. This represented around 45 per cent discount on the prospective flotation price of £6.50 per share. The expert witnesses arrived at very much the same required yield — 7½/8 per cent — but differed significantly on the capital appreciation factor so the valuation range was £2.50 - £5.50 per share. As this is the leading modern case on share valuation, it is also considered substantially later on.

***Salvesen* v *IRC* (1930)**

A 33 per cent influential minority holding in a large whaling company with extremely restrictive articles was valued at £3 per share, representing a dividend yield of 6⅔ per cent, an earnings yield of 73 per cent (based on £220 000 maintainable earnings) and 70 per cent discount on the £10 net asset value per share. Depreciatory factors included:

- the need for large reserves due to seasonal trading and vessel replacement;
- the low pay-out ratio (with a cover of around 11);
- the company's dependence on the deceased;
- the company's capital commitments (£300 000 for the latest season);
- the unusually restrictive articles;
- the prospective capital outlay of £152 000 implied by one Crown expert's valuation at £5.50 per share.

***Re Courthope* (1928)**

A 48 per cent influential minority holding in a company whose trading functions had effectively ceased so that it held essentially cash and loans and would be wound up in three to five years at the latest, was valued at one-third discount on the estimated liquidation proceeds, giving the purchaser a required profit of 50 per cent.

***McConnel's Trustees* v *IRC* (1927)**

A 99.8 per cent holding in a property company was valued uncontroversially on a full assets basis and the judge said:

> In my opinion it is a mistake to suppose that the value of a share in a company is to be ascertained with reference merely to the income which it yields and without regard to the capital value.

In fact the pendulum has since swung the other way so that even minorities in property companies are often valued on a discounted assets rather than a yield basis.

THE *LYNALL* CASE

The basis of the *Lynall* case in the House of Lords was that the flotation report prepared by Messrs Cazenoves (the so-called category B documents) constituted inadmissible evidence. It presented private treaty information standards and not open market information standards so that the lower valuation at £3.50 per share (rather than £4.50 per share suggested by Plowman, J.) at first prevailed.

Basic data on the company available as at the valuation date was as follows (trading year to 31 July):

	1959	1960	1961
Turnover	1 267 000	1 604 000	1 607 000
Pre-tax profits	156916	274713	268 077
Earnings for ords	90 697	141 343	135 496
Gross dividend (%)	15	15	15
Cover	6.1	6.4	6.1

The 241 700 £1 ords were held as to 28 per cent by Mrs Nellie Lynall (the deceased), 32 per cent by her husband, 20 per cent each by their sons and 200 only by the general manager.

Extracts from the transcripts of the *Lynall* case now follow, classified as appropriate; the names of the expert witnesses appear as headings. These extracts give the flavour of expert testimony at a public hearing on share valuation and therefore the kind of valuation process that occurs at a tribunal, whether the High Court or the Special Commissioners. The latter are now the normal appellant bodies for IHT as well as CGT and, with the simplified procedure, more cases may well go to appeal.

Basis of valuation

Benson

In the ultimate, a valuation usually comes down to three factors. The first is the dividend yield which is appropriate to that particular company. The second is the prospective dividend which the buyer can expect to receive in the future. The third factor is the possibility of some capital appreciation — in the case of quoted companies it is usually a takeover bid, in the case of private companies it can either be a takeover bid or it can be the company going public.

Comment

In fact for most private companies the capital appreciation will accrue to the shareholder on a winding up.

Andrews

Q. What factors does one take into account or would you, in your experience, take into account — in valuing shares? Do you relate the value to anything else?

A. The value of shares only has meaning in relation to the value of other shares.

Q. You do not relate it to old masters?

A. People have done, but I do not think it makes much sense.

Q. What, basically, is the major factor that you consider is relevant to share prices?

A. I do not know that I want to put it as high as 'the major factor', but a very important factor in determining the relative prices of shares is the profits of those companies.

Q. When you say 'the profits', do you mean the profits on the past five years or do you mean something different?

A. I mean anticipated level of profits. Maintainable profits would be an equally acceptable expression to me.

Potential purchasers

Benson

There were seven possible classes of purchasers, which are as follows. The first is the existing shareholders themselves, but I think that was unlikely because of the size of the holdings and the amount involved and in the light of what I have heard since, in this court, I think it can be ruled out.

The second class of purchasers would be the surtax payers, who would be glad to buy a share of this character in order to succeed to the capital profits which I referred to a little earlier this morning: but surtax payers are not very easy to find who are prepared to go into a transaction of this size, although they can be found sometimes by contacts with merchant bankers and the larger firms of accountants who sometimes have such among their clientele.

The third class of purchaser would be the investment trusts who specialise in industrial securities. Normally speaking, an investment trust prefers to have a quoted security; but there are investment trusts which are prepared to invest in high-class private companies in the industrial scene if they think there is a reasonable prospect of the company going public within a foreseeable time.

The fourth class of purchaser would have been a merchant bank which, either on its own account, or on its own account and with partners, such partners being his own clientele, but the merchant bank taking the lead, would be willing to make this type of investment because the company was high class and would have been a good investment for them to make and, of course, the merchant bank might expect, in time, to become an adviser to the company concerned and possibly to be concerned in an ultimate flotation.

The fifth class of purchaser would be an industrial holding company. There are several such companies in existence which are prepared and do —their object is to — buy blocks of shares in good industrial securities in order to get a good industrial spread.

The sixth class of purchaser would be another industrial concern of itself, not an industrial holding company — another industrial concern. There are several such who are anxious to buy into good other industrial companies, particularly if they are in a like form of trade, in order to broaden their base, and they are particularly anxious to do this if they see the possibility, as would have been the case here on the facts, that they might be able to increase their holding as the years went by.

There is a seventh class of purchaser, which is, of course, the public itself.

Q. That is the purchaser which would emerge if the company made a public offer?

A. Yes. The point about this is that this company, at this particular time, is ripe for a public issue and therefore this increased the marketability of the shares at the date of death. By 'marketability', I mean in the sense of being able to find a purchaser.

Size of holding

Benson

Q. What was your view about the effect, for valuation purposes, of the holding being of the size of 28 per cent?

A. It seemed to me that this was a factor which I must take into account because 28 per cent is an important proportion of a company's share capital. But it will not entitle a holder by right to a seat on the board. As quite often happens in cases of this sort, where there is a large holder, he is invited to join the board; but he would not, of course, have the right to do so. But there would be a rather more special factor of importance, which is that the company could not pass a special resolution, once he is on the register, without the board's approval; and to that extent, have a bearing on the value of the shares. The directors would not be able to ignore the outside shareholder, assuming it was an outside shareholder, not they themselves, who bought the shares. They would not be able to ignore the existence of the outside shareholder; and if he asked for reasonable treatment as an ordinary member of the shareholding public, I would expect the directors to take account of his wishes.

Q. Is that answer based on experience of what in fact happens?

A. Yes. It is not of course universal because some boards dislike outside shareholders; but where there are normal and reasonable men and there is a substantial holding, it is normal and reasonable for them to work as partners together and to behave as such.

Prospective dividend

Baynes

Q. After you looked at the profit record, what would you look at next?

A. The dividends.

Q. Perhaps you would say again the conclusion that you reached on that by looking at the pattern of dividends.

A. The pattern of dividends is what you would expect in a private company, especially where directors have expressed the view that this is a private family company. They do not want to take out of the company more than they need, and therefore the 15 per cent that had been paid for the last year or two was the figure that anyone would have to go on when he is considering the value of the shares.

Q. First of all, tell my Lord the guess, or inference perhaps, you would have made or drawn.

A. The inference is that the dividend of 15 per cent would be retained as long as possible. Now, it does not follow that the profits will be maintained at the rate they have been, although one would naturally hope they would be. It also follows that there would come a time when the Special Commissioners would say, 'We cannot any longer accept your plea that you have a great deal of further capital expenditure to perform to justify us in giving you a clearance certificate'.

Q. Have you from your consideration of these figures formed a view, or do you say it is not possible to form a view as to the possible timing of an increase in dividend — how long in the future it might be or how short?

A. This depends on the answer to the question Mr Lynall was not able to give. He could not foresee the profits, so all I can say is that if profits were to continue at the rate that they were, the estimated rate they were for the year ended 31 July 1962 — we have not got them but we assume that they are running roughly in line with the previous year — if we can assume that that is going on for two or three years, I would expect an increase in the dividend in two or three years time.

Benson

That has shown, as now well established, a steadily rising trend of dividends. I think in the light of that trend there was a clear expectation of further dividend increases in the future, having regard to three factors: firstly the strong liquid position of the company, which meant that there was no need, by reason of cash shortages, to restrict the dividend; secondly the rising trend of profits; and, thirdly, the encouraging views of the chairman in his speech to the shareholders on 7 June.

There is another factor of considerable significance, and that is the pressure which, in my opinion, would have continued to have been exerted on this company by the Special Commissioners in relation to Section 245. I have already given evidence to the effect that, in my experience at that time, the sort of distribution which the Special Commissioners required in a company with a strong liquid position was between 30 and 40 or about 3 × coverage, but the dividend at this time was over 6 × cover and I think that this factor alone would have meant that, apart from the channels to which I have just referred, the pressure on the Special Commissioners would have required or caused there to be higher dividends to be paid.

Q. In which year — if you are advising a potential purchaser in May 1962 — would you have advised him to expect a dividend of 32 per cent?

A. I would not have advised him to expect a dividend of 32 per cent. This is not the purpose of the document at all.

Q. What if the prospective purchaser whom you are advising wants to form a view as to what dividend he is likely to get in the future?

A. Yes.

Q. As he would pay a different price — supposing he had the gift of prophecy — would he not, if he was certain (looking at it now in May 1962), on a dividend of 32 per cent. In the year 1962, from what he would pay if he knew he was only certain of a dividend of 32 per cent in 1972?

A. Of course, if his view of the prospective dividends was different from this, the price would be different.

Q. Do you visualise a gradual increase in the dividends or do you visualise a situation in which the dividend will continue at 15 per cent until disaster occurs and then it is suddenly doubled to what — 32 per cent?.

A. I do not think that that is really how reasonable men would have behaved. They would have realised that the dividend would have had to go up for fear of Section 245 and they would try and have a discussion with the Revenue to see what indeed they could agree between them. That is how it would have been done.

Q. Yes, and they might well, when the axe fell, get away with a dividend of — I am not now expressing this as a distribution of available profits, but the rate of dividend on the shares — perhaps they might have been forced to put it up from 15 to 20 per cent and they might have held that line for three years, perhaps four, and then put it up to 25 per cent and held that line and then eventually put it up to 30 per cent. Is that wholly unreasonable?

A. It depends how persuasive they were. I think the liquid position of this company in relation to its capital commitments was such that the Revenue, judged by my experience in other cases, would have demanded a more immediate increase.

Q. You think that the right exercise is to take as a basis the yield on engineering, motors, and aircraft related to the existing dividend and reflecting all future prospects and to apply it not to existing dividends with our company, but to a projected future dividend?

A. I think that is the right way to proceed because you must have a firm and solid foundation on which to base a valuation and the firmest and solidest foundation you could find is what the market thought was the right dividend yield for this class of company.

Q. My suggestion to you is that you destroy the whole benefit of your firmer foundation if you then fail to compare like with like?

A. Respectfully, I do not think I would destroy it because the dividend yield on that class of company is an indication as to what the investor would expect when he expended his money. But he must of course apply it to the income which he can reasonably expect to derive.

Q. I thought I understood your answer a moment ago to be that so far as you knew, you knew of no case in which the price or value for this purpose had been ascertained by reference to a percentage of dividend yield applied to future dividend of future profits on a dividend?

A. This was the basis in the *Holt* case. That was exactly the point in the *Holt* case.

Q. In the *Holt* case the dividend was constant at 5 per cent, was it not?

A. It was the prospective dividend that was constant. This was the whole point of the case.

Comparable companies

Rose

Q. In some cases of this nature it has been sought by gentlemen in your profession to compare the yield and profitability of the company in question here, Linread, with the yield, profitability and market price of quoted shares in comparable companies. What do you say about that exercise?

A. I think that exercise is entirely profitable if someone wanted to test the accuracy of my valuation of £5.50 on the footing that it had been decided on 21 May 1962, to obtain a public quotation for the shares of Linread Ltd. One might then say that, since all investment is competitive — an investor puts his money, if not into one share then into another — that one must justify the figure of £5.50 by reference to comparable companies if those exist. But in the state in which Linread Ltd then was, as a private company with an uncertain future, so far as status was concerned, I think the exercise is wholly useless for the simple reason that, with private company status the dividend policy is so utterly different from that followed by the directors of public companies and the transfer restrictions existing in the case of private companies for other quoted public companies, that no comparison is possible, except by starting with some alleged comparison and making allowances for the private company factors; and to my mind this is an unsatisfactory method as it is common ground that some allowance must be made and no one can logically say how much.

Baynes

Q. I think you are accepting, are you not, that at any rate it is proper to look and see what the general yield of public companies in this sort of field — engineering and motors — is and obviously (if I may say so) an investor in a private company would expect a larger yield than he would get anyway on the Stock Exchange?

A. Yes.

Q. Do you agree that it is a legitimate start or approach — it is not yours in your book, but it is a legitimate start or approach — to look and see what the general yield at the relevant time is for public companies and then to make a discount (though it means adding to the figure) for the fact that it is more than lock-up investment?

A. Yes. I have used the word guidelines and I think that is the best way of describing my attitude.

Q. It is only because you were a little strenuous yesterday about the comparisons that I wanted to make quite clear what you meant.

A. Let us get this clear. I was making it abundantly clear, as I hoped, that I was talking about comparison with individual companies. That is the difference.

I have expressed fairly vigorously my views on using the Stock Exchange quotations. Now I am making an exception, and it may profit you to accept this, because it is in your favour. I am making an exception where shares are offered to the public by way of a placing or offer. There are no laws of supply and demand in operation. Some individual or group of individuals has to give his expert opinion as to what he thinks the shares are worth at the date on which the offer is made. That seems to be very important. Therefore I do pay some respect to the offers for sale that are made about the time or the date we are talking about.

Dividend cover

Rose

The average or typical cover of a company of this kind in 1962 would have been something of the order of 2¼ compared with 6 or 8 in this case. The significance of that exceptional cover to a purchaser of a minority holding is in view only twofold. First it promises him a pretty strong immunity from any reduction dividend, even if the profits should fall back, as in the history of any industrial company they are almost bound to do at some time or another, and I think the record of dividend distributions in this company, such as it is, bears that out. The other significance of the cover is that the investor might hope — it can be no more than that — that these high profit retentions would be invested in such activities as the company was authorised to carry on and would themselves, in the future, yield an additional profit return and — and this is where the argument becomes more speculative still — that if that additional profit return did materialise the directors would choose to apply some proportion of it in additional dividend distribution. On the basis of all this — and now, at last, I come specifically to the point you asked me to answer — I would have thought it to be a reasonable supposition that this company's dividend distribution, starting off with the figure of 15 per cent, and still ignoring all possibilities of a change of status, might double over a ten-year cycle.

Benson

Q. At any rate, that is the basis on which you arrived that the appropriate dividend yield for that company was 7½ per cent?

A. Yes, but with one very important reservation, and that is that that dividend yield and cover are closely related. This dividend yield of 7½ per cent which I arrived at would only be appropriate if it was applied to the prospective dividends concerning which I wish to give my views very shortly, but the point I wish to stress is that if the cover is increased then the dividend yield must go down. This point is of profound importance in looking at yields. They must be read in conjunction with cover. I found . . . there were 67 companies which had dividend covers of between 3 and 4 times earnings. Then I looked at all the companies where the dividend cover was between 4 and 5 times. There were 17 such companies and the average dividend yield dropped from 3.9 to 3.3. Then I looked at the companies covered between 5 and 6 times. There were only four such, and the dividend yield had again dropped to 2.8 from 3.3. There were only ten companies over 6 times cover and again the average dividend yield had dropped from 2.8 to 1.4.

Dividend yield

Rose

I would expect, or would have expected at that time, from an investment in a company of this kind, an effective return of 15 per cent. By the effective return of 15 per cent, I mean something which is by no means to be compared with the dividend yield on shares that one sees published in the newspapers every weekday. I mean a return which is compounded of that dividend yield, certainly, but, in addition to it, of that return which accrues to the shareholder in the form possibly of capital gain and which arises from future increments in earnings and dividend income.

I make these assumptions, that we start off with a dividend of 15 per cent, as in fact we do; that an investor might reasonably expect this dividend to double over a ten-year cycle. This latter portion can be converted into an annual increment of dividend, and it works out at 5 per cent. What I mean is that if a dividend doubles every ten years it is exactly the same arithmetically as if it went up by 5 per cent of itself every year; and from this annual compound increase of 5 per cent I derive an immediate required yield of 10 per cent, which is no more than 15 per cent less 5 per cent.

Q. And how do you apply that to an economic price to pay for the shares?

A. I apply that required yield of 10 per cent as so adjusted to the initial dividend of 15, and I arrive at a price of £1.50 per share, subject to all these other factors which we have agreed to ignore up to now.

Q. Would you agree that another approach to the appropriate yield is to find out what the yield is, not of a particular company's but the whole group of companies in this sort of field in a public quotation, and then affect that yield by a factor to take account of the fact that this was a private company with restrictions on transfer?

A. Yes, that is another approach to it, though not the one which I prefer. It is a perfectly proper one.

Q. I think you yourself said you would think it quite useless to compare with particular other companies, because there are so many variables?

A. Yes.
I do not condemn that method as wrong in the slightest. It is a perfectly

proper and correct method, but it runs into this difficulty, in my opinion, that when you have arrived at your required yield of 7½ per cent in the manner you have just described, to what actual dividend are you then going to apply?

Benson

Q. Would you kindly indicate to his Lordship what dividend yield you would think appropriate, and perhaps first of all by what method you would arrive at the dividend yield?

A. I first looked — and this, so far as I am aware, indeed, is the traditional method and the one which is applied in practice in my experience — and the dividend yields which were in fact being earned on quoted companies at about that time in this class of industry.

Baynes

Q. Starting from that position, from your 12 per cent, how do you adjust, so to speak, if you do, for this particular company?

A. This is a personal exercise and clearly I cannot give chapter and verse for each particular item that influences me, but eventually I arrived at a figure of 7 per cent in this company, with all its advantages, against my basic 12 per cent. Why stick at 7 per cent is because we are getting close to where a hypothetical shareholder were to say: 'Well, when I think of how I have to lock this thing up I might just as well see what I can do with the share that I can sell tomorrow'.

Q. As a comparable yield?

A. Yes.

Q. Would you expect (and again this may be a generalisation and you cannot deal with it) shares in a private company in any ordinary circumstances to change hands showing a dividend yield of less than 6 per cent?

A. It would have to be an extraordinary inducement for a shareholder, a hypothetical shareholder, risking so much money on a lock-up investment of this kind at a lower rate, for the simple reason that every year the expectation of whatever it is he is expecting does not come off he is losing so much income, which has to be set off against any future other benefit he may receive from the disposal of his shares.

Earnings

Andrews

Q. One has these profits, but if they are not distributed to shareholders does this matter?

A. The proportion of the profits distributed obviously creates minor variations in price, because different sections of the investing public have different income requirements; but to the extent that the profits are not distributed they are, by definition, retained in the company. If you assume that the company is competently run — and this was my assumption in this case — those profits will be in turn reinvested and, indeed, we have had ample evidence that this company had opportunities for profitable investment; that investment will, in turn, produce profits and enhance the capital value; and it is exactly this sort of petition that makes this investment attracted to a higher surtax-paying section of the community.

Earnings yield

Andrews

Q. How do you decide what is the right percentage factor?

A. Well, this is, as in any of these exercises, one of the figures that has to be a matter of judgement — this, in my view, against the values of private companies, of the shares in private companies, against such earnings yields of small manufacturing companies in the engineering field that appear to be somewhat analogous, against the quoted indices. I think it is interesting in this connection that the earnings yield on the *Financial Times* ordinary index at 21 May — this is the earnings yield, namely, the dividend times cover — was 8.9 and the earnings yield on the engineering section of the FT Actuaries Index at that date was 11.17. Now, I merely instance that to show comparisons with the sort of figure I am taking. I do not arrive at my figure by any direct relationship with them, but you can see from that, that I am approximately twice the earnings yield on a quoted company at that time, i.e. half the price. I am clearly not influenced in valuing the shares of a private company by any specific yield or indices on any specific date because otherwise one gets into the nonsense situation that your view of the shares of a private company would alter from day to day, and clearly does not.

Q. Because you value, in effect, not by what income your purchaser expects to get but by his public issue or flotation prospects; is that right?

A. Ultimately, in the very long term, and as an arithmetical exercise one is talking of a very, very long period. Profits ultimately get reflected in dividends or in liquidation or sale of the company, so in that sense I am influenced by dividends, but because here we were looking at a board with a policy of distributing a very low proportion of dividends and a policy which, in my judgement, was not likely to be able to be continued indefinitely, I have found it more convenient as a piece of arithmetic to look at the earnings yield because this is a shorthand way of dealing with this interminable argument we have had about dividend yields and cover. It is only saying that same thing in one expression.

Q. Except for this, that it does not matter what the profits are in the long-term, your investor is getting no benefit unless the dividends are paid, is that right?

A. No, these people are primarily in for the profit of flotation. They are not all that interested in the dividend position.

Q. And you disregard entirely, as I understand it, immediate dividend yield?

A. Immediate dividend yield, certainly.

Q. Because one of your answers to my learned friend, Mr Harman, I think was that you would have found buyers, your surtax payers, who would have been prepared in 1962 to accept an immediate dividend yield of 3.3 per cent.

A. Yes.

Q. How is that relevant if you wholly disregard the immediate dividend yield? I just want to know how I have got to deal with this piece of your evidence in addressing his Lordship.

A. Let me put it another way. If the question had been, 'Would you still have valued the shares at £4.50 even if the dividend yield had been zero in the first year? my answer would have been, 'Why yes'. Could I still have found buyers at this price with a dividend yield of zero in year one, answer, yes. To my mind that means I have disregarded it.

Restrictions on transfer

Rose

As a result of this article, I immediately exclude from the circle of potential investors all private individuals, as distinct from corporate bodies and trustees.

Q. Why do you do that?

A. I do so because of the very circumstances which Mr Milner put to Mr Lynall in cross-examination, that a private individual might die and his executor might have to pay duty on shares valued at £2, £2.50, £2.75, a share, whereas that executor might or would, as the articles seem to be, only be able to get £1 a share if he had to sell the shares to pay the duty. This would be a situation that I think would be a noose that no private individual would put his head into. The company which does not die has certain trusts, such as pension trusts, the assets of which do not in practice pass on a death, would not be deterred by this consideration.

Q. Have you as a matter of interest ever come across an article restricting the transfers of shares more stringent than this Article 8?

A. No, not more stringent, and very few which were equally stringent — perhaps one or two.

Q. Just assume for the moment that Mr Robertson-Durham was right in the *Salvesen* case in saying that the discounting factor for such an article should be 25 to 33⅓ per cent, would you expect in the present case the discount figure to be a higher percentage than that or lower?

A. I would expect the discounting percentage to be much higher because of the absence of freedom to transfer shares to a member of the family or a trustee of a family settlement.

Surtax directions (shortfall assessments)

Benson

Q. Is there, given a normal company, any sort of guideline to indicate the sort of level at which the danger of a surtax direction becomes serious?

A. Each company must be looked at on its merits, and this is in fact what happens in practice, but my experience at that time was that where the company was strong and fully liquid, in order to avoid the surtax direction, the sort of figure which the Inland Revenue used as a yardstick was a required distribution of between 30 and 40 per cent of the available profits; in other words, they required a distribution which gave a dividend of about 3 times cover.

Q. That is given everything else normal, but a company in a strong liquid position?

A. In a strong liquid position with a strong cash flow.

Comments

Trading companies are now no longer subject to shortfall assessments on their trading income.

Capital gain and flotation prospects

Rose

I came to the conclusion that I would have advised a purchaser to pay perhaps as much as £2.50 per share; that is to say £1 more than the figure of £1.50 that I arrived at by arithmetical processes, and that extra £1 is the payment for the possibility of a flotation or takeover bid in the future, less the burden of the transfer restrictions, my thinking, on this basis, is that over any given period of time — let us say ten years, though ten years has no merit as such — during those ten years a flotation may take place, or a takeover bid may be accepted by the family and, if that happens, then the purchaser of these shares, having paid £2.50 on my advice, is likely to receive £5.50 again in my estimation, and make a gain of £3. But if during that same period of ten years, no flotation takes place and no takeover bid is assented to by the directors, or perhaps never made, that a shareholder for some reason finds it necessary to dispose of his investment in Linread Ltd, he will, as I have understood Article 8, have to dispose of it at par and lose £1.50 per share, having paid £2.50.

It seemed to me (and this is a matter for subjective judgement if you want to be kind to it, or guesswork if you want to be unkind) that these figures of £1.50 loss and £3 gain per share are well matched, because there is one characteristic which I think is common to all investors, that their fear of making a loss is much greater than the desire to make a gain. Moreover, it seems to me also to reflect, to the extent to which one can say so, the probabilities of a flotation and takeover bid taking place, as against them not taking place and the investor having to sell his shares.

Baynes

Q. How would you go about advising the hypothetical purchaser on the possibility of appreciating through a public issue?

A. I would consider that a company of this size might be forced into the position of having a public flotation whether it likes it or not.

Q. Why do you say that?

A. There might easily come a time, with the expertise shown by the directors, that they themselves wish to expand by takeovers and so on and they might not have the funds to do it. That would be one reason. Another reason is that they might be forced into a position, if they were not careful about their disposition of their shares, that they would be faced with death duties which were difficult to pay.

Q. Those are the two considerations which you have in mind?

A. Yes.

Q. Would you ask the directors what their attitude was towards a possible public issue?

A. Yes; and I know the answer I would have been given. The answer would be: 'You have no right to ask that question. The board will not tell you', and from that I would have assumed that there was at any rate a possibility of considering it.

I considered that if the company were to be floated on the information available on 21 May 1962, I should probably want a dividend twice cover and that I would expect that brokers or finance houses would suggest a yield in the neighbourhood of 8 per cent on a public issue. Now, those two basic facts produced in the end, if my arithmetic was correct, a figure of about 5 guineas but — this, of course, is important — no one would have dreamed of paying that figure because in any case, however much Mr Lynall may have said, 'Well, we think it is likely that it may come off', we should adopt, of course, but supposing he had said, 'We have seriously decided we are going public as soon as we can', I would have expected the hypothetical purchaser to say 'I have had too many of these shocks and the profit may disappear and it may not be ripe, and, therefore, if I am buying with a view to capital profit on a public issue I should wish to make a 50 per cent profit'. In fact, Mr Justice Rowlatt gave that lead in the case of *Courthope*. In that case, of course, my figure would have been £3.50 or thereabouts in order to make a 50 per cent profit, that is all on the basis that Mr Lynall has said to me, 'I will tell you confidentially that we have everything lined up for public issue at the first opportunity when conditions are correct'.

Benson

Q. Tell his Lordship your view of an intelligent appreciation of these figures, the facts which obviously would be known with regard to the probability or possibility of a public quotation in this case, in May 1962?

A. I think there are four factors which would have been taken into consideration which will be material at the time. It is quite usual for shareholders of private companies to take the view that they will never become public companies, or only as a very last resort; but in point of fact there are many pressures upon shareholders of private companies, and I think that those pressures, to a greater or lesser extent, were present at 21 May 1962. The first of the four factors is that, before the date of death, and afterwards, there had been much public talk about the risk of Capital Gains Tax. In fact this had come to pass in part because in the Budget immediately before the date of death, in April 1962, the Chancellor brought into effect a short-term Capital Gains Tax.

The second factor which I think would have been present is the fact that the considerable burdens of taxation which have been imposed since the end of the war eventually began to have an effect on the holders of shares of private companies and sooner or later they wished to realise some spendable capital instead of being locked into large capital assets which are unrealisable. There is a third factor which causes private companies to wish to go public, sometimes earlier than they would think, and that is they very often want to expand by acquisition of other concerns. They cannot very well do this while they are still private companies.

The fourth factor is, of course, a more critical one and that is that they very often are forced to go public by the pressures of estate duty and this is something that the willing buyer in this case would have paid particular attention to. In other words, although shareholders of private companies may not wish to go public, the situation is very often forced upon them from outside.

The impact of that I think is plain to see, that by reason of the size of the holding and ages of both Mr and, if necessary, Mrs Lynall as such must have appeared probable as a public issue was also probable in the foreseeable future, and by 'the foreseeable future' I mean a short term of years, one, three, five years. But, of course, there is another factor there, and that is that if the shareholders foresee the possibility of a public issue arising they usually, or quite often, do not wait for the death, because it is a dangerous thing to do: you may be forced into making a public issue on a death at a time when it is inconvenient or unattractive because of the company's position. When this position is foreseen it is quite normal for the public issue to take place before the death, so that the situation on death is taken care of.

Andrews

Q. Is it your view that the time comes inevitably when any prosperous private company must have a public issue?

A. No, clearly not, because there are a very limited number of very large private companies. But if one is generalising, the probability — and in any investment assessment one is only talking about probability — is that successful family companies ultimately get quotations. I am sure there are exceptions.

Q. The extent must depend to some degree on the attitude of the family?

A. On the attitude of the family at the moment at which they make up their minds. But they can tell me, as here, 'We are never going to float' — I cannot believe they would, but they can say, 'We are never going to float this company'. Now, I hear what they say. I do not believe them. This is the policy that they have at this moment in time, just as they have commercial policies at that moment in time. As the facts change, as the companies develop, I would expect them to adopt a flexible policy, and in any given situation to take whatever steps are best for the company.

It is my assessment of probabilities that within a reasonable period —five to ten years — I mean, I would not want to be held down to a figure — there must be a high degree of probability that this company will be floated, yes, and this is one of the factors that I have put in in forming my judgement whether this discount is a realistic discount, the 40 per cent.

BUCKINGHAM v FRANCIS

Finally the recent case of *Buckingham* v *Francis* (1986) confirmed certain share valuation principles on the earnings basis for an influential minority shareholding.

Mr Buckingham was a director of a printing industry supplies company. He held 20 of the issued £1 ordinary shares of 40 per cent while the three defendants in the case each held 10 shares or 20 per cent each. The valuation date was 24 March 1981 at which time Mr Buckingham ceased to be a director. It was agreed that a going concern basis applied and the company was a quasi-partnership. The valuation of the 40 per cent shareholding was therefore to be the arithmetical proportion of the value of the whole company. The break up value was small or nil. However there was a net asset value of £39000. One accountant valued the company at £48650 goodwill (5 years' purchase of £9730 superprofit based on £13630 average of 3¼ years net profit less 10 per cent return on net assets) and £39000 net assets = £87650. The other accountant valued the company at a price earnings ratio of only 2 applied to a prudent purchaser's estimate of maintainable profit i.e. £6000 giving a valuation of £12000 for the company.

The Court agreed with the second basis of valuation (while agreeing the first method was possibly appropriate in other circumstances) but considered the multiplier of 2 was low. Substituting a multiplier of 4 a valuation at £24000 was determined.

15 Investment analysis and the stock exchange

INVESTMENT ANALYSIS

Investment analysts report for stockbrokers and their clients on share values, normally of quoted companies. They are concerned essentially with relative values and with timings of purchases and sales. There are two contemporary schools, fundamentalists, who analyse and project from available historic data, and company visits and chartists, who project from share price movements. Protagonists of the random walk hypothesis — that share prices are determined on a random basis and cannot therefore be evaluated by either school — reject both. Evidently, however, analysts' reports do influence share prices, and awareness of how they operate will give the valuer fresh insight in any comparability studies he undertakes. The information standard required, generally approaches that of a prospectus.

Analysts specialise in different sectors. The largest firms will have a team of analysts covering the leading companies in all the main *Financial Times* industrial and commercial sectors. They will supply periodic detailed reports on both the sector and individual companies within it for institutional and private clients. This expertise in equities and gilts is used by broker salesmen to generate the turnover from which the broking firm's commissions are derived. What is clear, however, is that both the company and the sector reports are goldmines of information and comment — far more detailed than would be seen in even the best-informed of leading financial journals devoted to gilt and equity investments. They bring together an invaluable amount of research into performance and prospects. Equally valuable is the perspective they provide by way of relative strength graphs showing how the different sectors interrelate at different times.

An example of the kind of coverage from a leading London firm is shown from the following list:

- building materials — 29 companies from Baggerage Brick to UBM;
- contracting and construction — 12 companies from AMEC to Wimpey;
- electricals and electronics — 52 companies from Acorn to Vinten;
- mechanical engineering — 54 companies from AE to Wolseley-Hughes;
- brewers and distillers — 24 companies from Allied-Lyons to Wolverhampton & Dudley;
- food manufacturing — 23 companies from ABF to United Biscuits;
- food retailing — 15 companies from Argyll Foods to Watson & Philip;
- health and household products — 19 companies from Amersham International to Whatman Reeve Angel;
- leisure — 16 companies from Comfort Hotels to Trusthouse Forte;
- stores — 51 companies from Aquascutum to Woolworth Holdings;
- chemicals and fibres — 15 companies from AAH to Yorkshire Chemicals;
- tobaccos — 5 companies, i.e. BAT, Carroll, Alfred Dunhill, Imperial Group, Rothmans International;
- financials — 9 companies, i.e. Bank of Scotland, Barclays Bank, Grindlays Holdings, Lloyds Bank, Midland Bank, National Westminster Bank, Royal Bank of Scotland, Standard Chartered, Exco;
- property — 53 companies from Allied London Properties to Warnford Investments;
- overseas traders and miscellaneous — 6 companies, i.e. Booker McConnell, Thomas Borthwick, Gill & Duffus, Hanson Trust, Inchcape, Paterson Zochonis.

Analysts are therefore the research arm of a stockbroking firm. They are ranked annually in the Extel (formerly Continental Illinois) survey conferring prestige arising out of institutional assessments of the analytical teams of the leading firms. Their profession is relatively new — the Society of Investment Analysts dates only from 1958 and the practice originated of course from across the Atlantic.

STOCK EXCHANGE INFORMATION

Influences on share prices vary on a day-to-day and even minute-to-minute basis from ill-founded bid rumours to major world events. The market frequently discounts profits and losses and many other positive and negative factors in advance. Hence the phenomenon that reported profits increases may result in a share price drop (as they did not match the forecast) while

Table 15.1
Share prices and corporate profits

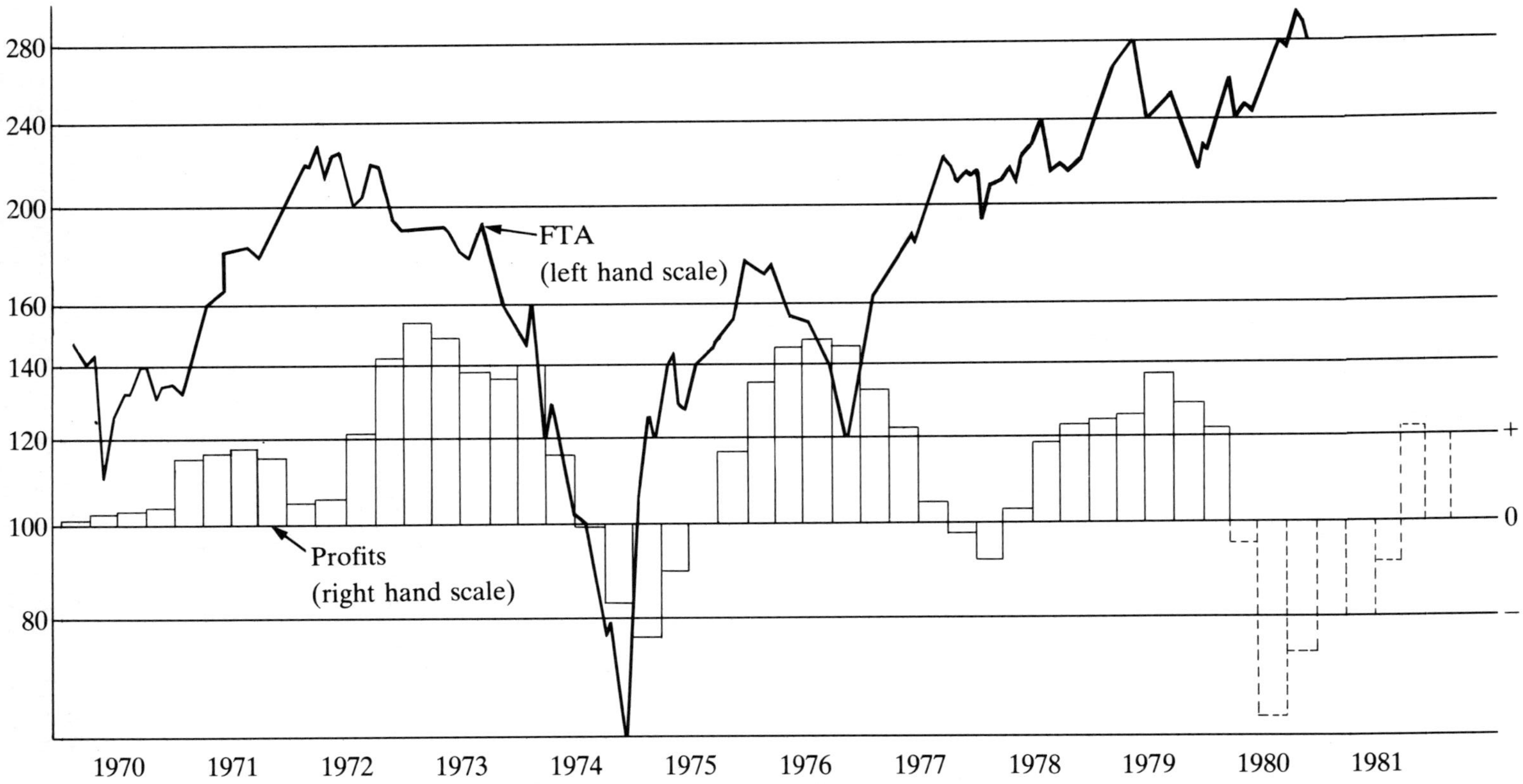

announced losses may result in a share price rise (as they were not as bad as anticipated). Broadly speaking, the macro-economic and socio-political factors and events will determine market trends while more specific incidents will affect the fluctuations in the share price of a given company. Either class of event may determine sector share prices since there can be events affecting a particular sector, such as a property tax like DLT, and there can be knock-on effects, notably the impact of bid speculation on to all possible candidates. Certainly the kind of information that leads to daily price fluctuations is unlikely to affect the far more stable price of an unquoted share. Indeed the valuer of unquoted shares must effectively discount such specific factors that cause movements in quoted equity share prices and think much more in terms of fundamentals. The reason is that investors in quoted equities are much more likely to be looking for short-term gains and the investor in unquoted shares is invariably looking to longer-term capital growth. Indeed his view may be gauged from the minimum five-year retention period required for investors under the Business Expansion Scheme to avoid loss of the top-rate tax relief obtainable from such investments. On the other hand, the unquoted share valuer is looking keenly at sector trends and market moods since he is required in all statutory valuations at least to examine the open market price a prospective purchaser would pay who is of course taking into account all the relevant information. It is here that the efficient market hypothesis should be invoked. The market's assessment of the company in its share price embodies the latest available information as between willing buyer and willing seller. The share valuer can use the ratios and yield embodied in that price, therefore, with some confidence. The market reports contained daily in the financial and other media illustrate the way new information feeds back on to the share price of quoted equities. On the other hand, fundamentals do count. In the longer term an asset situation will be reflected in an upward share price movement and, still more significantly in the long term, the broad movements of share prices do tend to follow the fluctuations in company profits. The graph in Table 15.1 shows this quite clearly.

The *Financial Times* Actuaries Share Indices cover virtually every industrial and commercial sector. There will always be small companies with some peculiar product that cannot be fitted exactly into such sectors, but even they can be valued by reference to approximate equivalents. Examples of the information given as at 13 November 1986 are shown in Table 15.2.

Information about the yields, ratios and price fluctuations of the individual companies in the Actuaries Share Index are to be found regularly in the *Investors Chronicle* on a quarterly basis. Monthly statistics on such matters in respect of unquoted companies can be found in *Venture UK* relating to USM/OTC companies. Detailed statistics on quoted companies can be researched from Extel cards or the company accounts themselves. Similar information can be found for unquoted companies from Data Stream or Jordan's, both specialising in this field. Private company accounts and other statutory documents can always be obtained from Companies House via the microfiche system, or again the services of Data Stream or Jordan's will supply

Table 15.2
Example of the *Financial Times* Actuaries Share Index

	EQUITY GROUPS & SUB-SECTIONS	Thursday November 13 1986						Wed Nov 12	Tues Nov 11	Mon Nov 10	Year ago (approx.)
	Figures in parentheses show number of stocks per section	Index No.	Day's Change %	Est. Earnings Yield% (Max.)	Gross Div. Yield% (ACT at 29%)	Est. P/E Ratio (Net)	xd adj. 1986 to date	Index No.	Index No.	Index No.	Index No.
1	**CAPITAL GOODS (211)**	679.77	−0.7	8.98	3.78	14.13	16.17	684.23	685.09	684.14	579.59
2	Building Materials (27)	827.05	−1.4	8.64	3.56	14.58	17.54	838.89	843.89	847.37	645.74
3	Contracting, Construction (30)	1163.00	−0.9	7.56	3.98	18.19	32.56	1173.65	1165.42	1163.76	951.72
4	Electricals (12)	1754.97	−0.9	8.38	4.78	15.44	53.27	1771.60	1805.19	1802.82	1561.37
5	Electronics (38)	1482.42	−0.9	9.58	2.74	13.91	29.90	1495.22	1490.40	1471.34	1377.86
6	Mechanical Engineering (60)	375.94	−1.4	10.47	4.42	12.18	10.42	381.27	379.88	377.72	333.58
8	Metals and Metal Forming (7)	339.83	−1.3	9.39	4.14	13.40	9.53	344.33	344.57	343.67	243.66
9	Motors (16)	258.17	−0.5	10.73	4.07	10.82	5.72	259.57	260.70	261.76	207.64
10	Other Industrial Materials (21)	1241.37	+1.4	7.20	4.35	16.48	30.19	1224.09	1232.44	1244.94	1055.75
21	**CONSUMER GROUP (185)**	941.51	−0.8	8.06	3.32	15.58	18.47	949.43	953.56	950.69	774.12
22	Brewers and Distillers (22)	970.00	—	9.05	3.31	13.59	14.91	970.02	966.70	961.54	809.38
25	Food Manufacturing (24)	724.83	−1.3	9.27	3.84	14.02	14.99	734.63	735.19	732.00	556.11
26	Food Retailing (16)	1874.19	−1.5	6.77	2.83	20.50	30.54	1901.92	1913.74	1896.11	1764.51
27	Health and Household Products (10)	1517.72	+0.2	6.20	2.50	18.85	21.37	1514.25	1532.83	1533.46	1184.69
29	Leisure (27)	965.47	−0.7	7.66	4.22	17.32	25.08	972.60	975.48	978.31	776.22
32	Publishing & Printing (15)	2605.46	−1.5	7.63	4.34	16.86	73.96	2644.30	2627.51	2589.55	1861.08
33	Packaging and Paper (14)	474.12	−0.8	7.12	3.47	18.25	10.54	478.09	472.93	468.03	373.27
34	Stores (38)	860.94	−1.3	7.16	3.05	18.95	16.10	871.95	880.31	877.79	818.61
35	Textiles (17)	543.79	−1.1	9.40	3.63	12.31	10.57	549.60	552.35	556.88	376.79
36	Tobaccos (2)	1297.08	−1.3	12.74	3.99	8.62	36.99	1313.76	1319.46	1325.16	821.23
41	**OTHER GROUPS (87)**	793.51	−0.7	8.48	4.04	15.20	17.50	799.24	799.13	797.61	738.64
42	Chemicals (20)	985.58	−0.1	8.92	4.39	13.64	29.15	987.05	982.18	985.13	732.50
44	Office Equipment (4)	238.15	−0.9	7.81	4.47	15.50	7.55	240.20	240.98	240.36	222.32
45	Shipping and Transport (13)	1574.08	−0.7	7.64	4.28	16.74	44.57	1585.29	1585.15	1575.83	1351.95
47	Telephone Networks (2)	780.38	−1.2	10.99	4.71	12.44	16.67	789.81	784.58	781.40	942.07
48	Miscellaneous (48)	1126.53	−0.6	6.00	3.02	20.93	16.87	1133.84	1144.39	1141.89	911.63
49	**INDUSTRIAL GROUP (483)**	843.98	−0.8	8.39	3.60	15.11	17.91	850.45	852.59	850.59	721.65
51	Oil & Gas (17)	1430.93	−0.3	11.42	6.26	10.79	62.83	1435.81	1432.79	1421.13	1209.48
59	**500 SHARE INDEX (500)**	893.37	−0.7	8.75	3.92	14.41	21.45	899.76	901.52	898.78	763.12
61	**FINANCIAL GROUP (118)**	605.42	−0.4	—	4.69	—	17.46	607.55	609.98	611.05	536.82
62	Banks (8)	655.07	−1.2	19.22	5.59	7.14	23.94	662.98	663.40	667.06	549.82
65	Insurance (Life) (9)	846.27	−0.8	—	4.60	—	27.29	853.37	854.68	853.02	418.00
66	Insurance (Composite) (7)	458.59	+1.2	—	4.73	—	13.49	452.96	463.43	467.46	1202.87
67	Insurance (Brokers) (9)	1267.82	−0.5	7.55	4.09	17.26	35.33	1273.91	1277.99	1289.25	287.37
68	Merchant Banks (12)	351.24	+0.7	—	4.08	—	6.37	348.85	345.35	343.57	693.34
69	Property (49)	799.15	—	5.66	3.55	23.21	15.17	798.71	802.52	797.13	307.93
70	Other Financial (24)	352.85	−0.8	9.32	4.53	13.08	9.06	355.64	353.94	352.90	639.23
71	Investment Trusts (98)	832.98	−0.2	—	2.73	—	14.22	834.46	830.65	828.15	263.46
81	Mining Finance (2)	344.93	—	9.11	4.65	12.91	11.30	344.81	348.25	337.02	587.27
91	Overseas Traders (13)	775.27	+0.4	10.36	5.68	11.65	29.17	772.21	768.04	765.51	696.04
99	**ALL-SHARE INDEX (731)**	815.85	−0.6	—	4.02	—	20.12	820.86	822.52	820.36	696.04
		Index No.	Day's Change	Day's High	Day's Low	Nov 12	Nov 11	Nov 10	Nov 7	Nov 6	Year ago
	FT-SE 100 SHARE INDEX ♦	1644.6	−9.9	1647.5	1634.7	1654.5	1660.9	1656.2	1662.6	1648.5	1443.1

these. ICC (Intercomany Comparisons Ltd) publish periodic detailed data on sector performance for every commercial sector.

Apart from influencing short-term fluctuations in share prices, analysts' reports can be of great value to a share valuer. In particular, they may well contain, in concise format, information and comment on a given industrial or commercial sector as well as invaluable research on the market leaders in that sector. This will undoubtedly assist in background and comparability studies that place the unquoted company in its proper market context and enable an appropriate evaluation of its past performance and future prospects to be made. Similar investment criteria will be found in the company analyses found in those leading financial journals, the *Financial Times* and *Investors Chronicle,* and the main quality daily and Sunday newspapers. Correctly collated, these sector and corporate dossiers will ensure an up-to-date economic basis from which the valuation of the company and the holding in it can proceed. Apart from statistical data, the analysts will usually supply charts showing past fluctuations in the relevant *Financial Times* Indices and movements in the price of the quoted share or shares in question. Normally, other comparative graphics such as returns on longer-dated gilts, relative strengths of quoted sector shares, and industry output and consumer demand figures will also be set out. In short, no professional valuer will overlook such a prime source of first-rate material for him to work on.

Examples of share-price determinants can be gleaned from Table 15.3 showing the leading share-price movements whether up or down in a single week. Such factors must always be taken into account if present in a given case, but at the same time they are likely to represent a special purchaser

Table 15.3
Leading share price movements in a single week
(Sunday Times 16 November 1986)

Company	Friday's close	Change on week	1986 high	1986 low	
AMS Inds	48	-15	125	46	Profit warning
Armstrong Equip	134½	+16½	141	69	Caparo stake
Bryant Hldgs	149	+31	149	80	Bid approach by EEC
Burns Anderson	109	+26	110	58	Offer from Dudley Ltd
Conroy Petrol	348	+47	353	23	Exploration hopes
Copson (F)	106	+51	118	32	Asset injection hopes after bid
Glanfield Lawrence	111	+20	116	50	Expansion potential
Glasgow Stock'ers	159	+15	161	115	Bid approach
Grosvenor Sq Prop	115	+20	130	85	Takeover approach
Helical Bar	473	+60	457	56	Property sale
Milford Docks	73	+18	88	36	Bid approach
Moorgate Merc	63½	+13½	63½	40	Brit & Comm increase stake
Morland	370	+32	385	215	Takeover speculation
NMC Invs	189	+23	198	14½	Revived speculative demand
Ocean Wilsons	82	+17	82	34	Bid approach
Redfearn Glass	256	+45	256	118	Good results
Saga Holidays	166	+30	230	129	Booming holiday bookings reports
Snowdon & Bridge	172	+27	145	97	Offer from Fitch Lovell
Vaux	452	+47	540	350	Revived bid hopes

element that must also be put into its proper perspective. The realisation of bid potential will nonetheless be likely to transform even a comparatively pedestrian unquoted share in a small private company into a top performer among penny shares. This is something that can happen overnight to unquoted as well as quoted shares.

This has been a bumper period for new issues with 100 companies a year joining the Stock Exchange Official List (three-quarters of these on the USM) in 1984–86. During this time the annual value of new issues exceeded £2 billion, excluding introductions to the market. The recent privatisations, easily constitute the biggest flotations ever. By bringing in millions of small private investors to the stock market as direct holders of shares these flotations have significantly increased the estimated shareholders to in excess of 8.5 million.

Apart from illustrating the market mechanism in action, the flotation and the necessarily detailed prospectus bring together into a convenient format a mass of information about the company, arguably more than is likely to be produced ever again in its lifetime.

Table 15.4
USM flotation prices

Name	Sponsor	Placing price	Price now	% gain/ fall
Petranol	Brown Shipley	125p	490p	292
Body Shop	Capel-Cure Myers	95p	320p	237
Valin Pollen	James Capel	110p	300p	173
CPS Computer	L. Messel	67p	147p	119
Norbain Elect	Simon & Coates	116p	220p	90
Meadow Farm Prod	Capel-Cure Myers	130p	235p	81
Scantronic	de Zoete & Bevan	78p	143p	83
CML Micros	Simon & Coates	130p	205p	58
Ramco Oil Serv.	Schroder Wagg	70p	113p	61
PWS Int	Sheppards & Chase	214p	332p	55
The 10 Worst				
North Sea & Gen	Hambros/Samuel Montagu	125p	80p	36
Xyllyx	Anglo Dutch/Kemp Mitchell	50p	33p	34
Wordplex	Hill Samuel	285p	212p	26
Pacific Sales	Laurie Milbank	60p	45p	25
Connells Est.	Kleinwort Benson	120p	92p	23
Spectra Auto	Hill Samuel	65p	51p	22
Ennex Int	Allied Irish Inv	41p	34p	17
Plan Invest.	Robert Wigram	62½p	53p	15
Piccadilly R.	Charlton Seal D.	28p	24p	14
Sangers Photo	A. J. Bekhor	23p	21p	9

The progress of the recent floats demonstrates the enormous profits built into some new issues — and indeed the exponential profits growth of some companies, even at the end of the severest recession to hit manufacturing industry since the 1930s. It is also significant to note the areas in which the successful companies operate. These are almost exclusively high-tech or fashionable service sectors. Table 15.4 is essentially self-explanatory in this context.

NEW ISSUES

These can be charted from the Singer and Friedlander Index of New Issues.

Flotations may be made by the following methods:

- Offer for sale — at a specified price often leading to substantial over-subscription or sometimes to under-subscription.
- Tender — introduced in 1961 when the public acted as their own share valuer with 886300 shares applied for in the price range 80p–£2 per share and initial transactions ranging from 94p–£1.05 per share compared with the allotment price of 87½p per share.
- Placing — normally used for smaller amounts of shares for which it may well be a more economical method.
- Public issue — when the issuing house acts as an agent, normally used by investment trusts.
- Introduction.
- Transfer from provincial Stock Exchanges.

The study by Vaughan Grinyer & Birley shows that for 1966/74 the popularity order of these flotation methods was:

1. offer for sale;
2. introduction;
3. placing;
4. transfer;
5. tender; and
6. public issue.

OVER THE COUNTER AND UNLISTED SECURITIES MARKETS

These are suitable for companies in perhaps the £1m/£20m capitalisation bracket. Markets for these shares are, apart from private treaty sales and capital institution purchases by ICFC or Charterhouse Development or so on:

- Stock Exchange rule 163 (2), Disposals by Stockbrokers. Rule 163(3) applies to natural resource companies.
- The over the counter sales by Harvard Securities and Granville & Co which make a market in some private companies with prices listed in the *Financial Times*. Disclosure is the minimum required under the Prevention of Frauds (Investment) Act 1958. The start-up fees are perhaps 10/15 per cent of the cost of an official Stock Exchange listing. Examples have occurred of takeovers by share exchange using OTC paper and no cash alternative.

THE UNLISTED SECURITIES MARKET

Origins

The unlisted securities market started in November 1980 and there were 61 companies with total market capitalisation in excess of £500m and an average price earnings ratio exceeding 20 by the end of the first year. Half the companies on the other hand were capitalised at less than £3m. Actively trading rule 163(2) companies are now expected to transfer to the USM. Companies with no trading record have been accepted (such as Hesketh Motor Cycles) though normally 3 years' results are expected.

Present position

USM companies now number well in excess of 250 and there are 3 to 4 new entrants each week. As at mid-June 1983 the main category breakdown showed the following distribution: *Building* (8); *Stores* (6); *Electricals* (36); *Foods* (6); *Caterers* (4); *Industrials* (36); *Motors* (4); *Publishers & Advertising* (6); *Property* (14); *Finance* (7); *Oils & Gas* (11).

Electricals and industrials overlap — computer companies may feature in either category. Most USM shares are not taken up by private investors, but by institutions. This is partly because entry has been predominantly by placing (in more than 50 per cent of cases) and introduction (in the case of some 30 per cent). Moreover only 10 per cent of the equity need be made available (in contrast with a minimum 25 per cent for a full listing).

Impact on share valuation

USM shares commonly show a premium of 50 per cent in dealings over the initial price and double or even treble that is not unknown. Average price earnings ratios are around 20 — as high as for many listed companies. Rapid long-term growth is clearly looked for by potential investors. The scope for the USM is enormous. NASDAQ (the US equivalent) has 3700 stocks and a trading volume equal to two thirds that of the NYSE. While the USM cannot escape general market influences, such as the temporary bear market of September 1981, it will tend to exemplify the general principle that unlisted company shares show usually less violent price fluctuation than their public company counterparts. The USM as a halfway house on the way to a full flotation (and once in the USM the progress to a full listing is that much easier) will embrace more and more of the faster-growing private companies. It will accordingly become a special valuation factor — the USM factor — which will have to be considered by the share valuer in evaluating the capital growth potential of the shares in question. It is also a counter-argument when the locked-in nature of private company shares is being discussed. Ideally a potential USM entrant should show the following characteristics:

- operation in a new technology sector;
- three year track record on a rising level;
- exponential profits growth;
- if a 'greenfield' company proven entrepreneurial talent and persuasive marketing possibilities;
- excellent longer-term prospects;
- a customer spread;
- diversity of product;
- reliable sources of supply;
- sound financial structures (gearing, liquidity and so on);
- depth of management;
- capitalisation at a minimum £5 million;
- proper reporting systems;
- adequate internal controls;
- identifiable services;
- long-term profits potential;
- USM motivation such as:
  - the need for permanent capital beyond the resources of the present proprietors;
  - shareholders actively seeking to unlock their investment;
  - a policy of expanding by acquisition facilitated by the availability of shares for exchange as opposed to cash offers;

- a desire to foster public awareness of the company's performance and standing in the market-place.

As regards any particular company some of these characteristics may be absent. However the presence of the majority of them should identify probable USM candidates and help evaluate the quality of USM shares on offer, using the valuation techniques described and analysed elsewhere in this book.

ANALYTICAL STUDY — Telecommunications (Plessey and Racal)

In 1961 Plessey became a multi-national enterprise with a three-way merger and doubled in size. The same year Racal went public. It had ironically been created by two former Plessey executives, Ray Brown and Calder Cunningham. Plessey has always been biassed towards manufacturing. Racal is primarily a global marketing organisation.

By 1980 Plessey's sales of £751 million were nearly treble Racal's turnover of £262 million. Racal's profits however stood at £63 million; Plessey's were only £60 million. The relative impact of these huge differences in profitability showed in the comparative growth in dividends and share price. Between 1969 and 1981 Plessey's earnings per share rose 142 per cent but Racal's increased 42 times. Plessey's dividends similarly rose 150 per cent while Racal's rose 27 times. The sum of £1000 invested in each company would over that period have risen to £1698 in the case of Plessey and £26308 if invested in Racal.

Since 1981 however Plessey has turned around substantially. Measures such as a new pricing formula, an innovative military radio programme and electronic office systems have effectively trebled the share price between 1980 and 1983.

Racal over this period started to lag rather. Intimately connected with this sudden slowdown in growth was the acquisition of Decca in 1980 for £106 million. This was after competitive bidding from GEC. Digesting Decca has meant resolving a variety of management and technical problems. These included: structural weakness, poor labour relations, over-manning, out-of-date product, inadequate servicing, loss-making colour TVs and so on. Racal's acquisition skills have however turned Decca around from £12.2 million pre-tax losses in 1979/80 to £18.4 million pre-tax profit in 1982/83. Decca is now proving one of Racal's best-ever acquisitions and for 1983/84 the pre-tax profit of the group is £120 million.

16 Share valuation practice

Reading this book has of course shown you different ways of valuing private company shares and business goodwill as well as more esoteric items of intellectual property, such as patents, trademarks and copyrights, in different situations and for different taxes. Getting it right is always an elusive target in this particular field. As a practitioner there will always be more people to tell you that you have got it wrong — whether client, the auditors, the directors, the shareholders, the executors, the beneficiaries, the other party's accountants, the arbitrators, or whoever. The ex-learned editors of the leading work on death duties (Dymond's *Death Duties*) suggested in their essay on the subject that the acid test of a share valuer's expertise is whether his chosen yield will stand comparison with quoted companies. This is clearly based on their long stint in the estate duty office/capital taxes office since this is evidently orthodoxy in the shares valuation division. However, there will be many situations where dividend yield or any yield basis is inappropriate as the principal, or indeed any yardstick, of valuation. In such cases the other valuation techniques must be utilised to the full. The trick is to identify the situations where each technique is appropriate and to what extent, bearing in mind that in many, if not the majority of, cases require the consideration and possibly application of more than one technique. At the end of that valuation process the facts and figures must be distilled into a cohesive whole expressed as at least a valuation range within which negotiations can take place.

The parameters are, of course, of acceptable values — recognising at the very least the normal 10 per cent valuation margin representing the expected range of expert opinion. If one is acting for the vendor one naturally starts with a value at the top of the range. The same would apply if one was a fledgling valuer in the shares valuation division. The purchaser's valuer will of course head straight for the bottom of the range. He may even go right down into the bargain basement, finding every possible depreciatory factor and lining it up for consideration as a deflator of the vendor's high-flying kite

— whether that is being flown as a notional statutory, or an actual market, value — in which case both parties will eventually have to be brought down to earth with a bump. The outcome is inevitably a more realistic consensus opinion that embodies more objectively all the relevant factors than the initial special pleadings. In the relatively rare case of being arbitrator with no axe to grind — whether in advising family parties to a sale or in deciding a valuation under the articles — the valuer will no doubt arrive at his own reasonably objective price and this is likely to be mid-point within his valuation range.

In summary, the valuation process is a series of practical steps that lead to a definite, but in most cases provisional, conclusion. This will generally be a range of potentially acceptable values. The final stage is the presentation of both the process and the conclusion in a proper format. Beyond that lies the area of negotiation and its special skills. These skills include such personal elements such as tact, diplomacy, pleasantness, charm and stamina that cannot be taught, only cultivated if one is fortunate enough to possess such highly desirable attributes!

The steps for those requiring a guide are very roughly as follows:

- Set out the basic facts about the company and its performance and prospects in tabular form (see Chapter 7).
- Note the occasion for the valuation and the particular taxes involved (see Chapters 2 and 12, respectively).
- Confirm whether a statutory or commercial valuation is required (see Chapter 5).
- Check whether any of the following apply:
  (a) takeovers or mergers or similar (see Chapter 6);
  (b) the company is not of the norm (see Chapter 10);
  (c) there is some sort of special situation;
  (d) the USM or flotation factor exists (see Chapters 11 and 15).
- Establish the size of holding to be valued (if not already evident from the second point above). Make sure you are clear where the holding stands in relation to the following:
  (a) company law (see Chapter 3);
  (b) the rest of the company's issued share capital;
  (c) the other shareholder's various holdings (is there a special purchaser element because of a triangular situation, for example);
  (d) special fiscal considerations (notoriously the IHT related property provisions) — see Chapters 3 and 12.
- Confirm the company's status as private or public (see Chapter 4).

- Test whether special goodwill considerations apply (see Chapter 9).
- Decide whether a full-scale comparability is required or not. At the very least, investigate the background of economic, political, social, commercial and technical developments at the time. This can be gleaned from such contemporary media as the *Financial Times* and *Investors Chronicle* at the relevant valuation date and, in addition, if the company's sector warrants it, the available technical literature — starting with the company's own product and design leaflets and brochures.
- Apply the appropriate valuation techniques (see Chapter 8).
- Draw up a range of values.
- Set out the valuation report to match the purpose in hand, using one of the examples in Chapter 13 as a guide to layout.
- State the assumptions on which the valuation is based. Qualify if necessary where full information has not been forthcoming.
- Sometimes where there is a mass of statistical data this may be usefully placed in a schedule or appendix for ready reference and to improve readability in the text.

Share valuation is both an art and a science. In both respects, experience counts a great deal in acquiring expertise and in cultivating judgement. The greatest single storehouse of such expertise and experience lies in the records and personnel of the shares valuation division. Beyond that there are the experts among the tax partners of the leading accountancy firms who will now presumably be free to advertise their professional competence. This book is intended to offer to them specific points of reference and much food for thought. At the same time it is hoped that the less expert, and even the complete beginner in this field — notably the company director, the estate planner, the insurance broker, the investor in unlisted companies and the business studies student — will find it of assistance and value, both as an introduction and as a handbook in their day-to-day work. It is the cross-fertilisation of that practical work wherever planning points impinge on company and business valuation with the theory and practice laid out here that will progressively develop their expertise in a hitherto somewhat esoteric field. Equally importantly, in the fast growing area of personal and corporate financial planning, it will be possible for the non-professional share valuer to decide on the feasibility of schemes without necessarily calling in the full-time expert. He will also become aware of the boundaries of his own competence and will therefore be better prepared when he realises the professional valuer is essential, both in presenting the brief to him and in evaluating the quality of the subsequent advice.

Example

Valuation of 500 shares in AB Services Ltd — An uninfluential minority in a small private company

Purpose of the valuation The valuation is of a 23.58 per cent holding for CTT as at 31 August 1979.

Previous valuation The last agreed valuation was made in 1971 based on the accounts for the year ended 31 January 1970. The holding was a 45 per cent influential minority holding. At that time the value was taken at £1.25, representing 40 per cent of the asset value.

The application of a similar proportion to the asset value at 31 January 1979 produces a figure of £20.65 per share based on net asset value of £43 778. However, in view of the size of holding under consideration, an assets-based valuation is not considered appropriate.

Profits and adjustments

	Year ended 31 January				
	1979	1978	1977	1976	1975
	£	£	£	£	£
Pre-tax profits	45 894	21 004	14521	9079	7 580
Less: notional interest at 15% on directors' balances at start of year	(14 480)	(12 750)	(10 404)	(9085)	(6 620)
	31 414	8254	4117	(6)	960
Less: allowance for corporation tax at 42%	(13 193)	(3 466)	(1 729)	3	(403)
Notional net profit	18221	4788	2388	(3)	557

Average net profit is £25951 ÷ 5 = £5190. Earnings per share are therefore £5190 + 2120 issued shares, or £2.45. The grossed up equivalent at 30 per cent is £3.50 or 350 per cent gross earnings. Details of prices, cover, dividends and dividend yields, and earnings yields as well as price earnings ratios for five quoted companies in a similar trading market are shown in Table 16.1.

Basis of valuation Having regard to the size of holding, the relative unmarketability of the shares, the increasingly heavy capital requirements of the company and all other relevant factors, it is suggested that a price earnings ratio of 3.5 is indicated and that a value of £12.25 per share is reasonable in this case. (This represents a gross earnings yield of 28.57 per cent and a discount of 76.26 per cent on the net asset value of £51.625 per share.)

Table 16.1
Quoted sector yields and ratios

					Div	*Cover*	*Yield*	*PLG*
360	288	FII Group.............	320	.....	†66.25	4.6	2.8	9.4
206	155	Garnar Booth.........	155	.....	10.0	1.7	9.1	9.3
218	168	Lambert Hth. 20p......	190	.....	5.75	3.4	4.3	7.6
80	68	Newbold & Burton	76	.....	3.08	1.1	5.8	22.5
114	82	Pittard Grp............	108	.....	3.72	3.5	4.9	7.5
158	120	Strong & Fisher	150	.....	†7.5	2.6	7.0	5.9

Bibliography

COMPANY BACKGROUND

'Small firms: Report of the Committee of Inquiry, Department of Trade and Industry,' H.M.S.O, 1971
CBI, *Britain's small firms*
Clarke, *Small firms – how they survive and succeed*
DTI, *Companies in 1974–84*
Jordan & Sons, *Britain's top 2000 private companies,* Bristol, 1985

BUSINESSES

Arnaud, A. A., *Investment trusts explained,* Woodhead-Faulkner, Cambridge, 1983
'The property boom, 1968–73, and its collapse: supplementary memorandum of evidence to the committee to review the functioning of financial institutions, RICS, 1978
Nevett, T.R., *Advertising in Britain: a history,* Heinemann, London, 1982
Retail directory, 36th edn, Newman, 1981

COMPANY FINANCE

Davis and Yeomans, *Company finance – the capital market*
Pitfield, R. R., *Business finance,* Gee, 1976

VALUATION

Eastaway, N., *Practical share valuation,* Butterworth, London, 1983

Eastaway, N., and Booth, H., *Share valuation cases,* Butterworth, London, 1985
English, *Valuation of shares in unquoted companies* (ICFC)
Hamilton-Baines, *Share valuations*
Merrett, *The valuation of ordinary shares*
Moon, *Business mergers and takeover bids*
Parry, R., *Valuation and conversion tables,* 10th rev. edn, A. W. Davidson, Estates Gazette, 1978
Sedgewick, *Valuation and development of petrol filling stations*
Samuels and Wilkes, *Management of company finance,* Van Nostrand Reinhold, 1982
Wood, *Farm valuations*

TAXATION

Dymond, R., *Capital transfer tax,* 6th rev. edn, A. L. Chapman, Longman Professional, Harlow, 1985
Hepker, M. Z., *Tax strategy for companies,* 2nd rev. edn, M. Gammie, Oyez, London, 1980
Ray, R. P., *Practical capital transfer tax planning,* 3rd rev. edn, Butterworth, London, 1985
White, P., *Law and tax for the family company,* Oyez Longman, London, 1982
Whiteman, P. G., and Wheatcroft, G. S. A., *Capital gains tax,* 3rd rev. edn, Sweet and Maxwell, London, 1976
Whiteman, P. G., and Wheatcroft, G. S. A., *Income tax and surtax,* 2nd rev. edn, D. C. Milne, Sweet and Maxwell, London, 1976

TAKEOVERS

Firth, M., *Share prices and mergers: study of stock market efficiency,* Saxon House, Aldershot, 1976
Knight, W., and Langford, J., *Acquisition of private companies,* 4th rev. edn, Longman Professional, Harlow, 1985
Moon, *Business mergers and takeover bids*
Pearson, B., *Successful acquisition of unquoted companies,* 2nd edn, Gower, Aldershot, 1986
Stacey, *Mergers in Modern Business*
Stacey, N., *Psychological attributes of mergers,* Scottish Academic Press, 1980
Weinberg, M. A., *Takeovers and mergers,* Sweet and Maxwell, London, 1979
Weinberg and Blank, *Takeovers*

FLOTATIONS

Merrett, Howe and Newbould, *Equity issues and the London capital market*
Birley, S. J., etc, *From private to public: analysis of the choices, problems and performance of newly floated public companies 1966–74*, Woodhead-Faulkner, Cambridge, 1977

GOODWILL

Kemper Simpson, *Capitalisation of goodwill*
Leake, *Commercial goodwill*
MacLean, *Accounting for business combinations and goodwill*
Wright, E. K., *Professional goodwill and partnership annuities*, ICA, 1967

COMPANY ACCOUNTS

Holmes, G., and Sugden, A., *Interpreting company reports accounts*, 3rd rev. edn, Woodhead-Faulkner, Cambridge, 1986
Jones, F. H., *Guide to company balance sheets and profit and loss accounts*, 8th edn, Barkeley Book, 1977
Greener, M., *Between the lines of the balance sheet*, Pergamon Press, Oxford, 1980

STOCK EXCHANGE

Briston, R. J., *Stock exchange and investment analysis*, 3rd edn, Allen & Unwin, London, 1975
Lorie and Hamilton, *The stock market: theories and evidence*
Nursaw, W. G., *The art and practice of investment*, 3rd rev. edn, Hutchinson, London, 1974
Rix, M. S., *Investment arithmetic*, 3rd edn, Pitman, London, 1971
Weaver, D., *Investment analysis*, Longman, Harlow, 1971

Index